MAY - - 2023

THE
COLORLESS
MAN

THE COLORLESS MAN

THE SPIRITUAL SAGA OF OBAMA

DR. GREGORY G. OGLE

Outskirts Press, Inc.
Denver, Colorado

The Colorless Man
The Spiritual Saga of Obama

Outskirts Press, Inc.
http://www.outskirtspress.com

ISBN: 978-1-4327-4253-9

Outskirts Press and the "OP" logo are trademarks belonging to Outskirts Press, Inc.

PRINTED IN THE UNITED STATES OF AMERICA

Contents

This is a true saying. If a man desire the office of a bishop, he desireth a good work.

A bishop then must be blameless, the husband of one wife, vigilant, sober, of good behaviour, given to hospitality, apt to teach;

Not Given to wine, no stricker, not greedy of filthy lucre; but patient, not o brawler, not covetous;

One that ruleth well his own house, having his children in subjection with all gravity

For if a man know not how to rule his own house, how shall he take care of the church of God

1 Timothy 3: 1-5

Acknowledgements

Nothing of merit is ever accomplished in a vacuum. This literary offering is no exception. The inspiration for this book is grounded in the pursuit of excellence, which was infused by my parents in their sons, Gregory, Kyle, and Henry. My father, Francis L. Ogle, a gifted teacher, and his wife Edythe E. Ogle, reared us with a spiritually egalitarian respect of the beautiful diversity of all races, both genders, and with the love for fauna and flora. Having lived my formative years in the fifties and sixties, my parents' ideals harshly contradicted the brutal realities of those racially fevered times. The brutal murder of Emit Till, the death of the three little girls in the Birmingham 16th Street Baptist Church bombing, the cowardly murder of the three civil rights workers in Lauderdale County, Mississippi, and the assassinations of Martin, Malcolm, John, and Bobby lit a smoldering angry fire that remained suppressed until my fifty-fifth birthday. The cognitive conflict between my enlightened rearing and contemporary reality became a sublimated and smoldering ordnance in my spirit. When life for me was confusing, my parents became a stabling force, and I didn't explode.

My father's bright smile and infectious laugh are gone, but the glow of his personality lives on in his sons, grandchildren, and great-grandchildren. He would be proud of his "young 'uns." In celebrating his boys he would be boldly boisterous, but in the quiet pensive hours of the night he was tearfully humbled by what God had allowed him to do with his children, his natural children, and his students. Dat Dat, nicknamed by my oldest daughter Khea, was my one and only hero. I love him and I miss him every day.

My mother, "Boppie," also nicknamed by my oldest daughter, still loves everybody. She is special. If only I could develop her tolerance of the faults in people. My mother never said anything negative to us. When I was a child she actually made me believe that with safe "practice," it was possible to fly. In maturity, and seeing the ravages of parenthood around me, I profoundly appreciate their love and commitment. I pray that in time I can develop into a parent like "Dat Dat" and "Boppie." I love them.

The New Pledge of Allegiance

A combination of the Lord's Prayer and The Pledge of Allegiance

Now I sit me down in school
Where praying is against the rule
For this great nation under God
Finds mention of Him very odd

If Scripture now the class recites,
It violates the Bill of Rights.
And any time my head I bow
Becomes a Federal matter now.

Our hair can be purple, orange or green,
That's no offense; it's freedom scene.
The law is specific; the law is precise.
Prayers spoken aloud are a serious vice

For praying in a public hall
Might offend someone with no faith at all.
In silence alone we must mediate,
God's name is prohibited by the state.

We're allowed to cuss and dress like freaks,
And pierce our noses, tongues and cheeks.
They've outlawed guns, but FIRST the Bible
To quote the Good Book makes me liable
We can elect a pregnant Senior Queen,
And the "unwed daddy," our Senior King.
It's "inappropriate" to teach right from wrong,
We are taught that such "judgments" do not belong

We can get our condoms and birth controls,
Study witchcraft, vampires and totem poles
But Ten Commandments are not allowed,
No Word of God must reach this crowd.

It's scary here I must confess,
When chaos reigns the school's a mess.
So, Lord, this silent plea I make
Should I be shot; My soul please take!

Anonymous, a fifteen-year-old Arizona teenager

Theoanthropology

"Theoanthropology" is a term coined by the author, which defines the harmonious interaction of God and man. Theoanthropology, Theo- meaning "God," anthro- meaning "man," and -ology meaning "study of," or more specifically, "discourse with." Theoanthropology is an attempt to dismantle the specious belief that there is a dichotomy between the belief in the science of man, his terrestrial position, and the belief in God.

This theoanthropological discourse will investigate man's creation, fall from grace, and subsequent redemption. Theoanthropology will explore theodicy, which investigates the appearance of God allowing evil in the world in contrast to His righteousness and agape. This investigation will examine binding human genetic ties that despite differences in color, phenotypical characteristics, cultural differences, and civil advancements, validate our homogenous brotherhood. This exercise is not an attempt to give decisive clarity to contemporary dilemmas. It is an attempt to narrow the perceived breach between God, science, and humankind. The study of theoanthropology is a modest attempt to develop a vehicle to lessen global acrimony.

Theoanthropological men and women are spiritually anointed by our Creator at specific points in history to lead the world through treacherously challenging times. Theoanthropological men, or *colorless* men, are chosen to lead the people of God to truth and blessings. Please read and determine for yourself.

"Parochial and provincial thought prevent progress."

Gregory G. Ogle

"The Greatest act of faith is
when man decides he is not God."

Oliver Wendell Holmes

"Wisdom is the quality that keeps you from getting
into situations where you need it."

Unknown

"The Man who does not read books has no advantage
over the man who cannot read them."

Mark Twain

"The man with a toothache thinks
everyone is happy whose teeth are sound.
The poverty-stricken man makes the
same mistake about the rich man."

George Bernard Shaw
In *Man and Superman*, in the appendix,
"The Revolutionist's Handbook and Pocket Companion."

"Only put off tomorrow what you are willing
to die having left undone."

Pablo Picasso

"There may be times when we are powerless to prevent
injustice, but there must never be a time when we
fail to protest."

Elie Wiesel
In "Hope, Despair, and Memory" (December 11, 1986)

"Man must evolve a method for all human kind
that rejects all revenge, aggression and retaliation;
the foundation of such a method is love."

Dr. Martin Luther King Jr.

"There is no fear in love; but perfect love casteth
out fear; because fear hath torment.
He that feareth is not made perfect in love."

1st John 4:18

A Helpful Hint

After reading my first book, *Let the Men Fight*, my family and several friends jokingly said they needed a Bible and a dictionary to understand it. Levity aside, information written or spoken is useless if your audience does not understand. To relieve this issue, "13-cent" words will be contextually defined before and after their use. For your convenience, the author will also include a glossary at the conclusion of every chapter with word definitions and concept explanations.

About the Author

Rev. Dr. Gregory G. Ogle is a Christian believer who is dedicated to removing the racial divisiveness and disunity of America and ultimately the world. He believes that the most recent DNA research shows that all of humanity has a common origin. He also believes that physical vicissitudes are divinely orchestrated environmental adjustments. It is Rev. Ogle's opinion, and the data shows, that there are no races or ethnicities that are more or less intellectually gifted than the others. Understanding that his writing may be controversial, his information is documented Biblically and secularly.

His primary motivation is the salvation of the unsaved. He addresses this charge individually and corporately by preparing ministers. Reverend Ogle understands that racism is grounded in ungodly fear, and he has associated America's spiritual salvation with the eradication of societal division. One of Dr. Ogle's major concerns is the confusion between religion and relationship. He will show that a true and healthy relationship with Christ precludes any societal divide, be it xenophobia, jingoism, racism, or gender bias. The ongoing campaigns for president of the United States gives Reverend Ogle a perfect opportunity to describe what a spiritual man and woman are, by highlighting examples of non-Christian and Christian behavior.

Understanding God's purpose for his life has brought Dr. Ogle to a comfortable position in the body of Christ. His self-assurance and spiritual anointing allows him to address issues that others are reluctant to confront. Some call him a renegade. Some call him a radical. Some call him paranoid. However, his three favorite secular quotes are: George Bernard Shaw, "All great truths begin as blasphemies," E. Franklin Frazier, "A successful person is a person who can build a firm foundation with the bricks they throw at him," and Woody Allen, "Being paranoid is knowing the truth." You will find these pearls of wisdom reflected in his writing.

Reverend Ogle has prepared himself thoroughly for his calling. He has a B.S. degree from Morgan State University, a Master's Degree of Administration from the University of Baltimore, a Master's Degree in Ministry from Family Bible Seminary, a Doctorate of Ministry from Family Bible Seminary, and a Ph.D. from the University of Maryland, College Park. Rev. Dr. Ogle continues to hone his spiritual skills as associate minister at the Berean Baptist Church in Baltimore, Maryland, and his academic acumen at the Philadelphia Seminary and the United Baptist College and Seminary, where he is Dean of Graduate Studies.

Understanding the necessity for an American spiritual revival, Reverend Ogle is driven to preach and teach the Good News of Jesus Christ and His gift of salvation. *The Colorless Man* accomplishes this in an interesting and unique way. Read, learn, and enjoy. God Bless.

Mrs. Debra A. Ogle

Preface

The Colorless Man has a message for all of America; however, as an African American male and minister of the Gospel of Jesus Christ, my obsession is the spiritual uplifting and education of especially those of African American heritage. Truth always has its collateral benefits, and I am praying that this offering will enlighten all people, national or international, who have been living in the miasma of ignorance. By exposing the genetic and spiritual homogeneity of man, my hope is that humanity will view itself with more tolerance, love, and humility. As in nature, by initially targeting the uplifting of the "socially maligned" underclass of our society, the resultant effect will engage a societal capillary action of love and unity that will rise to the top. Christ began at the "bottom." Shouldn't we? *"Come unto me, all ye that are heavy laden, and I will give you rest. Take my yoke upon you, and learn of me; for I am meek and lowly in heart: and ye shall find rest unto your soul"* (Matthew 11:28).

Strong buildings always have strong foundations. Nothing of worth is ever built from the top to the bottom. Unlike the "trickle down" theory, where the substance is diluted or weakens as it descends, osmosis has an opposite effect. In this case, in order for a substance to rise, osmotic motion is dependent on the volume and intensity of the substance at the bottom. The operation is similar to Darcy's Law of Hydrodynamics. Americans must intensify and increase our love for the socially and economically marginalized. The foundational substance of love is grace, mercy, and forgiveness. It will rise in uniform concentration until it reaches the top and is unable to ascend any farther, whereby the "love" liquid descends and re-strengthens the previously traveled path. That is how the love of Christ works. As it rises, it cleanses the unclean and then descends to re-cleanse and fortify that which it has already cleaned. Reciprocity is its beauty. My prayer is that the information contained in *The Colorless Man* will convince you of the beauty of the human race and its creator, and hopefully it will personally engage you in the process of Godly love. May God bless you and yours.

Glossary

Darcy's Law - having to do with the flow of water in a porous media
Hydrodynamics - the study of the flow of water

Introduction

Race, religion, and region, from the beginning of time, have been major determinants of social harmony. From the earliest of times, ethnocentrism, the favoring of one's kind over another, has been both the uplifting and the degradation of humankind. Please understand that ethnocentrism is neither good nor bad. Its relevance and effect is grounded in our attitude toward each other individually or between two or more groups. Differences are not inherently bad. All living creatures tend to live in like groups—lions with lions, robins with robins, elephants with elephants, snakes with snakes, ad infinitum. This homogeneity is necessary for survival of the species.

It is also natural to believe that one's group is superior to others; however, negatively degrading racially supremacist attitudes are not. The difference between humans and lesser animals is the ability of humans to think and reason. Animals separate by instinct, men separate by choice.

For example, most ancient civilizations treated slaves differently from American slavery. There was no attitude of racial supremacy. Moreover, there were no races. Race and its definition is a relatively contemporary phenomenon, which metastasized in the late 1500s (West, 1992). After investigation, you will deduce that the majority of the world's conflicts are waged because of racial differences, religious differences, territorial acrimony, and monetary conflicts. Animals will kill to eat or for the opportunity to mate. Humans will kill because one person's nose is broader and their skin is darker, or they worship different gods. Humans have the unique ability to reason and communicate with intelligence, but we often choose to revert to the behavior of lesser animals. Please remember, God made us in his own image. God is love. *I John 4:8: "He that loveth not, knoweth not God; for God is love."* The love to which this scripture is referring is agape love, or God's perfect love. The writer refers to this love as God's "just because love." God loves us "just because." Racism, *xenophobia*, and *jingoism* cannot exist in the atmosphere of love.

God has given us the gift of science, and contrary to what many think, there is no dichotomy between science and God. What this book endeavors to show, with the help of the most recent DNA research, is that there is little difference between races, ethnicities, and clans. Although these minor differences appear to be profound, the *vicissitudes* are divinely and genetically created for human survival.

To further cloud the issue of racial superiority is the belief that civilized communities, or people who live in cites, are inherently more intelligent than those who do not. The discussion will address domestication and how it is directly related to the specious perception of the greater intelligence of some ethnicities and races. All of the above will be wrapped in the author's term, "theoanthropology," or the personal relationship between God and man that is necessary to be a "colorless man."

Barack Obama, a metaphor for the title of this book, will be chronicled in his march to the presidency of the United States of America. Discussed will be the character of a colorless man and woman, and how the Word of God and its ethical immutable nature will lift one to a Christ-like character. Finally, God's gifts must be used. When one becomes a colorless woman or man, there is an added responsibility. You have been given much, and the word explicitly says, *"For unto whomsoever much is given, of him shall be much required; and to whom men have committed much, of him they will ask the more" (Luke 12:48)*. The more gifts God blesses you with, the more they will be noticed by men and God. Man will require more of you than God. The irony and hypocrisy of human nature is if a man gives you $5.00, he will want you to reciprocate with $10.00. The colorless man must understand this. He loves and prays for all. The supernatural power of the Holy Spirit is the colorless man's power.

References

Holy Bible, King James Version.

West, C. (1982). "Prophesy Deliverance." Philadelphia: Westminster Press.

Glossary

Ethnocentric - the tendency to look at the world primarily from the perspective of one's own culture

Jingoism - male chauvinist; also fear of foreigners with extreme nationalism

Vicissitudes - irregularities or changes

Xenophobia - deep dislike of foreigners

"And God said, Let us make man in our image, after our likeness: and let them have dominion over the fish of the sea, and over the fowl of the air, and over the cattle, and over all the earth, and over every creeping thing that creepeth upon the earth." Genesis 1:26

Wouldn't life be interesting if we all had opaque skin, minimally translucent and with no color or tone and void of all distinguishing characteristics? Would not life be more pleasant and tranquil if we all looked alike? Perhaps something akin to Gunther Von Hagan's "Body Works" exhibit, which is presently touring the nation? Wouldn't it be wonderful if there were absolutely no distinguishing features between us? The scientists call it "phenotypically *homogeneous.*" Perhaps something of an extraterrestrial look? Would not the inability to distinguish between clans, tribes, and races be preferable? Unquestionably, a homogenized human existence would rectify the entirety of our sociological situations of race, gender, religion, region, and economy. Imagine the benefits of not being distracted by the many voluptuous curves of the female frame or the rugged sculpture and raw masculinity of the male body. Imagine the freedom one would have if we didn't have to contend with creamy smooth coco, tan, or white complexions, curly, straight, or coarse hair. That would eliminate the need for hair products. Perhaps we should eliminate hair totally. There, end of problem. Everybody is bald. Uniformity and consistency will curtail, if not eliminate, all conflicts and problems.

Our intellectual abilities will be universal also. Everyone would have the same gifts and talents, creative abilities, opinions, morals, and ethical positions. There would be no need for politics. We would only need one leader, and we would only need to change upon his or her death. In regard to death, society would only need one type of physician, because everyone would die of the exact same illness. The greatest gift of all would be the irrelevance of attorneys, because acrimony would abate, everyone would agree. The collateral benefit would be no more lawyer jokes.

Do not forget nature and the environment. Perhaps we should make all flowers red roses. We could have identical shrubs and flowers adorning our many homes, positioned in the same symmetrical or asymmetrical manner as not to cause confusion. That would end the devilish competition between neighbors in regard to who has the prettiest yard and deciding who wins the community association's "Best Yard Trophy." There is no need for variety. No one would miss it. We only need one kind of tree. A variety would only be superfluous. Perhaps all evergreen trees, since deciduous trees would be too confusing with their many glorious colors. After further thought, perhaps we would need a few types of fruit trees. Our botanical and dietary intelligentsia could determine which three or four are the most nutritious, and we could eliminate the remaining several thousand. Dendrologists may fret, but who needs tree experts anyway?

Diet is an interesting issue. We could devise a low-calorie, high-energy meal; give it an acceptable flavor, which everyone will like. A common diet would eradicate the daily indecision of what to eat and how to prepare it. As an additional benefit, a strictly controlled diet would end the worldly dilemmas of obesity and malnutrition in the world. Even better, in the spirit of "Soilent Green," we could recycle human flesh. Do you remember the movie? If you haven't seen the movie, rent it. *Anthropophagi* certainly did not have a negative effect on Charlton Hesston. The movie implied that cannibalism could be nutritious. Wouldn't that be a tasty innovation?

The previous literary discourse is obviously absurd and an

exercise in extreme sarcasm; however, the paradox is glaring. The human species seems to crave and destroy diversity simultaneously. Our unwillingness to eliminate fossil fuels, aerosols, and pollutants from our social diet is gradually destroying our perfectly anthropic environment. The changes in climate already caused by the temperature rise are threatening the extinction of several species of animals. The Most High God gave us the ultimate in life's *vicissitudes* and unique variations to make life interesting and beautiful for us, but we seem to be destroying them with cavalier arrogance. In addition to having the intellect to appreciate God's varied creations, He gave us dominion over the things and animals that He made expressly for our pleasure. This earthly environment is *anthropic*, meaning specifically suited for the existence of humans. *"And God said, Let us make man in our image, after our likeness: and let them have dominion over the fish of the sea, and over the fowl of the air, and over the cattle, and over all the earth, and over every creeping thing that creepeth upon the earth"* (Genesis 1:26). Apparently if we cannot make money selling the "creepy" things, then we eliminate them.

My wife and I presently are living in Baltimore. In the 1950s, Baltimore was nationally known for the city's abundance of Oriole birds. It was the most recognized and proliferate bird in the Baltimore area. It is a uniquely beautiful black and orange bird with an unusual chirp and markings. Orioles were as plentiful as pigeons are now. The city named its professional baseball team after the Oriole bird. The Oriole is a neo-tropical migrant that summers in the jungles of the South American rain forests. Unfortunately, increasing housing and industrial development destroyed most of the jungle. Consequently, the bird has declined almost to extinction, due to the elimination of their breading habitat. Baltimore has lost its mascot and one of God's beautiful creatures.

We probably should rename our baseball team the "Baltimore Pigeons." For the last five years, they have been playing like pigeons anyway. It certainly would be a more appropriate name.

The abounding question is, if God gave us this abundance of

good things in such a bountiful cacophony of endless beauty, why do humans continually try to destroy, control, eliminate, quarantine, neglect, abuse, and ignore God's gifts? Our environment has deteriorated to the point where it may already be irreversible. In a few years, we will be sunbathing in January on the resort beaches in Northeastern America. Humans love variety, but because of greed we seem to be driven to destroy the things that we claim to love. Perhaps this cupidity is the result of a phenomenon titled *scientific imperative*.

Scientific imperative drives man to use profound scientific discoveries to their ultimate, often resulting in additionally lucrative, but frighteningly dangerous disadvantageous collateral inventions. Certainly it is not necessary for me to belabor the point, but a few examples should suffice. Nuclear fission was a tremendous scientific breakthrough. Its development has contributed to myriad advances. Antithetically, nuclear fission ultimately birthed the atomic bomb, which was the genesis of the razor's edge of nuclear holocaust on which we fearfully reside today. Ironically, the development of nuclear power plants for the production of power and energy, a commodity which this nation never attains satisfaction, has established in excess of 126 nuclear waste disposal sites throughout the nation. Of course, these sites are supposed to be safely hidden and ultimately secure from terrorist attack, but are they really?

The latest project, the Yucca Mountain Project, House Joint Resolution 87, will allow the Department of Energy to take the next step in establishing a one site "dump" for the nation's deadly nuclear waste. Even though Yucca Mountain is probably going to cost us twice the national debt that George W. Bush so graciously reestablished for us with the Iraq war, we have few alternatives. With 39 nuclear power plants and 126 waste sites throughout the country, many of them filled to capacity, who accurately knows how secure they are? Conscientious action must be taken. Frighteningly, the locations of these sites are easily attainable, as detailed from the Web site from which I garnered this information. Imagine the peril this nation will face when the new Yucca Mountain is complete and the mass waste exodus and relocation begins. It will not matter that Yucca Mountain is on federal land surrounded by 100 miles of desert in Nevada with impenetrable bunkers deep below the surface of the earth. It doesn't matter that there will be little or no chance of seepage to the surface. The danger is the transference of the deadly material from the satellite locations. Accidents are more of a deadly possibility than terrorists. My question is, how can we adequately protect an enormous amount of terminally fatal poison in trucks being hauled from 126 different sites? We were not able to protect the Twin Towers in the center of New York City, in the heart of a "No Fly Zone" on a crystal clear autumn September day. Please remember, exposure to this poison means irreversible contamination and certain death. It means, "Cancel Christmas."

Here is a personal example of scientific imperative. My daughter works for Merk, the drug manufacturer and distributor. For me, Viox was extremely effective, but potentially deadly. Unfortunately, I have congestive heart failure, but took the drug for more than a year before the recall alerted the nation to the danger of its use. It was fortunate that the drug did not kill me. It is little mistake that the enormous profits realized from the medication prolonged the divulgence of its hazard. Scientific imperative is more concerned with profit than persons. Who can name the exact number of products that have been recalled in the past five years? It has become an accepted practice. The issue is not to have a product recall, but to be the company that has the least number recalled. There have been issues ranging from toys, cars, flammable clothes, dangerous drugs, airplane parts, and even faulty space shuttle parts. Greed has become the cornerstone of corporate culture. What does the rapper, film producer, and actor "Ice Cube" say? "It's all about the Benjamins."

In light of the "polysylogistic" sarcasm of the previous text, humans seem to generally prefer variety in every instance with the exception of ethnicity. However, the hypocritical innuendo of race separation is exterior of the bedroom. Interracial and cultural intermarriage has been considerably more prolific globally than the American culture knows or will admit. In America alone, if everyone in this nation were to agree to a DNA test to determine if their genome had a completely pure racial makeup, I would bet the house that less than 5% of this nation is pure anything. American slavery alone is validation. The colloquial oratorical game we blacks play, called the "dozens," gets its name from the accepted practice that the average slave master had twelve African mistresses. In Chapter 2, we will give close examination to the genetic makeup of the entire human race and its corporate genome. The paradox is that to be a "colorless man," one must be "color full."

Every generation or so, God gives us an exceptional human being. They usually come from the least of us in an unexpectedly meteorically burst to the front, which is a sure sign of divine intervention. 1 Corinthians 1:27-28 reads, *"But God hath chosen the foolish things of the world to confound the wise; and God hath chosen the weak things of the world to confound the things which are mighty; And the base things of the world, and things which are despised, hath God chosen, yea, and things which are not, to bring to naught things that are."* False empty leaders use religion, stumbling through half-accurate scriptural quotes, while divinely chosen leaders show their anointing by their actions. Anointed leaders are empathetic, not sympathetic. They hear the people's pain. Great leaders taste the people's anxiety. Great leaders hear their people's frightening sights, while flinching under the sound of their agony. Great leaders are a percolating pot of *synesthesia*, and this gifted, homogenized intra-sensual ability allows the great leader to anticipate the needs of his people while being driven to protect and provide. Saint Francis of Assisi may have been the first to experience physical *stigmata*; however, this bleeding from the wrists, side, and feet is not the only stigmata that can be experienced. The writer is speaking of spiritual stigmata, the emotional pain when one witnesses the perilous plight of the people's pain as God did. George Washington, John Adams, Gandhi, Mother Teresa, Sitting Bull, Geronimo, Joan of Ark, Harriet Tubman, Mary McCloud Bethune, Nat Turner, Gabriel Prosner, Frederic Douglass, and more recently, Megner Evers, Malcolm, and

Martin experienced emotional stigmata. James 2:18 says it clearly: *"Yea, a man may say, thou hast faith, and I have works, and I will shew (show) thee my faith by my works."*

Sidney Hooks made an extremely profound distinction between two types of potential heroes. "There is the *'eventful man'* and there is the *'event-making'* man. The *'eventful'* is any man in history whose actions change the course of history. The *'event-making'* man is an *'eventful'* man whose actions are the consequences of outstanding capacities of intelligence, will, and character than of accident of position" (Hooks, 1943). Please remember that all men walk with a limp, but those that understand their deficiencies and give the glory to God accomplish profound things.

At the writing of this book, the writer is blessed to have the opportunity to chronicle the presidential campaign of Senator Barack Obama, presently the front-runner for the Democratic nomination and the first African American with a realizable chance to be president of the United States. The paradox is: A black man full of color, his mother being a white American and his father being a Kenyan, spending his formative years in Hawaii and the South Side of Chicago, has amalgamated this nation to the degree where color is now less of an issue. In the primary elections thus far, the irony begins with his victories in South Carolina, Georgia, and Mississippi, three of the most racist states of the Confederacy. South Carolina was the catalytic state of the Civil War and the hub of the Confederacy, and Mississippi was the most brutal slave state in the Confederacy. In contrast, he lost the free states of Ohio, and Pennsylvania and Connecticut in the primary elections. However, at this point Obama has a solid lead in popular and electoral votes, and the super delegate tally seems to be increasing daily. It can happen. The United States could really have an African American president.

In spite of my normally cynical attitude, I have cause for optimism. Very simply, an African American is a serious candidate to be president of the United States of America. That simple possibility gives validation and credence to the words I say to my grandsons:

"You can be president of the United States if you want to be."

The heavily criticized statement by Michelle Obama, "For the first time I can be proud of my country," is a statement only an African American can appreciate. It has nothing to do with patriotism, and everything to do with "All men are created equally with unalienable rights." It directly speaks to the 13th amendment, 14th amendment, 15th amendment, the abolition of slavery, the right to be a citizen, and the right to vote, with no concern for color, race, or gender. Barack Obama's candidacy and his acceptance by this country for his political position and character makes all African Americans feel like they, we, finally have the potential of becoming fully invested in the "American Dream." Barack Obama becoming president will elevate the corporate self-concept of African Americans, and begin to dismantle the self-depravation that have Black Americans in an increasing spiral of self-destruction. An African American president will move black America toward recapturing the positive cultural and racial self-image that slavery and "Jim Crow" stripped from our corporate and cumulative psyches. Obama's success will catalyze African Americans into catching, and outdistancing, the crippling assimilation/acculturation and normative gaze syndromes that Cornell West eloquently describes in his book *Prophecy Deliverance*. Barack is the personification of the colorless man. The colorful colorless man represents white men wearing Brooks Brother suits, white corporate women, black middleclass men and women, boys in the hood, Asians, Latinos, Hebrews, Arabs, and all in between. Obama is the "Audacity of Hope." He gives this country a fresh appearance of ethical American character to the world. This book will be written during the presidential campaign. It will be interesting to see how the threads of current events meld their way into the substance of the text.

Theoanthropology is the bringing together of the Holiness of God and the natural mechanical nature of man to form a relationship that results in divinely inspired behavior. Theoanthropologic behavior is always manifested in the colorless man by his relationship with the one and true God. There have been a few in the history of the world. Most recent examples have been Frederick Douglass, Gandhi,

Mother Teresa, Martin, and Malcolm. All were woefully inadequate reasonable facsimiles of Christ, but the best we can expect from mere flesh. Perhaps it's time for another?

Also, in an effort to give the reader an idea of the creative process, at this point I am not completely sure of the book's direction. It will be interesting to compare the notes of this chapter with the flavor of the epilogue. The writer will be as surprised as the reader. The tenor of this book will undoubtedly be influenced by the results of the election.

The boon is that the Holy Spirit has manifested a spirit in a man that may be the persona that gives this work a parallel example of a colorless man and the colorless society we deserve. The world will never be perfect until Jesus returns. Perhaps, we can make the world a little better so at least His church will faintly resemble a church without spot, wrinkle, or blemish. "That He may present it to Himself a glorious church, not having spot, or wrinkle, or any such thing; but that it should be holy and without blemish" (Ephesians 5:27). Pray for The Colorless Man.

For Further Discussion

1. What do you think about Sidney Hooks' definition of the "eventful man" vs. "the event-making man"?

2. What does theoanthropology mean to you?

3. In terms of stewardship, what is your position on ecology?

Glossary

Anthropic - an environment established for the specific survival of humankind and supporting fauna and flora

Anthropophagi - cannibalism

Phenotypic - normal physical characteristics of the face and body including skin color

Cupidity - greed

Homogenous - of the same kind

Polysylogism - reasoning in which a conclusion or conclusions are drawn from two or more assumed propositions. For example, the colors of the football team's uniforms were red and white. The cheerleaders' uniforms were red and white. The mascot's outfit was red and white, and the benches of the stadium were alternately painted red and white. Therefore, the school's colors are assumed to be red and white.

Scientific Imperative - Once mankind has made a significant discovery or invention, that discovery is developed to its maximum. There are often collateral benefits and liabilities; however, their development is always for profit, war, or a combination of both.

Synesthesia - a physical gift allowing the poser to actually smell what he hears, taste what he sees, feel what he tastes, hear what he feels, taste what he smells, feel what he smells, and various combinations of the above

Stigmata - the instantaneous bleeding from the wrists, feet, and right side similar to the wounds of Christ. The first known person to experience stigmata was St. Francis of Assisi circa 1200 A.D. There were no other documented events prior to the 13th century.

References

Holy Bible, King James Version.

Hooks, Sidney (1943). *The Hero in History: A Study in Limitations and Possibility*. New York: The John Day Co., 1943.

Percelay, J., Monteria I., Dweck, S. (1994). *Snaps*. 2 Bros. & White Guy, Inc.

CHAPTER **2**

"And if ye call on the Father, who without respect of persons judgeth according to every man's work, pass the time of sojourning here in fear." (1 Peter 1:17)

"For there is no respect of persons with God." (Romans 2:11)

"And God said, 'Let us make man in our image, after our likeness; and let them have dominion over the fish of the sea, and over the fowl of the air, and over the cattle, and over all the earth'" (Genesis 1:26). "God is a Spirit; and they that worship Him must worship Him in Spirit and truth" (John 4:24).

The Word of God says that man is made in the image and likeness of God. Genesis 1:26 obviously validates the points of the book's introduction regarding God's various assortment of earthly gifts with which He blessed humankind. There are three key words in this passage of scripture. The first is *dominion*, which is the Hebrew word "rada." It means "responsibility" and connotes stewardship. The second is *image* (Heb. tselem) meaning "something cut out from or similar to." The third is *likeness* (Heb. demut), which means "comparatively similar." In synopsis, the scriptures meaning is that we have been given the responsibility of stewardship for everything on earth and each other. God has made us a reasonable facsimile and a comparative likeliness to Himself with His gift of the Holy Spirit. "For to one is given by the Spirit the word of wisdom; to another the word of knowledge by the same Spirit; To another faith by the same Spirit; to another the gifts of healing by the same spirit;

To another the working of miracles; to another prophecy; to another discerning of spirits; to another divers kinds of tongues; to another the interpretation of tongues" (I Corinthians 12:8). We have been given specific responsibility for the stewardship of each of God's animate and inanimate creations.

The reader asks what does the "colorless man" have to do with the above? The colorless man is an attitude of Spirit. God is a Spirit, and His spirit is reflected in the behavior of the colorless or theoanthropological man. It is an attitude analogous to God's Word. *"For there is no respect of persons with God"* (Romans 2:11). It is an attitude that after hundreds of years America and the world is finally beginning to recapture. Today is Saturday May 10, 2008, and the nation is in a political struggle in its attempt to select party candidates for November's presidential election. The Republican Party's primary election process has concluded with John McCain the overwhelming victor. However, the democratic primary process remains a "dog fight." For lack of committed delegates, the political pundits are saying that Hillary Clinton is mathematically unable to win the nomination. As of today Barack Obama (266) has surpassed, for the first time, Mrs. Clinton (263) in super-delegates. The super-delegate support may be the deciding factor if the nominee is to be decided at the national convention. At this point, and according to the political experts, Mr. Obama seems to have won the nomination. However, let us not jump to conclusions. The contest is not over. There are several smaller state primaries and one larger state, Oregon, to be contested.

As a relatively cynical man, and obvious Obama supporter, I am guardedly optimistic. Who would have ever thought that an African American man would have a legitimate chance of becoming a frontrunner, much less a major party's nomination for president of the United States? *"But God hath chosen the foolish things of the world to confound the wise; and God hath chosen the weak things of the world to confound the things which are mighty; and the base things of the world, and things which are despised, hath God chosen, yea, and things which are not, to bring to nought things that are"* (I Corinthians 1:27). Admittedly, this nation has come a long way.

Similar to Michelle Obama's statement, this writer is now beginning to add pride to my love for this country.

The irony of the primary election process is that the slave states of North Carolina, South Carolina, Georgia, and Mississippi have voted for Obama, while the free states of Massachusetts, Pennsylvania, Indiana, and Ohio voted for Mrs. Clinton. Admittedly, the results show that race relations have improved in America, but bigotry and its metastasizing effects remain crippling to our country. As evidenced by public inquiry and media exposition, some Americans are reluctant to select an African American or woman as president. Race and gender bigotry remain, to the degree that the Ku Klux Klan has indicated that they will endorse Barack Obama before Mrs. Clinton. The KKK would rather see a black male president than a white woman president. The election of an African American president will do two enormously beneficial things for this nation. The amelioration will affect the corporate self-image of African America, by allowing African Americans to genuinely participate in the "American Dream." It will erase the crippling stigma of the 3/5 of a human being status that surreptitiously clouds and devalues the psyches of black Americans. This country now has the redemptive and healing opportunity to fulfill Barbara Jordan's dream, "What the people want is simple. They want an America as good as its promise." "We hold these truths to be self-evident, that all men are created equal, that they are endowed by their creator with certain unalienable Rights, that among these are Life, Liberty and the pursuit of Happiness."

Perhaps the fate, direction, and business as usual of this country are about to change. As a spiritual man and ordained minister, my belief is that brother Obama has been ordained by God as obvious and certain as Rev. Dr. Martin Luther King Jr. was divinely driven to eliminate racism, war, and poverty in America in the 1950s and 1960s. Mr. Obama is the light shining through the miasma of unrighteousness that mires America in injustice, greed, and sin, all of which relegates this country and its allies as the anathemas of the world.

Mr. Obama's mother is of European white decent and his father is of black African descent. Contrary to some criticism, he is genetically an authentic African American. He understands and has lived in both worlds. Understanding the African American Church and his close ties with it, Obama is the quintessential theoanthropological "colorful colorless man." He appears to have a relationship with God and a love for all people. Referencing Mr. Obama's parentage is an appropriate segue to our discussion of the oneness or homogeneity of the human race. Please remember, God said, *"Let us make man in our image, after our likeness" (Genesis 1:26).* He did not say that some men were made in God's image.

With the miraculous advancements in the investigation of DNA, we are now able to determine with relative certainty the origin of man in regard to time and place. It will be interesting to see how the information correlates with the Bible.

E Pluribus Unum: "Out of many, one" ▬▬▬▬▬▬▬

The discussion of genetics is baffling to many lay people, including myself. However, the rudiments of genetic enlightenment as is pertains to human development will be discussed, and a synopsis of the information will hopefully form a palatable nugget of understandable information. For a more detailed explanation, please refer to The Journey of Man: a Genetic Odyssey by Spencer Wells. Please remember that at the conclusion of each chapter there is a glossary, which defines theological, technical, and what the writer calls "13-cent" words for the readers convenience.

At its inception, the study of the racial diversity of the human existence was restricted to observation, i.e., skin color, height, body build, facial features, hair texture, and in many instances perceived intelligence. This apparent information appears to be valid, but its inaccuracy continues to influence racial relations today. Until recently, there was no accurate way to determine human variation, which tacitly perpetuated misinformation. Dr. Cornel West discusses in his book *Prophecy Deliverance* what he calls the normative gaze, which is tantamount to what we call today's racial profiling. Dr. West details the practice of physiognomy, which ranks humankind in reference to their proximity to the accepted ideals of "classical Greek" physicality—the ideals being those closest to the ancient Greeks' definition of beauty, which was fair skin, keen features, *mesomorphic*, straight hair, blue eyes, etc. Humans, minus these congruent physical characteristics, were not only considered to be physically deficient, but their apparent *phenotypical* deficiencies were assumed to contribute to intellectual, ethical, and psychological shortcomings. Seventeenth-century anatomist Pieter Camper *speciously* determined that the angle of the jaw was reflective of the beauty of one's face, and therefore was an indication of the intelligence and quality of an individual's character. Prognathism, Pieter Camper's pseudoscientific belief, posited that because Africans' facial angles were between 60 and 70 degrees, similar to lesser animals and less that the 97 to 100 degrees of Greek perfection, Camper surmised that Africans were less than human (West, 1982). As if that were not enough, John Gall's pseudoscience of phrenology held that the size and shape of an individual's head indicated their intelligence, moral fiber, and hierarchy in human development (West, 1982). Although obviously misleading, unfortunately at that time these "scientists" held the world's respect, and their specious opinions continue to feed racist and discriminatory practices. A great deal of this misinformation was accepted as truthful, and became the standard by which humankind was evaluated.

Samuel Stanhope Smith (*Essays*, 1787), former president of Princeton University and an honorary member of the American Philosophical Society and the first eugenicist, promoted intermarriage of races and the social interaction as a way to "upgrade" the black race. Intermarriage, or *miscegenation*, was Smith's solution whereby the theory of race mixing would improve the genome of Africans. In addition, the encouragement of social interaction between the races would promote civilized behavior by Africans. Cornell West titles this "strong assimilation" and "weak assimilation" (West, 1982). At that time Smith's position was radically liberal; however, it still erroneously validated African inferiority and spurious information. Unfortunately, similar misinformation has been used in several circles for nefarious purposes throughout history. This evil intent is not specific to one race or ethnicity; it seems to be grounded in greed, controlling power, and flavored with negative ethnocentricity. It also seems to have been promoted by both races, both black and white. White because of the obvious desire for racial superiority, and black due to the corporate devaluation of self-concept systematically taught to slave populations— the result being a mentality similar to the Stockholm syndrome (Freire, 1993). The combination of greed, power mongering, and the illusion of race superiority are the Achilles' heel of all mankind.

Let us look at American racism. Racial supremacy in this country is based on a construct named "hypodescent." There are two parts to the construct. The first is *the rule of recognition*. Anybody who looks black is black. The second is *the rule of descent*; anyone who is known to have African parentage is black, or "the one drop of blood" rule. America has become what the writer terms as "pseudo erudite" in its classification and stratification of racial suppression of bigotry. In order to fully comprehend, one must understand the attitude of the slave owner. The slave owner not only looks at the slave from a position of superiority. He perceives him/her as a movable possession, known as chattel. The irony is that this same attitude toward his slaves parallels the attitude toward himself. He sees blacks as his possessions and he also sees his whiteness as his possession. Therefore, he guards his whiteness as pure, and anything less is a graduated degree of less purity. By his "whiteness," or "purity," he is rightfully and lawfully mandated to suppress anything less than what he believes is a God-given mandate.

America still retains graduated degrees of blackness that even today determine the degree by which a black person is accepted by white America. For example, the designations are less formal in that they are no longer politically acceptable. Some of us may remember the old but well-used aphorism, "If you're light you're right, if you're brown stick around, if you're black get back." In the old days African Americans were categorized:

Mulatto. Mulattos are the offspring of mixed heritage irrespective of the number or percentage of the mixtures.

Named fractions. Mulattos are named by the amount of African heritage. Mulatto is usually one half white and one half black; a quadroon is one-fourth black and three-fourths white, a sambo one-fourth white and three-fourths black, etc. Today we are a little more politically correct. We call them all mixed.

Social continuum. The social continuum is considerably less stringent. Usually the lighter mulattos are more socially acceptable among blacks and whites, and fair better educationally and economically, oftentimes more successful than some whites (Gotanda, N., 1991).

Under the American system of racial superiority, hypodescent has generational grounding, and determines the degree of "human contamination" in a non-white person. Moreover, historically Africans were considered possessions simply because of their color. White people, on the other hand, considered their "whiteness" as a possession. Whiteness continues to provide certain privileges and entitlements not privy to non-whites, and are still guarded quite vigorously. The Civil War is an extreme example. This nation was willing to split this country and fight to the death in dispute of the African's "right" to be human. The remnant attitudes remain in the 2000s. Andrew Hacker, in his 1992 book *Two Nations*, discussed the querying of a group of college students concerning how much money they would require to allow themselves to be turned from white to black. Their response was that it would not be extreme to ask for $500,000 or $1 million for each coming 50 years.

The law requires the acceptance of all races, religions, colors, and ethnicities, and the law has been largely effective. However, there is still a racial divide in America as evidenced by this latest presidential contest. There are obviously millions of white Americans who have no difficulty in voting for an African American for president.

Unfortunately, remaining are still millions of people who say they will never vote for a black man for president or any other political office in America. That is resultant of ignorance, lies, and false information as to who African Americans are as human beings.

Our understanding of the human species has been tainted by information that appears to be true but is woefully inaccurate. Most of this specious information has been shown to be false; unfortunately, because of the sources and time, the information was considered scientifically sound. The "experts" were considered state of the art scientists and were not to be questioned. In the 1500s, 1600s, and 1700s, their information was considered sound, and the "scientists" who provided this information were regarded as experts. In the late 1700s Johann Ferick Blumenbach, the founder of modern anthropology, based his evaluation of humans on the physical characteristics of ancient Greek painting and statues. Anything that deviated in skin color, physique, hair type, and other phenotypical features was considered less than human. Louis Leclerc de Buffon, in his famous book *Natural History of Man* stated that the real color of man was white. Blumenbach later supported Buffon's position. Buffon was obviously a buffoon, but his opinions, even today, remain true to many. To reiterate, John Camper a Dutch anatomist, and world-renowned at the time, considered the proper angle of a human chin to be approximately 100 degrees. The average chin of Africans is between 60 and 70 degrees, similar to dogs and apes, therefore Africans are less than human. This pseudoscience is called prognathism. In addition, physiognomy is the pseudoscience that promotes the belief that if the physical attributes are not in keeping with Greek physical characteristics, all other characteristics of the individual are deficient. This included moral and ethical foundations, perverted sexual behavior, emotional stability, diminished intelligence, etc. (West, 1982).

Fortunately, modern science has shown this data to be spurious. Unfortunately, this information was relatively unchallenged for several decades, and became entrenched socially, academically, and legally in America and the world's psyche.

The following pages will show that all humankind has one genesis, and all minor variations are resultant of divine and normal morphology, in addition to environmental adaptation. With the advent of DNA research, perhaps the greatest genetic discovery in regard to the development of man has been that of Mitochondrial Eve. Eve is postulated to have lived circa 200,000 years ago in Africa, specifically in the Sudan region. Mitochondrial Eve was the originator of the 168 gene. Every human being is in possession of this gene, and therefore everyone is her descendant (Wells, 2002).

The Birth of Mitochondrial Eve

Alan Wilson is an Australian biochemist who was working specifically on an ingenious method of studying molecular biology at the University of California, Berkley. Using the previous information gleaned from the studies of Dr. Zuckerkandl and Dr. Pauly, Wilson and his students devised a method to accurately identify the date of the split between the lesser primates and man (Wells, 2002). Their continued research subsequently devised a method for pinpointing a considerably more accurate date and place for the origin of man.

Drs. Zuckerkandl and Pauling and Drs. Gilbert and Sanger in the mid-seventies, and independent of each other, discovered the technique for rapidly sequencing DNA. All four shared the Noble Prize, but the relative simplicity of the new process started a firestorm of DNA research.

This new discovery allowed Wilson and his staff to investigate the inner workings of human chromosomes and their parental combination to form a human offspring. Humans have 23 pairs of chromosomes. When the egg is fertilized, it receives a strand of 23 each from the mother and father. However, before receiving the chromosomes from the parents, the 23 donated from each parent morph, forming chromosome and gene differences exclusive of their parents. They are called polymorphisms. Wells describes the process as a series of photocopies with minor mistakes in each copy. The more you copy, the more and more profound the mistake. By the tine you finish one has a reasonable facsimile, but profoundly different from the original. That is why everyone has a unique fingerprint. Even identical twins are not totally identical.

In addition, this unique phenomenon allows for Darwin's natural selection, because these morphisms are adjustments to environment and may become dominant characteristics after several generations (Wells, 2002). Let us understand that mitochondrion has its own genome located outside of the nucleus of each cell. The polymorphisms, or genetic changes, are easier to track, because they are spaced every 100 genes, so the changes are easily identifiable. In addition, mitochondrial DNA (mtDNA) is specific to the female chromosomes and is passed from mother to daughter. Rebeca Cann, a research assistant of Wilson's, began a study of the pattern of mtDNA variations around the world by collecting the human placentas of women of different races and nationalities: Europeans, New Guineans, Native Americans, Africans, etc. Placentas are rich in mtDNA, and their study found that all of the different mtDNA stems from one woman who is thought to have existed approximately 200,000 years ago in Africa (Wells, 2002). What was interesting is that the greatest variation between mtDNA existed among Africans, which showed that they had been diverging longer. According to the data, Africans are the oldest group on earth. By DNA analysis, the data validates that our species originated in Africa from a single common ancestor. Through several hundred years of migration, environmental influence, and natural polymorphism, the resulting "races" have changed phenotypically to the degree that they do not resemble their original "mitochondrial parents." Well's example is analogous to a stone thrown into a pond. The ripples move further and further away and change, never again to resemble the original splash. The analogy seems to indicate that we are vastly different; however, we will learn later in the discussion that 85% of our human genomes are identical with the polymorphisms being the primary differences and accounting for the remaining 15%. In spite of our many visual differences, we are truly "colorless men."

What about the Brother's? Why the "Y" is Important ━━━━━

Before we discuss the significance of the "Y" chromosome, let us clarify the importance of polymorphisms and how they contribute to the diversity of the human species. Polymorphisms literally mean many changes. As identified earlier, when the parental genome forms the zygotic genome, the parental chromosomes morph slightly before forming the zygote offspring. The changes form a completely unique individual. The human genome for all races and ethnicities is 85% identical, and the remaining deviations are due to these polymorphisms. This ability is a safety valve that allows for the adjustment of environmental conditions and trauma, tacitly validating Darwin's theory of natural selection.

To be more specific, humans have a total of 46 chromosomes, two sets of 23. The gender chromosomes for each pair in the female are both X. However, the male has one strand of chromosomes with a female chromosome X and one strand with the male chromosome Y. When they combine, not only do they morph at approximately every 100 places, but upon combination there is a 50:50 chance that X will combine with X, forming a female zygote. If the female gender chromosome X combines with the male chromosome Y, a male zygote will form. That is how the baby's gender is determined. Simplified, when the two X chromosomes combine, forming a female, they combine uniformly along the continuum. In contrast, when the male chromosomes swap, the *autosomes*, chromosomes other than the gender chromosomes, combine uniformly along the continuum except for the gender chromosomes of X and Y. The male chromosomes only combine at both ends, forming a male zygote (Pseudoautoautosomal regions). This makes the male "Y" chromosome uniquely traceable.

Before going further, let us clarify the uniqueness and mechanics of polymorphism. Chromosomes are mainly composed of DNA, which are the building blocks and the genetic map of the formation and foundation of all life, flora and fauna. There are four primary human DNA proteins called nucleotides. These proteins are classified by letters: (A) adenine, (T) thymine, (C) cytosine, and (G) guanine. These letters are readable and help us discover our personal and corporate genetic development. The male gender chromosomes, because of the XY combination, do not exchange letters except at the pseudoautosomal regions or ends. Again, the uniqueness makes each "Y" chromosome special and traceable (Bradman & Thomas, 1998).

To be more specific, the polymorphisms are classified into four categories: indels, snips, microsatellites, and minisatellites. Indels are insertions of the DNA at specific locations on the DNA chromosome. Snips are "single nucleotide polymorphisms." Microsatellites are short groups or sequences of nucleotides repeated over and over again in tandem. The number of repeats in an area on a chromosome, allele, usually remains unchanged from generation to generation, which in most cases is also easily traceable. The fourth category polymorphisms are minisatellites. Minisatellites are larger and more defined, contrary to the microsatellites that are 3-4 nucleotided. The minisatellites are 10-60 base pairs, and the number of repeats may be several dozen (Bradman & Thomas, 1998).

The wonderful difference of the polymorphisms' change over time is that the chronological differences allow us to track the date of the changes. Therefore, science is able to determine time, place, frequency of migration, and genetic change. The advances in DNA research now allow scientists to track where, when, and possibly how the human species became diversified phenotypically and regionally with some degree of accuracy. Underneath the cosmetic differences caused by God's genetic changes, we are all identical and made in His image. Our physical theoanthropological relationship is confirmed by our own anthropocentric scientific acumen. *"And God said, 'Let us make man in our image, after our likeness'"* (Genesis 2:26). Genetics define the theoanthropological relationship that each human has with God and the diversity of mankind. We all are made in Christ's physical image and the Father's spiritual image, therefore genetically and spiritually identical with the exception of the phenotypical variations. If God is also love, then we have the capacity to love like Him. The decision to choose is also a divine characteristic. Racism, *xenophobia*, *jingoism* are attitudinal choices. We have the divine capacity to choose to be "colorless men." What is your choice?

What is Your Pedigree?

Understanding that all of mankind is 85% identical and the remaining 15% is contributed to mitochondrial and "Y" chromosome polymorphism, how did we end up "out of Africa" in many places and myriad looks? Please remember, one of the primary functions of polymorphism is the phenomenon that allows genes to morph in response to environmental conditions and the challenging survival process of Darwin's natural selection. As the humans migrated farther from the African human epicenter, the necessity for adaptation increased, ergo, polymorphism and genetic change.

The analogy illustrated by Spencer Wells describing the tossing of a stone into a pond is a good example. The original splash has little resemblance to the outermost ripples. Similarly, the size and the intensity of the ripples change as the frequency of the ripples increases (Wells, 2003).

Francis Cress Welsing, in her book *The Isis Papers*, posits her theory that the white race developed from African albinos who, because of their lack of melanin, migrated north, seeking a less tropical, sun-rich climate. As a result, and perhaps over several generations of polymorphic mutations, they developed long hair for warmth, narrow noses because of the less humid air, and fair skin because of the lesser sun intensity.

In addition to all humans having the M168 gene, the greatest numbers of polymorphic changes occur in Africa, which validates that all life originated there. Scientists have been able to track the sequence and position of the outward polymorphic ripples (Wells 2003). An interesting, but not particularly relevant "Did You Know," is that of the "Hot in Tot"/ Bushman South African tribe's women have an especially distinctive characteristic. Their glutei maximi are large and sit high and round on their backs. The irony of the matter is that a Russian czar became so overwhelmingly enthralled with one of their women that he married and made her queen. Her derriere was so attractive to the Russian populace, the *bustell* was invented to compensate for the lack of voluptuousness of the Russian women. Stenophigia contributed to the fashion of the Victorian period in Europe and America and is a prevalent physical characteristic in African American women today. Viva genetic heritage and polymorphism.

The ability to trace, track, and tabulate polymorphic occurrences has given scientists the ability to date, locate, and calculate the arrival of man in specific locations of the world. Henry Harpending, an anthropologist at Pennsylvania State University, with his colleagues conducted a study that scientifically validates congruent dates when mankind began migrating out of Africa with the beginning of the Upper Paleolithic epoch. The Upper Paleolithic era is the third and final period of the Old Stone Age. Humans (i.e., *Homo sapiens*) are understood to have emerged circa 130,000 years ago in Africa. However, this humanlike species were kin to the hominid Neanderthal man, whose remains were found in the Neander Valley in West Germany. Neanderthals were a local, extremely primitive population specific to the area. In addition, they were believed to have never come in contact with the African modern man of circa 50,000 B.C. (Wells, 2002, pp. 92-93). The Neanderthals and early *Homo sapiens* were tacitly not modern humans.

"The Great Leap Forward"

God said, "Let us create Man"

It gets spiritually interesting now. The "Great Leap" was a period in the Upper Palaeolithic epoch when man made exponential growth in human development. Humans unexplainably began to develop tools, master the use of fire, and the first remnants of art appear.

For example, human artifacts could be sorted into several different categories, i.e., projectile points, engraving tools, knife blades, drilling tools, piercing tools, and a variety of others. At the same time "modern man" was experiencing a period of rapid growth, Neanderthals simultaneously, mysteriously vanished. Modern man's tools are significantly different and more refined than the primitive instruments used by the now extinct Neanderthals. The modern man, or Cro-Magnons, formed settlements, and they are even thought to have begun domesticating animals.

Harpending and his staff analyzed their data from several worldwide populations and the results indicated that exponential growth began circa 50,000 to 60,000 years, with the growth beginning in Africa. In addition, the populations seemed to have expanded almost independently of each other. Africa was the leader (60,000 yrs. ago), followed by Asia (50,000 yrs. ago) and Europe (30,000 yrs. ago). The dates are perfectly congruent with the "Great Leap."

As a point of conjecture, let us speculate that the Neanderthals and all hominid species are not considered human. Perhaps God was experimenting with humankind before the final product. Scripture says that God spoke the universe and mankind into existence. *"In the beginning God created the heavens and the earth. And the earth was without form, and void; and darkness was upon the face of the deep. And God said, let there be light: and there was light. And God saw the light, that it was good: and God divided the light from the darkness...And God called the dry land Earth; and the gathering together of the waters called he Seas" (Genesis 1-10).* When one examines the scientific points of *Darwin's Theory of Evolution and Natural Selection* in conjunction with the latest data in reference to the origin of man, the two can theoretically exist in harmony. The *hominids* essentially validate the theory of evolution. Creationism (the Bible) is validated by the most recent DNA research.

This speculative position is also consistent with Ockham's razor, which says that the least complicated path is most likely correct. God's way is most times the simplest. The problem with man is that we consistently try to make ourselves the center of the universe, instead of God. *Paul says, "Beware least any man spoil you through philosophy and vain deceit, after the tradition of men, after rudiments of the world, and not after Christ (Colossians 2:8).* Understanding who we are requires faith in God and the belief in his divine sacrifice that allows God to be the center of one's existence and the universe. *"For God so loved the world, that He gave His only begotten Son that whosoever believeth in Him should not perish, but have everlasting life" (John 3:16).*

Man's Achilles' heel lies in scientific belief that everything has a cause and effect, which precludes God from being a sovereign entity. God has no cause. He is completely sovereign. Gordon Clark distills God's creation into three distinct possibilities. First, God is caused. If God is caused, there must be a causal entity. If that is so, then God is not sovereign and cannot be God. Second, God caused Himself. That is physically impossible. For God to cause Himself would violate the first law of thermodynamics. If one does not exist, then one cannot cause Himself. Matter cannot just "pop up." Finally, God is uncaused. God just exists. To an empiricist that is unfathomable. However, God confirms this to Moses when Moses asks God, *"When I come unto the children of Israel, and shall say unto them, The God of your fathers hath sent me, what is thy name? What shall I say?" (Exodus 3:3).* God responded, *"I AM THAT I AM."* God was not trying to be flippant. God was simply telling Moses you cannot box me in. To name God would be to consider God finite. *"I AM THAT I AM."* It is not likely, but perhaps God is unable to explain His existence? Certainly appears that way. However, we continue to try to justify, evaluate, and legitimize God using our limited finite facilities. A finite being cannot understand an infinite being. Therefore, man's arrogance and limited intellect limits one from knowing God, or developing a theoanthropologic relationship. We must know God by way of His son Jesus the Christ. *John 14:6 says, "Jesus saith unto him, I am the way, the truth, and the life: no man cometh unto the Father, but by me."* As long as man is arrogant to the point that he thinks that his intellect is comparative to God's infinite intellect, we will continue to be confused and lost. Blaise Pascal said, "Human beings must be known to be loved: but God must be loved to be known."

There is no dichotomy between science and God. It a nefarious evil illusion created by the enemy to trick humanity into spiritual defeat. Even Albert Einstein, the world's quintessential paragon of scientific mastery, believed that God was the creator of heaven and earth. Einstein's Theory of Relativity $E = mc^2$, imply theorized, and now is confirmed by quantum physics, that time and space are "warped" outside the gravitational pull of the earth. An example is the term "warp" time used generously in the '70s T.V. series and movie *Star Trek*. To further explain: In the absence of gravity, time and mass "warp" or change. A simplistic example is that if it required ten units of energy to walk across your room, outside of gravity it may take that same amount of energy to travel from Earth to Pluto and back. Chronologically, it may only require two years of space travel time to reach Pluto and return; however, 20 years may have elapsed according to Earth time. There is a difference between (Gk. kronos) and (Gk. kiros) time. Kronos time is Earth's finite time, and kiros time is God's time. God's time is eternal, meaning from whatever was the beginning time to whatever is the end time may be. God operates along this incomprehensible continuum simultaneously, which allows God to affect His ubiquitous nature. God's ability to be everywhere at the same time allows Him to effect all time along this kiros continuum. The concept is unimaginably difficult for the human mind to synthesize. Simply stated, God's time seems akin to time minus gravity.

Moreover, Einstein, before he died, was working on what he named "The Universal Field Theory." Initially, he was trying to show that the truths of physics were perfectly congruent with the truths of mathematics. Einstein was a religious man, and rumor has it that his ultimate goal was that God's truths were synonymous with scientific truths. One of his most revealing religious quotes is, *"Science without religion is lame. Religion without science is blind."*

Scientists are skeptical of the Bible, but Einstein's theory validates the following scriptures. *2 Peter 3:9 says "that one day is with the Lord as a thousand years, and a thousand years as one day."* Also, *Isaiah 40:22 says, "It is He that sitteth upon the circle of the earth, and the inhabitants thereof are as grasshoppers; that stretcheth out the heavens as a curtain, and spreadeth them out as a tent to dwell in."* Our environment is anthropic, meaning especially designed for human existence. For example, if the earth deviated from its specifically calibrated orbit less than an inch either way, the earth would burn up or completely freeze over. What keeps the seas from stagnating is the natural phenomena call the *thermohaline* flow of the oceans. In addition, as the moon orbits around the Earth in an *elliptical* orbit, moving simultaneously with the Earth's rotation on its axis, the moon's distance from the Earth varies. As the distance changes, so does the gravitational pull of the moon. As the pull changes, the gravitational pull alters the flow of the oceans and forms the *ebb tides* of the Earth's waters. The phenomenon literally washes the ocean's waters back and forth across the Earth's surface, which keeps our oceans from stagnating and the Earth fresh.

Our air without human pollution is the perfect combination of gases, and is in perfect harmony with the flora and fauna of the world. Land-dwelling animals including humans inhale oxygen and exhale carbon dioxide. There is a perfect symbiotic relationship between plants and animals. Plants absorb carbon dioxide and give off oxygen, animals absorb oxygen and give off carbon dioxide— perfect harmony. How could one think this is coincidental and not of perfect design from an infinite, perfect, and divine mind? *"For my thoughts are not your thoughts, neither are your ways my ways, saith the Lord. For as the heavens are higher than the earth, so are my ways higher than yours, and my thoughts than your thoughts. For as the rain cometh down, and the snow from heaven, and returneth not thither, but watereth the earth, and maketh it bring forth and bud, that it may give seed to the sower, and bread to the eater"* (Isaiah 55:8-10). The previous scriptures give perfect meaning to the definition of the word anthropic.

"The Big Bang": God's Thunderous Voice ━━━━━━━

The most recent theory is that our universe was formed from a "Big Boom." This theory posits that a random massive thermonuclear explosion created the universe we previously described. The "Big Bang" theory attempts to convince us that atoms came mysteriously together, "rubbed" up against each other, and created enough heat to explode and form the many massive planets and stars that form our universe. To continue, the contemporary scientific minds of today consider the "Big Bang" theory as an acceptable explanation for the creation of the universe, which is not antithetical to creationism. Thomas D. Williams states in his book Greater Than You Think, "The 'Big Bang' theory cries out for a divine explanation" (Williams, T., 2008). To satisfy the scientific community, there needs to be a cause for the "Big Bang." The Bible says that "In the beginning God created the heavens and the earth. And the earth was without form, and void; and darkness was upon the face of the deep. And the Spirit of God moved upon the face of the waters. And God said. Let there be light: and there was light. And God saw that light, that it was good: and God divided the light from the darkness" (Genesis 1:1-4). The previous Bible verse infers that God spoke the world into existence. Therefore, God's Word explains the "Big Bang" and satisfies the scientific need for causality. These Bible verses may give further clarity. "At this also my heart trembleth, and is moved out of His place. Hear attentively the noise of His voice, and the sounds that goeth out of His mouth. He directeth it under the whole heaven, and His lightings unto the ends of the earth. After it a voice roareth: He thundereth with the voice of His excellency; and He will not stay them when His voice is heard. God thundereth marvelously with His voice; great things doeth He, which we cannot" (Job 37:3). That says it all. Robert Jastrow writes that "the astronomical and Biblical accounts of Genesis are the same; the chain of events leading to man commenced suddenly and sharply at a definite moment in time, in a flash of light and energy." The two accounts, scientific and biblical, are congruent (Jastrow, R., 1992). Also, Nobel Prize winner

Arno Penzias' biblical support is reflected in his statement, "The best data we have are exactly what I would have predicted, had I nothing to go on but the five books of Moses, the Psalms, and the Bible as a whole" (Penzias, A., 1978).

In addition, without intelligent design, every one of the Earth's anthropic conditions was created by chance. Scientists expect us to believe that this happened *ex nihilo* or out of nothing. The irony of the entire discussion between the "Big Bangers" and the creationists is that the proponents of the "Big Bang" theory expect us to accept their fairy tale, while calling the Holy Bible an interesting story written by delusional prophets.

To further extrapolate, Fred Hoyle, an astronomer, calculated that the chance of DNA assembling by chance is one in 10 to the power of 40,000 (Hoyle, F., 1981). Hoyle said, "That the probably of life originating on earth is no greater than the chance that a hurricane, sweeping through a scrap yard, would have the luck to assemble a Boeing 747" (Dawkins, 2006). Similarly, mathematician Rodger Penrose estimated that the probability of our universe being randomly formed with its particular physical properties is one part in 10, first to the exponential power of 10 and then to the power of 123 (Penrose, R., 1989). Whoever can compute that number will require Einstein's 225-point I.Q. However, you can be certain it's pretty small. To make it clearer, begin with the primary number (1) and divide it in half 30,000 consecutive times. Your concluding number is a reasonably accurate probability of the possibility of our universe forming randomly. In its frustrating attempt, science would rather foster spurious and specious information rather than to acknowledge God's sovereignty. Some of history's greatest scientists—Newton, Pasteur, Galilei, Lavoisier, Kepler, Copernicus, Faraday, Maxwell, Bernard, and Heisenberg—were all Christians (Williams, 2008, p. 82).

America Morphs

Earlier in Chapter 1 we discussed the polymorphic tendencies of the human DNA molecule, specifically the process of fertilization when the reproductive chromosomes combine to form the zygote. To maintain the uniqueness and diversity of future generations, with the ability to adapt to environmental change, there are a total of 30 genes that morph randomly. The issue of racism in America is much like the chromosomal process of morphing.

In October 1562, the African American Holocaust began when the first slave ship arrived on these shores. The ignominious passage of America's first African slaves was ironically booked on a ship named *The Good Ship Jesus*. John Hawkins, the captain and a Christian with a little "c," brought the slaves from Sierra Leone, which subsequently became a hub of the Atlantic slave trade. From its beginning in 1562 until 1865, when the 13th amendment was passed, this country was mired in slavery and brutal American apartheid. Slaves were treated as chattel, a movable possession. During that period, most non-Africans favored slavery or were ambivalent to its existence. However, during that 302 year period, small sociological morphs were taking place contrary to the established anathema of accepted human bondage. The Religious Society of Friends, formally known now as the Quakers, was an egalitarian group who favored equal rights and gender equality. In the early 1700s John Wollman, a Quaker preacher, convinced the denomination to become abolitionists. They became instrumental in setting up the "Underground Railroad" and maintaining it in the northern states, especially Philadelphia and Pennsylvania. The northern Methodists were especially involved in the abolitionist movement. Led by Lucius C. Matlack, the northern Methodists were so adamant about the abolition of slavery that it led to a schism between the northern and southern Methodists.

Perhaps three of the more profound morphs were the aborted slave rebellions by Gabrial Prosser on August 30, 1800, and Denmark Vessy on July 14, 1822, followed by the successful revolt of Reverend Nat Turner on August 20, 1831. The most violent abolitionist was John Brown, the white son of an Ohio frontier man. Brown actually formed a militia funded from northern sympathizers. Slave   and plantation owners feared John Brown for his violent aggressive raids in freeing slaves in the South and Midwest.

Let us not forget Harriet Tubman, a six-foot pistol-packing woman, who after her escape from bondage, escorted more than 300 slaves to freedom and served as a Civil War nurse. Another tireless female sojourner for abolition was Sojourner Truth, a former slave, who because of a divine anointing suffered great pain, hardship, and danger in her tireless efforts to rid America of the bondage of slavery. National attitudes also changed because of the heroic fighting men of the 54th who sacrificed their lives in the Civil War. Please remember the character, determination, and courage displayed by many black soldiers who fought in our World Wars. They are all examples of metaphoric polymorphisms that deviated from the spurious negative stereotype of Africans. Under great opposition, there were presidents who made limited contributions to the abolishment of slavery and racism. The most noted were Lincoln, Roosevelt, Kennedy, and Lyndon Johnson, who signed the Civil Rights Act of 1964.

There are countless African American heroes and heroines. Perhaps the most famous include Thurgood Marshall, Rosa Parks, Irean Morgan, and especially Megar Evers, Martin and Malcolm, who made the ultimate sacrifice. The litany is endless. Moreover, it is an injustice to try to name everyone, because the most effective soldiers for the cause are little known or unknown. Thousands of Americans of all ethnicities sacrificed to produce these changes in the nation's racial attitude. It is the consistency of the divine spirit of freedom that produced these innumerable socially genetic morphs. They all contributed to the present American genome of liberty, and birthed an America that would support a black man in his bid for the presidency of these United States. *"But God Hath chosen the foolish things of the world to confound the wise; and God hath chosen the weak things of the world to confound the things which are mighty; And the base things of the world, and things which are despised, hath God chosen, yea, and things which are not, to bring to nought things that are."* God does not lie. Obama is the culmination and amalgamation of former colorless men. However, like every one of God's believing children who strive for ultimate good, one must expect attacks from the ultimate evil.

When we pause to look at where the attacks emanate, it should be no surprise. The attacks are from the media, our communicative airways. It is no wonder that the prince of the air is Satan. *"Wherein in time past ye walked according to the course of this world, according to the power of the air, the spirit that now worketh in the children of disobedience"* (Ephesians 2:2). However, God's Word says, *"No weapon formed against thee shall prosper; and every tongue that shall rise against thee in judgment thou shalt condemn. This is the heritage of the servants of the Lord, and their righteousness is of me, saith the Lord"* (Isaiah 54:170).

Speaking of weapons, this may be the greatest day in America. Today, June 3, 2008, Barack Obama secured the Democratic Party's nomination for the president of the United States of America. This is an epic milestone in American history, despite the frivolous attacks of the media and Obama's less than gracious opponents. The media attacked Mr. Obama for what his former pastor, the Rev. Jeremiah Wright of Trinity United Church of Christ, said from his pulpit ten years prior. The media, with obvious nefarious intent, colored the preacher's intended meaning by taking his words out of context. When that settled, after about a month of senseless "hype," the media attacked the comments of Rev. Michael Pfleger, the controversial and outspoken pastor of a predominately Catholic African American church, for his words spoken from the same pulpit. In my opinion, his comments were accurate and not deserving of the subsequent reprimand and punishment he received from his superiors.

What is flagrantly clear is the obvious lack of attention given by the media to the faux pas of other candidates. For example, John McCain's reference to the Vietnamese as "gooks" got little attention. Perhaps Hillary Clinton's lies concerning being under fire in Bosnia is not as critical a mistake as unsolicited comments by your former pastor spoken several years prior? Remember the media and Ephesians 2:2.

Theoanthropology is not religion. It is the spiritual relationship one has with God. Religion is empty doctrine and useless tradition, whereas theoanthropology is relationship with God through the Holy Spirit and Christ. How can one know when a person is theoanthropologic? *"Yea, a man may say, Thou hast faith, and I have works: show me thy faith without thy works, and I will show thee my faith by my works."* Unlike Mr. McCain and Mrs. Clinton, Mr. Obama has maintained the high road and has refused to sink to negative campaigning a la his opponents. When Mr. Obama had a clear opportunity to take advantage of an opportunity to crush Mrs. Clinton in their final debate, he declined to do so.

Perhaps you saw the debate. They were allowing videotaped questions to be asked of Mrs. Clinton and Mr. Obama. Mrs. Clinton was queried concerning her exposed lie concerning her alleged attack in Bosnia. She answered with a canned response. When Mr. Obama was asked his opinion he responded, and I paraphrase, "Everyone makes mistakes and misspeaks from time to time," and he suggested that we stay with the political issues. After picking myself up and off of my floor in shock at the opportunity he let pass, the magnitude of this man's character became gloriously apparent. If you recall, only a few weeks earlier there was a Clinton ad that asked whom you would want to answer the phone at three o'clock in the morning in reference to the safety of America. A crushing response by Mr. Obama would have been, "In light of the recent disclosures concerning Mrs. Clinton's truthfulness," would you feel safer with my alleged inexperience or her confirmed tendency for untruthfulness? That was a magnanimous example of his integrity. Senator Obama has written several books. One who has written one book knows that manuscripts are scrupulously proofread and each word is measured before printing. Without question, Mrs. Clinton knew exactly what she was writing and selling to the public.

After displaying my anger at Senator Obama's apparent lack of aggression, and mentioning to my wife that the right Reverend Dr. Gregory G. Ogle would have put her "feet to the fire," my wife made a profound statement. She very simply said, "That is why he is running for president and you are not." Wives can be a real pain, but she was right! Perhaps my theoanthropologic attitude needs a slight adjustment? Obama is a special man. We can tell by his behavior and his divine desire to strive for ethical correctness and trueness to his word. Obama is divinely and timely placed in history. If he is true, as suspected, his election as president can begin to heal this country and the world. Pray that the colorless man lives.

For Further Discussion

1. Considering the information above, what do you think about the genetic homogeneity of the "races"?

2. Does the "Big Boom" theory make sense to you? Please explain.

References

Bradman, Neil & Thomas, Mark (1998). "Why Y? The Y Chromosome in the study of Human Evolution, Migration and Prehistory." Center for Genetic Anthropology at University College, London. http://www.ucl.ac.uk/tcga/ScienceSpectra-pages/SciSpect-14-98

Colson, Charles (2001). *Science and Evolution*. Tyndale House Publishing, Inc. Wheaton, Illinois 60189.

Dawkins, Richard (2006). *The God Delusion*. New York: Houghton Mifflin. p. 36.

Freire, P. (1993). *Pedagogy of the Oppressed*. The Continuum International Publishing Group, Ltd. Tower Building, 11 York Road, London SEI 7NX.

Hoyle, F & Wickramasingle, C. (1981). *Evolution from Space*. J. M. Dent.

Holy Bible, King James Version.

Crenshaw, K., Gotanda, N., Peller, G., Kendall, T. (1995). *Critical Race Theory*. "A Critique of Constitution is Color Blind" New Rose

Press, New York, New York. pp. 258-260.

Hacker, A. (1992). *Two Nations*. First Scriber Publishing, 1230 Avenue of the Americas. New York, New York 10020.

Jastrow, Robert (1992). *God and the Astronomers*. New York: W. W. Norton, 1992. p. 14.

Penrose, Roger (1989). *The Emperor's New Mind: Concerning Computers, Minds, and the Laws of Physics*. Oxford: Oxford University Press.

Penzias, Arno (1978). Quoted in M. Browme's *Clues to the Universe's Origins Expected. New York Times*, March 12, 1978. Cited by Francis Collins in *Language of God*, p. 76.

Wells, Spencer (2003). *The Journey of Man a Genetic Odyssey*. New York, Random House Publishers.

West, C. (1982). *Prophesy Deliverance an Afro-American Revolutionary. Christianity*. Philadelphia, Pennsylvania. Westminster Press.

Williams, Thomas (2008). *Greater Than You Think: A Theologian Answers the Atheists About God*. Faith Words Hachette Book Group USA. 237 Park Avenue New York, NY 10017. p. 75.

Williams, Thomas (2008). *Greater Than You Think: A Theologian Answers the Atheists About God*. Faith Words Hachette Book Group USA. 237 Park Avenue New York, NY 10017. p. 82.

Glossary

Acumen - the keenness and quickness of mind or intellectual ability

Anthropic - an environment especially suited for the existence of man

Anthropocentric - considers man as the central figure in the universe

Autosome - any chromosome other than a gender chromosome

Chromosome - threadlike cellular structure that carries the genetic information in the form of genes

Cupidity - greed

Darwin's Theory of Evolution and Natural Selection - the belief that all life formed from the beginnings of single cell life; Natural Selection - the stronger and wiser are naturally selected and because of this will survive environmental harshness

Ebb Tides - the in and out flow of the oceans of the world

Elliptical - the oval shape

Empirical - the science of observation through controlled experimentation

E pluribus Unum - Latin phrase meaning "out of one many, or we are all in this together"

Eugenics - the science of improving the human population by controlling inherited characteristics

Ex Nihilo - formed out of nothing

Gamete - a reproductive cell that can unite with a similar one that can form into a new individual

Homogeneity - of the same kind

Hominid - an underdeveloped prehistoric, humanlike primate

Jingoism - fear of women and people of different nationalities

Mesomorph - person with a compact muscular body

Miscegenation - interbreeding of races, especially of whites and non-whites

Nucleotide - special proteins which comprise a portion of DNA

Phenotypic - the normal physical characteristics of the body, especially the face

Phrenology - the study of the size of the cranium as a supposed indicator of character and mental facilities

Pseudoautosomal - the ends of the male chromosomes that combine; the ends of the male X and Y chromosomes

Sovereign - supreme ruler, independent of all outside influence

Specious - plausible but wrong information

Theoanthropology - the spiritual relationship between God and man, more specifically the spiritual awareness of God in man. It is the "knowing God" in contrast to "knowing of God." Pascal said, "Men must be known to be loved; God must be loved to be known."

Thermohaline - the flow of the oceans and seas of the earth

Xenophobic - the fear/hate of people of different nationalities

Zygote - any union of two gametes

"Having a form of Godliness, but denying the power thereof; from such turn away." (2 Timothy 3:5)

"Beware of false prophets, which come to you in sheep's clothing, but inwardly they are raving wolves." (Matthew 7:14)

"Ye shall know them by their fruits." (Matthew 7:14)

"Even so every good tree bringeth forth good fruit; but a corrupt tree bringeth forth evil fruit." (Matthew 7:15)

Why Does America and the World Need a Colorless Man?

"But God hath chosen the foolish things of the world to confound the wise; and God hath chosen the weak things of the world to confound the things which are mighty. And base things of the world, and things despised, hath God chosen, yea, and things which are not, to bring to naught things that are" (I Co 1:27).

As mentioned in the introduction, Barack Obama is our living metaphor for the colorless man. The colorful colorless designation is a perfect oxymoron in that he is a man of color but his parentage is mixed. The black washes the white—ergo, colorless. Obama is the perfect African American. His father is Kenyan and his mother is a white American. Several have challenged his "classification" as African American, but who better qualifies?

He is supremely experienced in domestic issues, and contrary to the prevailing rhetoric, understands international affairs better than he is given credit. If Obama was not African American and looked upon in the classic African American position of pajority, his international experience would not be questioned. To this point, the leading candidates, both Hillary Clinton and John McCain, displayed class and character by the limited playing of the "race card." However, Obama's persona and impeccably positive campaign does not allow for the easy intervention of negative racial or bigoted discussion. We will see if the race card remains mute.

In the midst of many scurrilous attacks on his character, Obama remained steadfast in his refusal to acquiesce to the pressure of negative political ads and negative conversation. Remaining ethical at all costs is what the colorless man will always strive to accomplish. His apparent naiveté is actually a positive characteristic, because it gives merit to his not being a part of the "business as usual" domestic and international political loop. Let us examine America's present domestic and international position.

Unfortunately, there are vast numbers of critical problems vexing our world. The crises range from economic complexities, environmental concerns, religious and ethnic wars, and diseases that threaten us with distinction. The global threat is compounded by hate, social oppression, and imperialism. The travesties are manifested in the behavior displayed by the many evil demagogues and despotic leaders, greedy corporations, and power-hungry leaders who are willing to sacrifice the world for their greedy gain. This *cupidity* goes relatively unnoticed by the American people because of the layperson's constant pressure for survival. There are C.E.O.s in this country whose annual salary is in excess of $500,000,000, while the *proletariat*, or middle class, is earning a mere $25,000 to $50,000 and trying to support a family of four. Let us not consider college tuition.

We are rapidly losing the middle class as evidenced by George Stephanopoulos' question to Hillary Clinton and Barack Obama concerning taxes. Stephanopoulos referenced the middle class as earning between $97,000 and $250,000 per year. Perhaps Mr. Stephanopoulos is a little out of touch? This country is becoming a population of the "haves and the have nots." There is a significant population in this country who live at the level of destitution. All of their resources have been exhausted. Some are living on the streets; some are living with their families, some in their cars and in shelters. They are the *lupenproletariat* or working poor, Americans who are minimally employed for various reasons. The sad reality is that a considerable majority of these Americans are suffering undeserved consequences. Their slumbers were soothed by the images of the American Dream, but they awakened to the American Nightmare.

America's malignancy will continue to fester until we are shocked out of our spiraling descending ethical standards. A racial divide shackles America and drowns our nation in bigotry, classicism, and gender bias. It is sinful hate and cruelty. Hate and cruelty seem to be the rule, not the exception. At present, The Top Ten List of the World's Worst Dictators for 2007 is a litany of evil. Heading the list is Kim Jong-il, the notorious dictator of North Korea. He is most notable for his possession and testing of nuclear weapons, but his domestic abuses are *nefariously* legendary. Kim Jong-il purposefully isolates his citizenry from the remainder of the world to keep them ignorant. This allows him to use his dogma and *patriarchic* persona to rule North Korea. He may appear to be a weirdo, a joke, or cartoon, but please do not let the *animatronics* fool you. He was trained by his father, and is a well-educated and competent politician who wields complete and brutal power. Number two on our list of infamy is the supremely savage Omar al-Bashir, who orchestrated the brutal genocide in Darfur, Sedan. Over the last five years, an excess of 500,000 people have been killed in addition to 5.3 million who have been driven from their homes. Number three on our index of infamy is Than Shwe, the dictator of Burma (Myanmar), who is a more recent top "fiver," with a bullet and rising to the top. His social policies are similar to those of Kim Jong-il; perhaps less clandestine but equally as brutal. This year Shwe ordered the firing into a crowd of protesting Buddhist monks and ordered the detaining and torture of several hundred more. Number four is most interesting, the sadistic Saudi, King Abdullah of Saudi Arabia. There are several interesting things about King Abdullah. His country has been deemed one of the top offenders of religious freedom in the world. The king is anti-Christian and anti-Semitic. Women in his country have been stoned to death for simply being accused of adultery, and recently there have been reports of men being hanged for homosexuality. Rounding out the top ten are:

5. Hue Jintao, China
   Controls all media and represses religion

6. Robert Mugabe, Zimbabwe
   Unemployment high, food supplies low

7. Sayyid Ali Khamenei, Iran
   Officials carry out public hangings

8. Pervez Musharraf, Pakistan
   Suspended Pakistan's constitution

9. Islam Karimov, Uzbekistan
   Government engages in torture of its citizens.

10. Isayas Afewerki, Eritrea
    No national election, no constitution (The World's Worst Dictators, 2008).

Most interesting is the relationship Saudi Arabia has with the Bush family. Saudi Arabia is a suspected haven for several terrorist groups and the home and family base of Osama bin Laden. Some "suspect" that Saudi Arabia trains and harbors international terrorists, yet America remains its ally. Why? Because Saudi Arabia is the leader and heaviest influencer of the Organization of Petroleum Exporting Countries, O.P.E.C. Who has ties to Saudi Arabian oil, and the presidents Bush? It is documented with relative accuracy that the Bushes have personal and business ties to the bin Laden family through at least two organizations that are known to have funded Osama bin Laden's terrorist group. Perhaps the most infamous is the Bank of Commerce and Credit International (BCCI). The BCCI is known to have defrauded depositors of $10 billion in the late 1980s in what many called the largest bank fraud in world financial history. The second is the Carlyle Group, an investment group that specializes in the buyouts of defense and aerospace companies.

Former president George H. W. Bush, representing the Carlyle Group in a 1981 trip to Saudi Arabia, met with King Fahd and the bin Laden family to establish a mutually beneficial relationship between the three. Tacitly, when the Carlyle Group makes money, so does the bin Laden family. Is there monitoring of the clients to whom the Carlyle Group sells arms? Could it be that the Bush family business investments are supplying, or did supply, arms to our enemies? His grandfather did. Moreover, do any of these arms companies sell goods to countries that support or harbor terrorists? If this is factual, obviously the money would benefit the bin Ladens and potentially Osama.

As expected, the bin Laden family has divorced themselves publicly from Osama. However, James Barth, who was deeply involved in the BCCI scandal, brokered for the Bush and bin Laden families. To further "step in it," Barth also brokered for Khalid bin Mahfouz, a Saudi Arabian banker and BCCI principle. Perhaps it's only a coincidence, but Mahfouz's sister is Osama bin Laden's wife.

Please understand that Osama had already been determined by the C.I.A. to be a "bad man" years before 911. America funded him, trained his men, and hired him as a mercenary to fight successfully for Afghanistan freedom fighters against the Russians. Our government knew that business with Osama was like walking on a razor's edge. We slipped and our gonads were cut off.

Please do not be naive. One must understand that where there is profit, the lines between wrong and right are often blurred and sometimes ignored. A sad litany of ironies: The president who initiated the war on terrorism by attacking a nation who had nothing to do with the 911 attack, the president who knowingly had the world look for the phantom Weapons of Mass Destruction, the president who entered America into a war that took us from a budget surplus of three trillion dollars to a deficit of eleven trillion dollars, the president who contributed to gas prices presently at 4.00 plus, the president who plunged America into an un-winnable war that is killing our young men and women daily, is the same president responsible for the sad, sickening satire that indirectly, and in some cases, directly contributed financially to the terrorist attack that prompted the entire fiasco. Perhaps it is becoming a little clearer why we can't catch bin Laden. There could not be a more interesting novel. It is obviously a quagmire of interesting international intrigue. Don't forget Katrina!

Did you see the movie *Sleeping with the Enemy?* That is not unusual for the Bush family. Prescott Bush, George W's granddaddy, was a Nazi sympathizer. In 1942 Prescott Bush was the managing partner of Brown Brothers Harriman Bank. Prescott's son, the 18-year-old George, the future president of the United States, was training to be a fighter pilot. On October 20, 1942, after Pearl Harbor the United States government seized the banking records of Nazi Germany in New York, which was being personally managed by granddaddy Prescott. The law, Trading with the Enemy Act, was passed specifically for Prescott Bush's arms sales and money laundering operations for the Nazi regime (Tarply & Chaitkin, 1992). The presidents Bushes' relationship to Saudi oil and their suspicious ties to terrorist are hardly surprising considering Prescott Bush's World War II legacy. The Bushes were unscrupulous then and they remain so. Let us not forget how the entire family stole the presidential election from Al Gore.

The interesting element in all of this is that by most international opinions, George Bush is the most hated man in the world. If one were to take an international poll, one might expect President Bush to be atop the most hated list of several Middle Eastern and African countries. Internationally, President Bush may be the most hated American president ever.

On a more auspicious note, Barack Obama today, June 3, 2008, with his win in the Montana Democratic Primary, secured the Democratic nomination for the presidency of the United States of America. Inauspiciously, Hillary Clinton did not give a conciliatory speech in support of Mr. Obama as was expected. It is characteristic of a defeated opponent, who is interested in a victory for their party in the November national election, to offer words of healing and unity. It seems that the Clintons, who have the image in America of being pro-diversity and champions of African Americans, seem to have a different attitude when beaten by a soul brother. Their attitude is congruent with white entitlement, racial subordination, and the privilege of having "ownership of being White" (Cheryl, H., 1995). To synopsize, the "ownership of being White" is the perception of some white folks that their "whiteness" is a possession that entitles them to subordinate those who are not white. Mrs. Clinton's insolence in refusing to graciously concede gives validity to the statements of Rev. Michael Pfleger. Pfleger hit the nail on the head when he said, "Out of nowhere came 'Hey, I'm Barack Obama,' and she said, 'Oh damn, where did you come from? I'm white, I'm entitled. There's a black man stealing my show!'" Pfleger was summarily reprimanded and punished for telling what is now the obvious truth.

More perplexing is who is going to be Mr. Obama's running mate. There was talk of a "dream team" of Obama and Clinton. However, with the attitude and acrimony in this campaign stoked by Mrs. Clinton and her husband, perhaps that would be a mistake, especially with her refusal to gracefully accept Mr. Obama's victory. There is some discussion that Mr. Obama may be considering retired General James Jones. General Jones is a Vietnam War veteran with 40 years military experience. He is the former head of the U.S. and *NATO* (North Atlantic Treaty Organization) forces in Europe. He was the head of the independent commission assigned by Congress to investigate the Iraq war. General Jones retired in 2006. It is also "rumored" that General Jones was asked to retire by the Bush administration for his opposing opinions concerning the Iraq war. General Jones' prognostications were eerily accurate. He anticipated every aspect of the war. The general's choice would quell the misgivings that some voters have with Mr. Obama's perceived lack of international experience and would greatly improve his position with military voters.

Theoanthropology, as discussed earlier, is the relationship believers have with God through the tender, gracious, and redeeming mercies of Christ. In ancient Greek there are three words that Paul uses for redemption. The first is (Gk. agorazo), which means "bought at full market price." Christ did not bargain for our salvation. Christ did not go to a discount store. Christ did not put us on "layaway." Christ did not go to the Dollar Store, K-Mart, Target, or Wal-mart. Christ paid full price with his unblemished life. The second is (Gk. exagorazo), which means "bought at market price but not for resale." The third word is (Gk. apalutrosis), which means "bought at a ransom." Christ paid the price for our kidnapped souls. Believers cannot even sell themselves back into Hell. *"My father, which gave them me, is greater than all; and no man is able to pluck them out of my Father's hand"* (John 10:29). I Peter 2:9 says, *"But ye are a chosen generation, a royal priesthood, a holy nation, a peculiar people: that ye should shew forth the praises of Him who hath called you out of darkness into His marvelous light."* The words "peculiar people" (Gk. peripoiesin, peri- po-ay-sin) are in the genitive or possessive tense and mean " a company of people for my possession. All believers belong to God. We are His special possessions for eternity.

How Can One Discern God's Chosen?

Luke 6:45 reads, *"A good man out of the good treasure of his heart bringeth fourth that which is good; and an evil man out of the evil treasures of his heart bringeth forth that which is evil; for of the abundance of the heart his mouth speaketh."* One can tell an evil man from a good man simply by observing his behavior and listening to him speak. Do not be deceived. Scrutinize the person's deeds. Look at what his/her life has spawned. *"Ye shall know them by their fruits. Even so every good tree bringeth forth good fruit; but a corrupt tree bringeth forth evil fruit."* (Matthew 7:14-15). "People may doubt what you say, but they will always believe what you do" (Lewis Cass, God's Little..., 1994).

For the next several pages we will discuss the nine Fruits of the Spirit, which is located in Galatians 5:22-23 of the Bible: *"But the fruit of the Spirit is love, joy, peace, longsuffering, gentleness, goodness, faith. Meekness, temperance: against such there is no law."* Please understand that the number nine is of extreme importance. The numbers 3 and 7 are God's Holy numbers of perfection and completion; any multiples of these have the identical spiritual significance. Therefore, these gifts are the perfect and complete identifying characteristics of the spiritual and "colorless man." These are the gifts, the *"tells"* that identify a man of God from an imposter.

Often as believers we do not use our spiritual discernment to our full advantage. We ignore the subtle hints that the Holy Spirit provides, and we neglect to study Scripture as diligently as we should. This hobbles us, and the crippling effect makes us vulnerable to negative influences.

Tools to Teach Truth

We will engage in two processes, *exegesis* and *hermeneutics.* Exegesis is the spiritual gathering of scriptural and natural truths that expose the literal meaning of the Bible's text. They may include chronology, language, customs, secular history, religious doctrine, and the personalities of individual characters in the scripture passage. Exegesis contrasts *eisegesis,* which is the personal infusion of the opinions and attitudes of the person doing the research.

Hermeneutics is the culmination and amalgamation of these spiritual and secular truths gathered through exegesis and placed in a package of contemporary understanding. The first hermeneutists were Hebrew scribes: Ezra, Jamin, Serebiah, Azariah, Jeshua, Barni, Hodjah, Maaseiah, Kelita, Jozabad, Hanan, Pelaiah, Akkub, and Shabbethai. These *metaturgemen* translated the Holy Scriptures from Hebrew to Aramaic for the formerly exiled Israelites (Nehemiah 8: 5-9).

To reiterate, the Fruit of the Spirit are love, joy, peace, longsuffering, gentleness, goodness, faith, meekness, and temperance. The latter eight fruit are all grounded in the first, agape love. Agape is God's perfect love. It requires no prerequisites, qualifications, or *reciprocity.* This writer calls agape (a-ga-pay) " the just because love." I love you just because you are. The second Fruit of the Spirit is joy (Gk. xara, key-ra), meaning great happiness. Often it is expressed idiomatically: "My heart dances because I'm happy." Perhaps a better example would be to equate the felling of spiritual ecstasy one feels when one becomes "happy" with the Holy Spirit in church. *"And the people with one accord gave heed unto those things which Philip spake, hearing and seeing the miracles which he did. For unclean spirits, crying with loud voice, came out of many that were possessed with them; and many taken with palsies, and the lame, were healed. And there was great joy in that city"* (Acts 8:6-8). Peace, (Gk. eirene, e-ray-nay) is the feeling of tranquility. The spiritual characteristic of peace is that it can be experienced when faced with great stress. It is to be without trouble or vexing of spirit. *"Peace I leave with you, my peace I give unto you: not as the world giveth, give I unto you. Let not your heart be troubled, neither let it be afraid"* (John 14:27). Longsuffering (Gk. makrothumia, ma-cro-thu-mia) is the state of maintaining patience when provoked or agitated. Perhaps better stated, "When someone gets on your last nerve." *"But thou, O Lord, art a God full of compassion, and gracious, longsuffering, and plenteous in mercy and truth"* (Psalms 86:15). The connotation of the word is to practice patience in the face of negativity, but also returning good in the place of bad. Kindness (Gk. crestotes, cray-to-tays): this interpretation is reflective of benevolence or the unfretted willingness to serve and give cheerfully. *"But after that the kindness and the love of God our Savior toward men appeared. Not by works of righteousness, which we have done, but according to His mercy he saved us, by the washing of regeneration, and renewing of the Holy Ghost; which He shed on us abundantly through Jesus Christ our Savior"* (Titus 3:4-6). What is stated above is a special type of mercy. This kindness of gifting is too valuable ever to approach repayment. The value of this gift, and the magnitude of the giver's kindness is unquestionably a *macrothumasonic* gesture. Goodness (Gk. agathosune, a-ga-tho-su-nay) refers to general positive character qualities. Goodness is an intuitive sense of pleasantness, which translates into a desire to always do good for your neighbor.

"Let your light so shine before men, that they may see your good works, and glorify your good works, and glorify your Father which is in heaven" (Matthew 5:16). What we also must remember is that multitudes of people talk "good" games, but few play the "good" games. *"Show me your faith without good works, and I will show you my faith by my good works" (James 2:18).* Faith may be the only way we can show God how much we love Him. *"But without faith it is impossible to please Him: for he that cometh to God must believe that He is, and that He is a rewarder of them that diligently seek Him."* If you love someone and the love is reciprocal, then there is a mutual trust between the two. Blaise Pascal said, *"To love a man one must know him first. To know God one must love Him first."* When one trusts another person, the trusted individual can do one of two things. He or she can honor the trust or violate the trust. Deserving and honoring trust is the best way of learning how to trust. Pistos is the Greek word for faith/trust. The denotation of the word is "complete belief"; however, the connotation reveals a different but more profound meaning. *"Now faith is the substance of things hoped for, the evidence of things not seen."* Paraphrasing, to believe will occur despite the appearance of apparent physical impossibility. As mortals, what we neglect to do is wait for God to do His "God thing." God's time (Gk. kiros) is infinite and eternal, unlike our time. Our time (Gk.kronos) is finite and imperfect. God's time is eternal, meaning it has no definable beginning or end. God's time is not only perfect, but also perfectly timed. He gives a believer what he needs exactly when he needs it. God's timing is never early and never late. Man's problem is that in our ignorance, we want to preempt God. The natural tendency of man is to think he can anticipate divine action. The Word says to wait on the Lord. *"Wait on the Lord: be of good courage, and He shall strengthen thine heart: wait, I say, wait on the Lord." (Psalms 27:14).* *"But they that wait upon the lord shall renew their strength; they shall mount up with wings as eagles; they shall run, and not be weary; and they shall walk, and not faint" (Isaiah 40:31).* Contrary to what some may think, meekness and gentleness are not synonymous with weakness.

Gentleness (Gk. praotes, pra-o-tays) and meekness mean having the ability to be harsh and aggressive, but choosing not to. The African proverb which "Teddy" Roosevelt made famous, "Speak softly and carry a big stick," demotes the posture a gentle man will assume. "Teddy" Roosevelt wrote, "I have always been fond of the West African proverb: Speak softly and carry a big stick" (Hoyt, 2002). President Roosevelt used the quote twice. In each instance he said "speak" and not "walk."

Is the ability to bench-press 400 lbs. strength? Perhaps? However, strength, or better said, temperance or self-control (Gk. egkrateia, eg-kra-teea), is spiritual self- constraint. *"And every man that striveth for mastery is temperate in all things. Now they do it to obtain a corruptible crown; but we an incorruptible."* The meaning is that the unsaved strive for temperance to please man; however, the believer strives for temperance to please God.

In summary, *"And to knowledge temperance; and to temperance patience; and to patience godliness; and to godliness brotherly kindness; and to brotherly kindness charity (love). For these things be in you, and abound, they make you that ye shall neither be barren nor unfruitful in the knowledge of our Lord Jesus Christ"* (II Peter 1:6-8). Please notice that the *confluence* of the nine fruit is a perfect description of the character of Christ. Believers who strive to be Christ-like need not look any farther than duplicating and bringing together the Fruit of the Spirit.

Does America and the World Have a Chance?

Can anyone answer the question? With myriad contemporary domestic and international ills, the world needs divine intervention. Only prayer can help at this point. However, there is a modicum of solace that may minimize one's skepticism. Perhaps a positive change is imminent. A colorless man has a chance of leading this country and the world.

Please take inventory of the last four administrations. With the exception of Mr. Obama, has there been a president, vice president, Democratic, Republican, Independent, Communist, Socialist, or candidate who has displayed the Fruit of the Spirit to the degree of Mr. Obama? He seems to genuinely experience joy by helping people, as evidenced by his record of public service and his accomplishments in public office. He appears to be a man at peace, comfortable with himself and his spirituality. That grounding is referenced in his paraphrasing and accurate quotes of the Bible.

Mr. Obama is obviously longsuffering, as evidenced by his handling of the media during their disingenuous attacks. Fortunately, the tricky spin by the predominately partisan media and political pundits actually accentuated the positive elements of Mr. Obama's character. One must remember. Generally, with the majority race, diversity will be championed until it challenges the majority's position of racial subordination the majority race enjoys. This applies to all of America's minorities to varying degrees (Harris, C., 1995). Mr. Obama has pricked a nerve. He has surprised the world! Mr. Obama has politically challenged the white world's assumed position of superiority, and it is apparent by the media's reaction. The media is trying to be politically correct; however, the racial "backlash" is oozing between the printed lines. In spite of the negative innuendo, Mr. Obama has handled himself in a divine manner. Moreover, not once did Mr. Obama retaliate with negative diatribes when attacked by his opponents. However, his responses were defensive when appropriate. He always showed kindness by being non-aggressive regardless of how irrelevant, inaccurate, and deriding the comments and questions directed at him. His temperance is impeccable. If he ever was harried in this campaign, his demeanor certainly did not reveal it.

As a living and contemporary metaphor, Mr. Obama's behavior seems to be a clear example of a colorless man's behavior. His actions are driven by his love for this nation and its suffering citizens. Moreover, Mr. Obama realizes that America's weakest citizens reflect the combined strength of our nation and perhaps the world. Of course, his colorlessness does not approach that of Christ, but his candidacy gives reason for "the audacity of hope."

There is a caveat. Everything in the universe operates by rhythm, from our heartbeat to the *thermohaline* and *ebon* flow of this planet's seas and oceans. Here is an interesting "Did You Know?" As the earth rotates on its axis at 1,026 miles per hour and around the sun at 200 miles per hour, the moon revolves around the earth in an elliptical motion. The varying angles of rotation combined with the elliptical rotation of the moon result in the moon rotating around all portions of the earth. The elliptical orbit of the moon brings the earth closer to it at specific times. During these times, the gravitational pull of the moon draws the oceans and seas toward it, which causes the *ebon* flow of the oceans. This rhythmic motion keeps our oceans and seas from becoming stagnate. Do you remember the definition of anthropic? God has created an environment especially suited for the existence of man.

Rhythm affects the physical, psychological, emotional, and spiritual behavior of human beings. One of the more perplexing physical phenomena that affect all of the above is entrainment. *Entrainment* is the uncanny tendency of two or more independently oscillating objects to adjust their rhythms to form one rhythm or work in complex harmony. First written about in 1665 by Dutch scientist Christian Huygens, entrainment was first noticed while working on the design of a pendulum clock. Huygens noticed that two independent pendulums swinging at different rates would automatically synchronize in rhythm. The phenomenon is universal. It has been shown that individual heart rates will synchronize when in close proximity, and the menstrual cycles of women living in the same house will often harmonically adjust. The flight pattern of Canadian geese is another example. The leader will fly point for a specific time period, and right on queue the next gander in line will assume the lead, and the former leader will retire to the rear to rest. This practice in addition to the aerodynamics of the "V" formation enables the flock to fly longer and more efficiently. This gives more meaning to the well used aphorism, "Birds of a feather fly together."

However, there is a caveat. Entrainment is the reason why believers must pray for Mr. Obama; that if he becomes our leader, he will not be influenced by the pull of negative politics and politicians. Mr. Obama's mantra is "change." Change is only good if it is positive, and it is only effective if it is frequent and consistent. The acrimony he has suffered thus far as a candidate will wane in importance compared to the opposition he will receive from entrenched "old boy" politicians, Democrats and Republicans. Pray that the "colorless man" will stay steadfast in the face of corrupting opposition. There are plenty of places for the enemy to hide and attack, especially in Washington, D.C.

For Further Discussion

1. Understanding the author's definition of the colorless man and theoanthropology, do you think the world is in need of a leader that fits the definitions, or a complete atheist or agnostic? Please explain your answer.

2. How can entrainment affect the spiritual soundness of a colorless man?

References

The Holy Bible, King James Version.

God's Little Instruction Book (1984). Honor Books, Inc. Tulsa, Oklahoma 74144.

Grenz, S., Guretzki D., Nordling, C. (1999). Pocket Dictionary of Theological Terms. InterVarsity Press. Downers Grove, Illinois.

Harris. C. (1995). Critical Race Theory. "Whiteness as Property" New Rose Press. New York, New York. pp. 276-290.

Hoyt, E. (2002). Teddy Roosevelt in Africa. Stackpole Books, 5067 Ritter Road, Mechanicsburg, Pa. 1705.

Tarply, W & Chaitkin, A. (1992). George Bush: The Unauthorized Biography. Executive Intelligence Review P.O. Box 17390. Washington, D.C.

"The World's Worst Dictators" (2008). http://www.parade.com/dictators/2008/

Glossary ━━━━━━━━━━━━━━━━━━━━━━━━━

Confluence - the coming together of a minimum of three things (usually describing rivers)

Cupidity - greed

Ebon Flow - the tidal flow of the oceans and seas

Eisegesis - is a derogatory term used to designate the practice of imposing a preconceived or foreign meaning onto biblical text (Grenz, S. Guretzki D. Nordling, C. 1999)

Entrainment - the tendency for two oscillating bodies to lock into synchronization or two or more rhythmic cycles

Exegete - to exegete is the process of seeking the meaning of a biblical text on it own or literal meaning, using verifiable information (Grenz, S. Guretzki D. Nordling, C. 1999)

Hermeneutics - the discipline that studies the principles and theories of how biblical texts ought to be interpreted (Grenz, S. Guretzki D. Nordling, C. 1999)

Lupenproletariat - the bottom rung of the sociological chain; the unrecognized underclass

Macrothumasonic - a gesture or gift that is too valuable to repay

Metaturgemen - translators of God's Word from Hebrew to Aramaic

Proletariat - the common workingman

NATO - The North American Treaty Organization was formed on April 4, 1949 to prevent the spread of Communism. With the fall of the USSR, its role has changed.

Nefarious - evil; of bad intent

Patriarchic - fatherly

Tell - a subtle idiosyncrasy of that person that reveals a specific behavior

Thermohaline - the natural movement of the oceans and seas according to water temperature and weather

CHAPTER

"The rich man's wealth is his strong city, and as a high wall in his own conceit" (Proverbs 18:11)

A quick exegesis of this chapter's title reads, *"The rich man's sufficiency is the belief in the impregnability/inaccessibility of his city. This anthropocentric attitude is idolatrous and offensive to God."* Proverbs 18:11 tacitly expresses how man reveres structures, monuments, and his own limited abilities as opposed to the reverence and dependence on God. "The greatest act of faith is when man decides he is not God" (Oliver Wendell Holmes, *God's Little*, 1994).

Proverbs 18:11 also implies that those who live in cities are more cultured, intelligent, and industrious than those who enjoy a *bucolic* environment. In ancient times, if one didn't live in a city, one was considered a *pagan*. Is that so? "Civilized" simply means those who live in cities, and "pagan" means those who live in the country. As time progressed, the *denotative* and *connotative* meaning of pagan deteriorated into the assumed belief that country folk were less educated, cultured, and intelligent.

To this point we have discussed theoanthropology in terms of one's personal relationship with Christ. We continued the discussion with an expanded conversation of the importance of diversity, and how genetics, environment, and natural polymorphism contribute to the diversity of human beings. Understanding this, we learned that 85% of the physical and mental makeup of all races and ethnicities is identical, and the remaining 15% is purely phenotypic or superfluous physical differences. We investigated the anthropic nature of the world, and that the universe was not created randomly, or –by chance. Finally, we packaged the discussion in the definition of a colorless man, using Barack Obama as a living metaphor.

Assuming that the above is accurate, what is the cause of the diversity in cultural development? Is a society's state of technology a determinant of a superior population? What separates industrial countries from *agrarian* societies? Jared Diamond specifically addresses the issue in his book *Guns, Germs, and Steel*.

History widely accepts the beginning of formal writing as Egyptian Hieroglyphics circa 3200 B.C. However, some scholars attribute writing to a joint collaboration between the Egyptians and the Ethiopians (Sudanese known as Ethiopians in biblical times). From that point until the present, there have been several societies with centralized governments, laws, punishments, economic systems, *mores*, inventions, and traditions that were and are specific and *endemic* to its culture. The question is, what allows Western and European nations to subjugate the world when Europeans are the minority population of the earth? Why are there different rates of technological development on different continents?

The answer may be hidden in a question asked by one of Jared Diamond's New Guinean friends. His friend, Yali, asked him a question, "Why is it that you White people developed so much cargo and brought it to New Guinea, but we Black people had little cargo of our own? Cargo is a general aphorism meaning "stuff." Seemingly, this "stuff" gave the white "masters" a sense of superiority and reason for the subordination of the New Guineans. In his opinion, the attitude of the white imperialists resulted from the natives less that technological prowess. The natives were considered lesser humans, and to the whites are most likely vestiges of apelike *hominids*. The New Guineans were assumed to be less intelligent because of the sparseness of their technological development or "cargo" (Diamond, 1999). Even the *miasmic* façade of political correctness cannot hide the reality of social, political, and economic subordination universally practiced by Western countries.

The interesting twist is that there is little correlation between technological development and the degree of human intelligence. Ironically, the opposite may to be true. It seems that to be a successful hunter-gatherer, one must be more intelligent than the average person living in a technologically advanced society. It is no secret that in an effort to support racism, psychologists have been trying for decades to affirm that African Americans are innately less intelligent than peoples of European descent (Diamond, 1999). It is only in these latter years that IQ tests have been confirmed to be a measurement of culture, not raw intelligence. Paradoxically, the lack of technology is contributory to the greater mental acumen of the New Guineans.

According to Jared Diamond, "In the average American household, the TV set is on for seven hours per day. In contrast, traditional New Guinea children have virtually no such opportunities for passive entertainment and instead spend almost all of their waking hours actively doing something, such as talking or playing with other children. Almost all studies of child development emphasize the role of childhood stimulation and activity in promoting mental development, and stress the irreversible mental stunting associated with reduced childhood stimulation" (Diamond, 1999, p. 21). Please take note of the spiraling downward trend of academic proficiency of American children compared to other nations.

In 1964 the first cross-national assessment was conducted in regard to the mathematical competencies of children ages 13 and 17 in 12 industrial nations. It was shown that American teenagers were among the most poorly educated of the 12 nations. 13-year-old American adolescents ranked a poor 10th and 11th in math and science respectively. An assessment of 17-year-old pupils was based on students who completed two intense college preparatory classes in math and science. The American students scored last. Subsequent to that initial assessment, an additional cross-national test of a similar nature was completed in 1995. The students assessed were students ranging from middle through high school. Forty-five nations were involved. U.S. students ranked 28th out of 41 nations in 8th grade and 24th out of 39 nations in the 7th grade. This is inexcusable considering the United States is the wealthiest and most industrialized nation on earth. For your information, the country receiving the highest scores was Singapore. By the time of the publication of this book, there may be more recent data. Unfortunately, at present the United States has the reputation for having some of the least educated students in the world!

If it is not physical or mental, what is the contributing factor or factors causing the differences in the technological advancements of many societies of the world? What differentiates the nomadic rat from the country rat from the city rat? Jared Diamond may have the answer.

Scientists always know that if there is an effect, there is always a cause. There must be a reason for technological advancement and the accumulation of Yali's "cargo." Many scholars dispute the accurate date when most of the world had organized settlements and governments. The earliest villages, cities, and governments are widely believed to have begun on the continent of Africa circa 11,000 B.C. (Diamond, 1999). In minor contradiction, there is documentation that by 13,000 B.C., the walled city government paradigm was commonplace. As an interesting "Did You Know?" concerning cities, Flavius Josephus gives an account of a major military victory by Moses in circa 13,000 B.C.

Most of us know the biblical story of Moses being rescued from the river by Pharaoh's daughter and being reared in the palace. What most of us do not know is that Pharaoh hated Moses, and his daughter was the only person keeping Moses from the Pharaoh's ire. What most of us also do not know is that Moses had two wives. His first wife's name was Tharbis (Josephus, F. Jewish Antiquities: 12 1-4). Pharaoh knew Moses was a Jew, and he and the chief Egyptian priests wanted him dead. Pharaoh and his cohorts maintained that acrimony well into Moses' adulthood. However, Moses was a great general, a brilliant military tactician. That, combined with his surrogate mother's influence, kept him alive.

The immediate southern neighbor to Egypt was Ethiopia, not Abyssinia or what we contemporarily call Ethiopia, but Sudan. The Ethiopians were called Cushites, named after one of Ham's sons and one of Noah's grandsons. The specific area is closer to Darfur, where the manic genocidal Omar al-Bashir has murdered in excess of 500,000 people and displaced an additional 700,000. All of this has been done under the watchful eye of the Bush administration. Ethiopia, as named in the Bible, was a more powerful nation at that time, and had just completed a successful and embarrassing military campaign against Egypt. In fact, the Ethiopians had moved into Egypt as far as Memphis. Their position strategically threatened the Egyptian empire. Pharaoh's daughter, as a bargaining tool, offered the military service and talents of her son, Moses, in exchange for his lifetime clemency.

In his brilliance, Moses devised a masterful plan. There were two paths to Meroe, the capital of Ethiopia. One path went by the sea; however, it was a military death trap, similar to the topographical situation the Assyrians faced in fighting the Spartans and Leonitis at Thermopylae. The second way was through the jungle, which was perhaps worse, because the jungle was infested with king cobras and flying cobras. The Egyptian army would suffer more casualties from the serpents than the battle.

Moses, with his brilliance, had a plan. An Ibe is a crane-like bird that is the natural enemy and predator of snakes. Moses marched thousands of Ibes to the jungle route and released them, which safely cleared the way for his army. During one of the battles at the wall of Meroe, Tharbis, the Ethiopian king's daughter spied Moses and fell in love. A compromise was struck. Tharbis would become Moses' wife and a truce met. Tharbis is the Cushite wife, not Zipporah who caused Aaron and Miriam to come against Moses. *"And Miriam and Aaron spake against Moses because of the Cushite woman whom he had married; for he had a Cushite woman"* (Numbers 12:1, ASV). In ancient times Ethiopia was what Sudan is today, and the people of *that land were called Cushites.*

God found Miriam too rambunctious and punished her with a brief bout with leprosy. *"And the anger of Jehovah was kindled against them; and he departed. And the cloud removed from over the tent; and behold, Miriam, was leprous, as white as snow: Aaron looked upon Miriam, and behold, she was leprous"* (Numbers 12:10). If you remember your Bible stories, Jethro, Moses' father-in-law, sent Zipporah back to Moses. This obviously implies that she left. Apparently, Zipporah got an attitude. This makes sense, because Tharbis was the first wife, and when Moses returned to Egypt she had opportunity to reclaim him and their marriage. In other words, Tharbis became "big mama." Moses was a player!

Hopefully that little side bar will help you with your understanding of scripture and give further insight into the lives of the prophets. The more things change, the more they stay the same. However, the prime issue is that there were villages, towns, and major walled cities well before 3,000 B.C. Returning to the question, "Why are some societies more technologically advanced than others?"

& City Life "Was It God's Plan?"
The Great Leap Forward, Last Ice Age, Village ▬▬▬▬

Coincidentally, the last major Ice Age ended approximately the same time as "The Great Leap Forward," which marked the beginning of man's tendency to establish villages and walled cities. In addition, the origin of the #168 gene, the mitochondrial Eve gene, is dated at approximately the same time.

With the most contemporary equipment, one can only determine approximate dates for these occurrences; however, they seem suspiciously close in time. For example, several scholars believe that the development of cities began circa 11,000 B.C, but we have already determined from the most respected biblical historian, Josephus, that there were walled cities during Moses' time circa 13,000 B.C. With the ending of the Ice Age and the melting of the glaciers, the ocean levels increased. As a result, the number of continents increased and were separated by great ocean divides. Consequently, human evolution began to genetically and environmentally adapt to newly established living conditions. The obvious result was that people developed specific physical idiosyncrasies necessary to survive in their environments, i.e., different races.

Please understand that this is purely conjecture. However, *"In the beginning God created the heavens and the earth."* Genesis 1:1 is certainly more logical than the universe, the world, man, and animals being created by chance, especially when the "Big Boom" could have been God's voice. My doctoral advisor, Dr. Seppo Iso-Ahola, would always say, "Greg, you must have evidence." Perhaps there will never be any definitive evidence, but Creationism seems more empirical than Evolution. Moreover, considering the above documentation, Creationism and Evolution can coexist. Please consider. God spoke the heavens and earth into existence. All men are created in God's image and 85% homogenous. God allowed man to migrate to several different and specific parts of earth. The genetic makeup of man allowed humans to naturally morph and adapt to their specific environmental conditions, which satisfies the evolution and natural selection *treatises.*

Village and City

Now that we have everybody placed in different parts of the world, again, why did different societies develop at different technological rates? If it was not intellectual prowess, what was it? Jared Diamond, in his book *Guns, Germs, and Steel*, fosters a thought-provoking thesis. According to him it was the domesticating of plants and animals that contributed to the many advancements in technology.

Initially, humans were hunters and gatherers. We moved as the seasons changed or the available game migrated. Hunting and gathering predominated human existence until circa 28,000 to 18,000 B.C. (Diamond, 1999). About this time food production became common, largely by accident. Conjecture postulates that farming initially was an insurance mechanism for sparse hunting and gathering conditions. Hunting and gathering as sustenance providing is often an all or nothing condition. However, even minor farming will yield substance for survival. Sufficient rain and cultivation may provide bountiful yields minus the erratic success of hunting and gathering. The two food-producing practices counteract the negatives of both. Droughts will occur and people perish. Hunting depends on skill, opportunity, and availability of game. If one is fortunate and kills a deer, everybody eats, but only for a short time. In Diamond's opinion, *"There often was not even a conscious choice between food production and hunting-gathering. Specifically, in each area of the globe the first people who adopted food production could obviously not have been making a conscious choice"* (Diamond, 1999, p. 105). By trial and error, food production was mastered and became an accepted practice. In most cases farming augmented a staple diet of various herbs, berries, tubers, and small game.

After a period of success, an interesting sociological phenomenon began. The autocatalytic process is self-reciprocating. For example, as the farmers improved food production, the population had more discretionary time. The discretionary time resulted in a larger birth rate. With the availability of a consistent food supply, the infant survival rate was higher, which ultimately required greater food production. As the cycle continued, more and larger farming communities were established, which led to the eventual demise of the hunter-gatherer population. The hunter-gathers had two options. One, become food producers, or two, be eradicated.

The Khoikhoi tribe of South Africa is an example. The Khoikhoi (men of men) people are the aboriginal people of the region. They are also called the Khoisan, and Bushmen or Hotentots, by the white South Africans. The Khoikhoi were formally hunter-gathers. Around 500 B.C. the Khoikhoi acquired livestock and became herdsmen (food producers). However, the San, a small segment of Khoikhoi, wanted to remain hunter-gathers. Eventually, through intermarriage the Khoikhoi and San became one tribe. As a result of miscegenation and the blending of tribal *mores* and traditions, the practice of hunting and gathering dissipated. The combined people named themselves

Khoisan. The concepts of personal wealth, territory, property-ownership, and sedentary villages subsequently became common.

On the European side of South Africa's development, we have the interesting story of the Trekbores. In 1647 a Dutch vessel was shipwrecked in what is known now as Table Bay at Cape Town. The crew built a fort and remained for a year before they were rescued. Subsequently, the Dutch East India Company established a permanent settlement there only for the purpose of providing a way station for their ships traveling the spice route to the east. Initially the small settlement attempted to do business and employ the Khoikhoi as farm laborers. As one would expect, the relationship was volatile and intolerable for both. To remedy the problem, the Dutch East India Company released several Dutch settlers from their indentured servant contracts and encouraged them to establish farms, which would provide the staples that the settlement required. The Dutch settlers grew in numbers and expanded their territory to the dismay of the Khoikhoi, who used the same land for their farming. The Dutch settlers were known as Free Burghers, a rough independent bunch, highly religious, who distorted Bible scripture to justify the attempted *subordination* of the Khoikhoi. After years of violent battle, the Free Burghers were ultimately successful because of superior weaponry and the introduction of European diseases, which the Khoikhoi could not tolerate. The Khoikhoi finally succumbed to the subordination of the Free Burghers by working on their farms and in their mines for slave wages.

The Trekbores (wandering farmers) were unique. Their practice was to wander the hinterlands, often with no more than a wagon, a few guns, and a Bible. They farmed where they found rich soil and returned to the city only to sell their harvest. Often if they found a desirable piece of land, they would erect a small mud cottage and mark the land as theirs.

Under the guise of thwarting Napoleonic colonization, the British at the close of the 18th century (1795) temporarily took control of South Africa. They returned South Africa briefly to the Dutch when the Napoleonic threat subsided (1803), but the British inability to discipline their imperialistic fervor re-conquered South Africa in 1806. Britain received sovereignty of the area when it was recognized at the congress of Vienna in 1815. Initially, Great Britain, like the Dutch, had little interest in South Africa other than as a nautical way station. However, to quell the continued bickering between the Bores and the Khoisan, British colonists were imported to settle the land between them in the hope of forming a demilitarized zone. The idea was a complete failure. The British determined that it was not their fight, and moved into the cities where they practiced their previous professions. Please understand, now there were two distinct white nations living simultaneously in South Africa, assuming sovereignty with two distinct languages. This will cause problems in the future.

To complicate matters, Shaka Zulu had united the many divided and quarrelsome Zulu factions into one mighty tribe and was giving the British imperialist grief. Shaka was convinced that to keep Zulu independence, the Zulu had to use force. His half-brothers Dingaan and Umthlangnna disagreed. The Zulus remained a dominant force in South Africa, fighting both the British and the Bores until Shaka was assassinated by his brothers. Dingaan's rule was despotic like his brother's, but he succumbed to greed. While continuing to terrorize the Bores, he attempted to establish political and economic relations with the British. The British and the Bores were at odds, and Dingaan's attempted alliance with the British further aggravated the Bores. Dingaan weakened the Zulu nation's military posture and the Zulu's resolve to remain independent. The ultimate result was the demise of the Zulu nation. The Zulus are another example of the more domesticated society dominating a lesser one.

The British allowed the fighting between the Bores and the Khoisan to continue and the fracture between the British and the Bores widened, especially with the abolition of slavery by Britain in 1833. Abolition was totally antithetical to the Bores' belief in the "God-given" ordering of the races. The British wanted to avoid any radical sociological reforms and acquiesced to the racist Bores. The Masters and Servants Act was passed in 1941, which overtly supported white control and ultimately developed into the anathema of apartheid.

The numbers of British were increasing in Cape Town after the discovery of diamonds and gold in the neighboring provinces, which the Bores and Khoisan farmed and thought they controlled. The British flexed their muscles and commandeered the land, gold, and diamond mines. The British had a problem. The Khoisan could be easily handled; however, the Bores were enraged, especial when the British refused to compensate them by sharing the wealth. It was on!

The first Anglo-Boer war "popped off" in 1880 at what the Afrikaners (Bores) call the "War of Independence" with a crushing Bore victory at the Battle of Majuba Hill. Even with the victory, the British maintained dominance in the region. The second Anglo-Bore war was a different story, with the British soundly defeating the Bores. The British were in complete control by 1902. Under the Treaty of Vereeniging, the Bore republics were united under British control. After World War I, the British and Bores coalesced into a government that completely marginalized the native Africans and coloreds.

South Africa subsequently gained its independence from Great Britain in 1934, and because of its fervent participation in support of the allied cause in World War II, gained equal international status with former British colonies like Canada, Australia, and India. South Africa subjugated the non-white population and subsequently, under the leadership of Prime Minister Dr. Hendrik Verwoerd, instituted the Grand Apartheid Policy in 1958. The *subjugation* of the African and colored population had nothing to do with white genetic superiority. The best food producer at that time was Great Britain. The advantage allowed the British the sedentary time to develop technologically, which ultimately contributed to greater wealth, greater military force, and eventually the domination of less technical societies. The imperialistic tentacles of Great Britain reached deep into Africa with political control of Swaziland, Zambia, and Zimbabwe. Even the European British and Dutch initially fought among themselves to determine superiority, but the subsequent winners were the British.

Native Africans were totally subjugated. The native Africans eventually gained political parity, but after the nation had been drained of the majority of its wealth and natural resources. The African National Congress, formed in 1912, finally came into power in 1994 when the first multiracial, multiparty election was held and Nelson Mandela was elected president (*History of South Africa*, 2008, *The World Fact Book 2008*, *Brief History of South Africa*, 2008).

Native Americans are a graphic domestic example. Native American tribes were affected by America's policy of Manifest Destiny, homesteading, and the gold rush. Their inability to sociologically adapt was a hindrance to this nation's technological development and its westward migration. As a result, Native Americans were deceived, purposely diseased, and brutally forced into submission. There is a word for that. It's called genocide. Food producers will subjugate or eliminate hunters and gatherers every time.

Domestication Is the Key to Food Production ▬▬▬▬▬

"Planned domestication may be defined as growing a plant/animal and thereby consciously or unconsciously, causing it to change genetically from its wild ancestors in ways making it more useful to human consumers" (Diamond, 1999, p.14). Historically, plant and animal domestication is a long process; however, with the contemporary advances in science, i.e., genetic engineering and cloning, it appears that man can create any type of plant or animal he wishes. In terms of domestication, there have been natural restrictions. Some animals and plants cannot be domesticated, or the difficulty precludes the attempt. Interestingly, Diamond notes the almond. It seems like a harmless enough nut. However, there are several wild varieties, which are all loaded with cyanide and lethal upon consumption. Makes one think a little longer about that dated Almond Joy jingle, "Sometimes I feel like a nut, sometimes I don't." If that information were widely known, think how that would affect the candy and pastry industries.

Animals are domesticated primarily for two reasons. The first is for food. The second is for work. Usually the larger animals are used for work, the smaller animals for food. Examples of large animals are oxen, horses, hogs, camels, and mules. Examples of smaller animals are chickens, rabbits, capons, sheep, and goats. As with some plants, some animals cannot be domesticated. A lion will never be domesticated. Cheetahs cannot be domesticated because their mating ritual requires vast acres of open area. Several males chase the female. She may run for days. The winner gets to mate, if he has the strength. That keeps the species strong and fast. How many animals can run with a cheetah? When we find an animal that can run as fast, then perhaps we can crossbreed them. The zebra is another animal that cannot be domesticated or tamed. They will attack, bite, and not let go. If a horse does that, one can always grab his ear and they will let go. Not a zebra; he will bite it until it comes off. They're tricky too. Get your best rodeo champion and he will not be able to lasso a zebra. Their eyesight, quickness, intelligence, and ability to follow the rope with their eyes make it impossible to get a rope around their necks. Zebras injure more zookeepers per year than tigers (Diamond 1999). Up until the postmodern era, domestication of plants and animals was dependent on nature, with a guiding hand from man. With scientific advancements things have changed.

Scientific Imperative

Cloning brings an entirely new dimension to food production and farming. There are four types of cloning: somatic therapy, germline therapy, somatic enhancement, and germline enhancement. Somatic therapy is the altering of the genome to heal diseases. For example, somatic alterations could heal cancer, sickle cell anemia, diabetes, cardiovascular diseases, and other more exotic maladies. Germline therapy is the altering of the reproductive DNA in an attempt to eliminate the future genetic potential for diseases, i.e., breast cancer. There is extensive significant data indicating the proclivity of mothers with breast cancer passing the disease to their daughters. Germline therapy is an attempt to eliminate diseases permanently by altering the cancer gene or removing it. Somatic enhancement, on the other hand, is an attempt to create a super being by replacing inferior genes with "super" ones in the individual. This process is tantamount to creating Michael Jordans or Albert Einsteins. Germline enhancement is permanent somatic enhancement. Germline enhancement's purpose is to genetically "breed" a generation of Michael Jordans and Albert Einsteins. Cloning is a serious issue, and one can see how its handling could affect the future of the world's diverse food production in terms of plants, animals, and humans.

Unfortunately, there is a sociological construct called the scientific imperative. The scientific imperative, as a result of profit and greed, will carry new inventions and discoveries to their maximum development regardless of the damaging effects they may have on society. Cupidity will always be the Achilles' heel of man. Imagine what uncontrolled cloning of plants, animals, and humans will have on the food production industry. Put that in your autocatalytic process formula. Uncontrolled, there would be bigger, better, longer living humans, eating better food, and having more children. The world's population would increase exponentially. God would have to speak another world into existence!

Thus far, we have explored the genetic sameness of the human species while explaining the obvious but largely superfluous differences in appearances. We have determined, contrary to specious information, that no race of people is inherently more intelligent, more creative, more ethically sound than the others.

It appears that the domestication of plants and animals contributes to a more sedentary lifestyle, which ultimately allows more discretionary time for technological development. Historically, technologically advanced societies have been shown to consistently supplant hunter-gather societies. It has nothing to do with the intelligence of the individual peoples, and everything to do with the domestication of plants and animals. History shows that the availability of larger domesticated animals gave the Eurasian societies an advantage in sociological development. However, once the less technological societies became exposed to the larger domestic animals, adaptations were made, exemplified by the American Indians and their mastery of horses and the Bantu tribes of sub-Saharan Africa becoming accomplished cattlemen (Diamond, 1999).

Domestication established a consistent food supply, and consequently enabled the military to concentrate less on food gathering and more on developing battle strategies, fighting techniques, and improved weaponry. Starving armies will lose. Malnourished armies will lose. The country with the most food usually has the most money. The country with the most money usually has the bigger guns. The country with the bigger guns usually has the most power. The country with the most power can subjugate whom they please. Global subjugation of nations and peoples has nothing to do with a divine right as the Bores (Afrikaners) of South Africa or American slaveholders preached. Societal dominance purely rests on the environmental availability of plants and animals that can be domesticated. Eurasians had more animals with the potential for domestication, so their societies advanced more quickly.

Germs Win Wars, Guns Don't

As profound as the domestication of plants and animals and its precipitous effect on social establishments, germs had an equally great impact. The domestication of animals and the resultant close proximity of animals, humans, and their waste resulted in disease. The tendency of people to keep pets, urban population, and the lack of sanitary health practices all contributed to massive epidemics, especially in European cities. The closeness would allow the animal germs to naturally mutate into human germs, causing what is termed zoonotic viruses, ergo the problem. The epidemics were devastating. Even today, the potential for contracting germs from pets and animals exists. Do you remember the "bird flu?" Many initial animal germs have mutated into major infectious human killers: small pox, influenza, tuberculosis, malaria, plague, measles, and cholera, to name a few. Here is an interesting note. Our common everyday flu mutates yearly. The flu vaccines we take every year are educated guesses. The flu germ mutates, requiring the vaccines to adjust every year. That is why the vaccine often has varying degrees of effectiveness. Disease has been the biggest killer in history. Disease killed more people in WWII than battle wounds. The winners of battles and wars are not always the folks with the best generals; they may be the armies that carried the deadliest germs.

Disease, as defined by *Webster's*, is "any departure from health or a particular destructive process in an organism; a corrupting effect." Germs cause diseases, and germs spread in several different ways. They can be spread passively or actively. An example of passivity is the salmonella problem we are presently having in America. Eating infected eggs or meat or anything the infected eggs or meat come in contact with spreads *salmonella*. *Trichinosis* is similar. The cause of the sickness is a parasitic worm ingested by eating poorly cooked pork. Anisakiasis is a disease transmitted by a worm in sushi or improperly cooked fish. To interject a great "Did You Know?" laughing sickness (kuru) experienced by highland New Guineans is contracted by the cannibalistic practice of eating the brains of humans. Children transmitted it as a result of playing in the brains of dead humans and licking their fingers. *Anthropophagi* is an extreme example; however, it is a clear example of germs non-aggressively attacking humans (Diamond, 1999).

Some germs are more aggressive and do not wait for an animal to be killed or die to attack. In this instance, insects play an active role in disease spreading. They bite the infected host, and the germs hitch rides and are subsequently transmitted when the insects bite and infect new hosts. Notorious insect vectors are fleas, mosquitoes, lice, and tsetse flies. These pestiferous vectors are the cause of the plague, malaria, typhus, and sleeping sickness.

Venereal diseases spread germs more aggressively through lesions and open sores. More dangerous are diseases spread by physical contact or through the air. A prime example is smallpox, which was nefariously used by the U.S. military to eliminate Native Americans when the American military cruelly issued the Indians blankets infected with smallpox microbes. Germs also may be transmitted in the air by coughing or sneezing. Influenza is an example.

The strange thing about some diseases is that their survivors develop antibodies or resistance to the disease. Generally, that is how vaccines are made from the blood of surviving victims. Of course, it's considerably more technical now, but that was the initial method. However, when diseases are introduced into virgin populations, the results are devastating. For example, please do not be confused. In 1519 when Cortes landed on the coast of Mexico with his contingent of 600 soldiers, he did not defeat the million or so fiercely combative Aztec warriors. With his advanced weaponry Cortes barely managed to survive. However, shortly thereafter a slave infected with smallpox subsequently devastated the Aztec population, killing or weakening half of the population, even killing Emperor Cuitlahuac. By 1618 the indigenous population of Mexico had spiraled downward from 20 million to one million and a half (Diamond, 1999). Smallpox was the Spaniard's biggest and most powerful weapon.

In 1540 when Hernando de Soto became the first European to explore the interior of the United States, in addition to encountering several viable and populous Mississippian mound-building Indian tribes, he also came across several sites which were abandoned because of disease. The diseases had been contracted from infected coastal Indians who had made their way back into the interior. The Mississippian mound-building was firmly established throughout the Mississippi River Valley, the Tennessee River Valley, as far east as North Carolina, west to California, and north to the Dakotas. Before the arrival of European and Old World disease, the population was estimated to have been in excess of 20 million Mississippians. By the 1600s, virtually all of the major Mississippian societies had vanished. Archaeologists estimate a 95% decline in the Indian population after Columbus' arrival to the New World. Again germs are the ultimate weapon, whether purposeful or by accident (Diamond, 1999).

More Obama Drama

The media is at it again. Again unfortunately, one of the folks throwing stones at Mr. Obama is supposed to be an ally. Jesse Jackson, not knowing that he was on a live mike, made an unseemly comment to fellow panelist Dr. Reed V. Tuckson. Dr. Tuckson at the time was the executive vice president and chief of medical affairs for United Health Group. Mr. Jackson said, "See, Barack been, um, talking down to black people on this faith based…. I want to cut his nuts off…Barack….he's talking down to black people." Jackson appeared to make a stabbing or cutting motion with his hand as he made the remarks. This seems to be a strange behavior from a former presidential candidate, and one who should understand the gravity of this nation having a black president. Jesse's own son, Jesse Jackson Jr., was appalled at his father's comments and released a statement describing his father's comments as ugly rhetoric. Jesse Jackson has done marvelous things for African Americans, and I respect his accomplishments, but sometimes Jesse should keep his mouth closed.

The second media controversy is Bernie Mack's "off color" joke. The joke by Bernie Mack is nothing unusual. He is Bernie Mack. What did they expect? If they didn't want to hear anything off color, they should not have allowed Bernie on stage. Bernie Mack is a comedian, not a politically correct politician. He makes his living by being politically incorrect. Frankly, it's my opinion that perhaps a few of the folks who bought the $2,300 a plate dinners are taking themselves a little too seriously. My question is, would it have been as much ruckus if Don Rickles had presented one of his "off color" jokes at one of Mr. McCain's fundraisers?

In contrast, the caricature of Barack Obama and his wife in *The New Yorker* magazine is inexcusable. The cartoon has Mr. Obama dressed like an Arab, a la bin Laden, and his wife characterized as Angela Davis carrying an assault rifle. The inference is that he is a terrorist and she a revolutionary. The magazine's explanation was that it meant to mock right-winged depictions of the U.S. presidential candidate and his wife. The media knows better than anyone else that the American public is visual. That image alone will leave a lasting damaging impression and will obviously have a negative effect on the Obama presidential campaign. Moreover, since when did *The New Yorker* magazine become liberal? They are big business. Let us not be fooled. *The* New Yorker may appear to be liberal, but behind closed doors they are as conservative as pin stripes and wing-tipped shoes. If you believe The New Yorker's explanation, you will believe that slaves were brought to America so they could have a better standard of living. This was plainly just another "crackerish" trick to undermine Mr. Obama's campaign.

Pray for Mr. Obama. His hardest fight will be after he becomes president. Fareed Zakaris had three of the world's most prominent economists discussing the state of the United States economy. The unanimous consensus was that this country needs a long-term fix. A positive turnaround will not be quick. It's doubtful that the next president, even with an eight-year tenure, will be able to correct this mess in which America is mired. In the short term, it will be impossible to make any significant improvements. With the several crisis situations with which America is faced, this nation will be fortunate if the incoming administration, whoever it is, can positively affect any kind of significant improvement.

The housing market is corrupted and collapsing, the value of the U.S. dollar is in the toilet, there are millions of people without health care, gasoline gets more expensive by the minute, we have irreversible environmental damage, and we are in an "unwinable" war. Let us not forget that our national debt went from 3 trillion dollars to over 10 trillion dollars in the red. How is the election of one man supposed to disinfect the stench of the outgoing Bush administration? With all that is happening in the world, how can one man possibly think that he can affect consistent positive change? There are too many fires ablaze, and our feet are not big enough to stamp them out. Theoanthropology, knowing God is the answer. How does one know God? We will examine prayer in the next chapter.

For Further Discussion

1. Do you think, as Jared Diamond's book explains, that domestication had a significant effect on civilization and ultimately religion? If so, please explain.

2. What is the scientific imperative and how can it potentially effect religion and ultimately theoanthropology?

References

Bible, King James Version.

"Brief History of South Africa." http://www.southafrica-travel.net/history/eh

Diamond, Jared (1999). *Guns, Germs and Steel.* W.W. Norton & Company, Inc., 500 Fifth Avenue, New York, NY 10110.

Geary, David & Carmen Hamson (2007). *Improving the Mathematics and Science Achievement of American Children: Psychology's Role.* University of Missouri-Columbia.

Herald Sun (2008). "New Yorker slammer over cartoon of Barack Obama and wife…" hhp://www.news.com.au/heraldsun/story/0,21985,24017100-663,00.html

The World Factbook (2008). "Brief History of South Africa." https://www.cia.gov/library/publications/the-world-factbook/geos/sf.htm#Intro

"History of South Africa." Wikipedia (2008). http://en.wikipedia.org/wiki/History_of_South_Africa

Whiston W. & Mailer P. (1999). *The New Complete Works of Josephus.* Kregeil Publications, Grand Rapids, MI 49501.

Glossary

Agrarian - farming

Anthropocentric - the interpreting of the world in terms of human values

Anthropophagi - cannibalism

Bucolic - concerning pastoral shepherds, country living, peasant living

Connotative - addition to the literal (dictionary meaning); an emotional meaning

Cracker - an ignorant white raciest American, often mistakenly thought to be poor and uneducated, but more often found in the highest political, economic, religious, educational, and social circles. Please understand that one can come in contact with "Black Crackers" also. I call them "Wheat Thins."

Denotative - dictionary meaning

Endemic - only found among a certain people or specific area

Hominid - member of the primate family including human, underdeveloped human

Miasma - musty swamp stench, offending smell

Mores - the fixed moral binding customs of a group

Pagan - country living, uneducated of the gods, usually peasants

Tells - the subconscious behavior which precedes or is done in conjunction with an individual's actions

Treatise - a written work or thought dealing formally and systematically with a subject

Salmonella - a bacterium causing food poisoning often found in poultry

Subjugate - to bring under control/subjection

Subordination - to make lesser or control

Sustenance - nourishment

Trichinosis - disease caused by hair-like worms ingested in undercooked pork

"Watch and pray so that you will not fall into temptation. The spirit is willing, but the body is weak."(Matthew 26:4)

"God allows man to participate in the honor of the execution of His will; God's institution of prayer lends to His creatures the dignity of causality." (Blaise Pascal)

One of the most profound statements concerning prayer that I have ever heard is the following by Blaise Pascal: "God allows man to participate in the honor of the execution of His will; God's institution of prayer lends to His creatures the dignity of causality." What does that mean? It means that God in His, and in spite of His perfection, treats us like He would treat himself. As He sees fit, God allows us to participate in the workings of the world. Through prayer, He allows us to help him effect change for the good of the universe.

For us old school folks, think of how much fun it was when your father allowed you to help him work on the family car, or when your mother allowed you to help prepare dinner. As children, we really did not know what we were doing, but just handing our parents the wrench or the spoon was exciting. That's what our heavenly Father does for us when we pray. To a great extent, our Father often allows us to determine our own fate. That is why the old folks say, "Be careful what you pray for." To teach you a lesson, God will often give you what you ask for even if it's not the best thing for you. Most of us do not appreciate or understand the true power of prayer.

Ultimate Theoanthropololgy ━━━━━━━━━━━━

Prayer is the ultimate expression of theoanthropology. Prayer above anything else is responsible for the quality of our personal relationship with God. Prayer is more important than scripture, because prayer is what ignites the divine Spirit of discernment necessary for understanding God's written Word. By the Holy Spirit, prayer allows us what little ability we have to operate in the preternatural. Contrary to what some people think, prayer does not, and in most cases should not, be magniloquent. God does not care about flowery bombastic pontification. God wants you to talk to Him from your heart and spirit. He only asks that you be true and not pretentious. Matthew 6: 5-7 says, "And when thou prayest, thou shalt not be as the hypocrites are: for they love to pray standing in the synagogues and in the corners of the streets, that they may be seen of men verily I say unto you, They have their reward. But thou, when thou prayest, enter into thy closet, and when thou hast shut thy door, pray to thy Father which is in secret; and thy Father which seeth in secret shall reward thee openly." Effective prayers are not ostentatious, loquacious gestures of human ego. False prayers will not make it past the Holy Spirit. God only hears the simple, plain, short, and sincere adorations, concerns, or requests. In fact, "Help, Lord" will suffice. God knows what is in your heart. God already knows what you need. He just likes you to ask Him. God likes for you to talk to Him, but He doesn't like **B**ilingual **S**ignification. Consider this parable. "And He spake this parable unto certain which trusted in themselves that they were righteous, and despised others: Two men went up into the temple to pray: the one a Pharisee, and the other a publican. The Pharisee stood and prayed thus with himself, God, I thank thee, that I am not as other men are, extortioners, unjust, adulterers, or even as this publican. I fast twice in the week; I give tithes of all that I possess. And the publican, standing afar off, would not lift up so much as his eyes unto heaven, but smote upon his breast, saying God be merciful to me a sinner. I tell you; this man (publican) went down to his house justified rather than the other:

for every one that exalteth himself shall be abased; and he that humbleth himself shall be exalted" (Luke 18: 10-14). The Pharisee was filled with false righteousness. His hypocrisy and lack of humility negated his prayer. However, the publican's brokenness, humility, and total belief in God's salvific love ultimately justified him.

Religion continues to make that same mistake. Religion and Pharisee are synonymous. Religion is *anthropocentric,* meaning man centered, or man's way of finding God. Relationship is *theopocentric,* meaning God centered. Please understand, we do not find God, God finds us when we acknowledge His son Jesus. Remember the words of Pascal: "To love a man one must first know him, to know God one must first love Him."

Unfortunately, most people do not understand the difference between religion and relationship. Religion is a generic term. After studying the major religions of the world, my definition of religion is "man's way of acknowledging corporate and personal belief in God or gods with varying degrees of pomposity, irrelevant doctrine, and pomp." The operative words are "man's way." Man's way is often encumbered with worthless tradition and mindless false doctrine. God's Word says, *"but the hour cometh, and now is, when the true worshippers shall worship the Father in Spirit and in truth; for the Father seeketh such to Him" (John 4:23).* As an ordained Baptist minister, my experience has shown me that often religion has nothing in common with Christ-like behavior. The simpler and uncluttered the adoration of God, the more spiritually pure it is.

The Maher Confusion

One of my favorite T.V. shows is the Bill Maher show that airs on Friday nights at 11:00 p.m. Maher routinely has interesting guests who often have provocative and insightful discussions on contemporary issues. Oftentimes the discussions skirt the issue of religion, which Maher is almost always violently against. He professes to be an atheist; however, Shakespeare's character Gertrude's response, "The lady doth protest too much," gives me cause to question his devout atheism. All humans are subconsciously or consciously looking for the meaning of life. Why am I here? What am I supposed to be doing? Atheists and agnostics are no different. In order not to believe in God, minimally one must tentatively believe in God. It's a paradox: one must first acknowledge the idea of God to reject God. Moreover, one rejects information because of ignorance, or because the evidence is defined improperly, insufficiently, or made to appear contradictory. According to what Maher understands religion to be, his antagonistic reaction to religious people, religious doctrine, and especially religious history, and the preternatural nature of scripture, is justified. The irony of the matter is that he is exactly right. In his vernacular, religion does "suck." Maher is absolutely correct. Religion is the mutant bastard of true Christianity. Christianity is Christ-like behavior; religion is not. Like many people, Maher gets religion confused with relationship. They are two independently separate things. He is 100% correct in his assessment that all religions, to a greater or lesser degree, have been used for various dastardly and nefarious things. We need go no further than the exploration of Vatican history and the popes, or the history of American slavery and its institutionalized social justification by domestic religion. Religion is so "wack" that some black people thought slavery was Christian! Is there a need to discuss the Catholic support of Hitler, Nazi Germany, and the Vatican's aid in protecting Nazi war criminals? Perhaps some discussion concerning the Spanish Inquisition or the Crusades, Christian and Muslim atrocities, are necessary? It would take two texts to adequately discuss the *progenitorial* relationship between the Roman Catholic Church and Islam. Big hint. Mohammad's wife was a filthy rich Catholic nun. Perhaps a study of the contemporary Baltic mess will be enlightening?

Maher has a valid point. Religion has nothing to do with God. Relationship with the one and only true God is Christianity, not the spiritually contaminated religions that profess to be Godly. Our job as true believers is to bring people like Bill Maher to the true realization of God, Christ, and the Holy Spirit. Again, prayer is the key. People like Maher are tough sells, because they are angry and bitter, and frankly they should be. Keep trying. Please remember, *"I can do all things through Christ, which strengthens me" (Philippians 4:13).*

Again, What Is Prayer?

Prayer is simply talking to God with the expectation that your conversation will be understood and acted upon. It is spending time with Him like you would any other loved one. Dialogue flows both ways, God speaks, we listen, we speak, and God listens. Prayer is the center of a believer's spiritual power. Perhaps the difficulty in understanding prayer is in comprehending its process? Before one completely understands prayer, one must understand the power of the Trinity, the Father, the Son, and the Holy Spirit. The word "Trinity" is never mentioned in the Bible; however, its divine members are gloriously and generously spoken of, from Genesis to Revelation inclusive.

John 1:1 says, "In the beginning was the Word, and the Word was with God. The same was in the beginning with God." Spiritually, when one sees the Word in scripture, it means Jesus Christ. Consequently, the scripture passage means that in the beginning was Christ and in the beginning Christ was with the Father. Where was the Holy Ghost/Holy Spirit? *"And the earth was without form, and void; and the darkness was upon the face of the deep. And the Spirit of God (Holy Spirit) moved upon the face of the waters" (Genesis 1:2).* From this we infer that the Holy Spirit was at the very beginning with God the Father, and God the Son. From these two scripture passages, we can conclude that all three forms of the Christian deity were present at the beginning, whenever that was. The problem was Adam's disobedience and the imputation of sin on all following generations.

Adam's spiritual fall required a *propitious* or restorative plan. God the Father satisfied that need with the sacrificial, redemptive, and justifying help of His son Jesus, and the salvific and protective power of the Holy Ghost. Some call it the three "P's." God the

Father planned salvation, God the Son provided salvation, and God the Holy Spirit promotes and protects salvation. It is the Gospel or Good News of Jesus Christ. The sacrificial Blood of Christ and His resurrection justified all of humanity. However, all who wish to be saved must request of God this justification and salvation by repentance and acknowledgement of their sins. *"If thou shalt confess with thy mouth the Lord Jesus, and shalt believe in thine heart that God hath raised Him from the dead, thou shalt be saved. For with the heart man believeth unto righteousness; and with the mouth confession is made unto salvation"* (Romans 10:9-10).

The three "P's" are located in Ephesians 1:3-14: *"Blessed be the God and Father of our Lord Jesus Christ, who hath blessings in heavenly places in Christ. 4. According as He hath chosen us in Him before the foundation of the world, that we should be holy and without blame before Him in love. 5. Having predestinated us unto the adoption of children by Jesus Christ to Himself, according to the good pleasure of His will, 6. To the praise of the glory of His grace, wherein he hath made us accepted in the beloved. 7. In whom we have redemption through His Blood the forgiveness of sins, according to the riches of His grace. 8. Wherein He hath abounded toward us in all wisdom and prudence; 9. Having made known unto us the mystery of His will according to His good pleasure, which hath purposed in himself. 10. That in the dispensation of the fullness of times he might gather together in one all things in Christ, both which are in heaven, and which are on earth; even in Him. 11. In whom also we have obtained an inheritance, being predestinated according to the purpose of Him who worketh all things after the counsel of His own will. 12. That we should be to the praise of His glory, who first trusted in Christ. 13. In whom ye also trusted, after that ye heard the Word of truth, the gospel of your salvation: in whom also after that ye behaved, ye were sealed with that Holy Spirit of promise."*

In the above scripture God acknowledges His blessed plan, and explains what it is. Christ's sanctified blood will cover all that believe in His sacrifice and resurrection, and all believers are redeemed according to the riches of Christ. For example, if an ordinary person were to take a group to dinner, when the bill came the waitress or waiter would be tipped according to the amount of the bill and what the host could afford. In contrast, if Bill Gates, the multibillionaire, were to take a group to dinner, "according to his riches" means that Bill Gates would be more likely to give a much larger tip than the average person. Imagine what "according to His riches" means in reference to Jesus.

Christ has also given us a modicum of spiritual discernment enabling believers to live a Christ-like life, and He will reveal special pearls of wisdom that only believers can understand. When the time is right he will gather all believers together, dead and alive, and the righteous will be rewarded. Best of all, because of our belief and love for Christ we are sealed, protected, and preserved for heaven by the Holy Spirit. No one, or nothing, can take your salvation.

Don't "Diss" the Holy Spirit

It is common for believers to celebrate God and Christ, but often acknowledgement of the role of the Holy Spirit is neglected. Some Christians totally eliminate the Holy Spirit from their doctrine, which is contrary to Scripture. Big mistake. The Holy Spirit just doesn't float around in the sky pouncing when He wishes. In Old Testament times when the Israelites worshiped and sacrificed in the tabernacle, the innermost section, the Holy of Holies, was reserved for the high priest only. Once a year, he and he only could go into the inner sanctum. Yon Kippur, or the Day of Atonement, was the festival when the Hebrews offered sacrificial prayers and animal blood for the forgiveness of sins. God is meticulous about who enters His Holy of Holies. The high priest needed to be spiritually and physically cleansed or he would be struck dead. The other priest tied a belled rope around his waist when he went into the sanctum. If the bell stopped ringing, it was an indication that he was dead and they would pull him out. That is how serious the Day of Atonement was to God and the Israelites.

The Holy of Holies was separated by a veil, which was torn upon the death and resurrection of Christ. The tearing of the veil from the top to the bottom signified that now it is not necessary for a high priest to intercede. Every believer has personal access to God through the Holy Spirit, who is spiritually in all that are saved. "*Ye are of God, little children, and have overcome them: because greater is He that is in you, than he that is in the world.*" Simply stated, the *Holy Spirit who is supernatural and spiritually carried in the natures of all believers is greater than any man or anything of this natural world.* Every believer in Jesus Christ spiritually carries the Holy Spirit, and every believer has the opportunity and the privilege to talk to God. The intercessors are the Holy Spirit and Christ. When Christ ascended to heaven, He didn't leave us without protection. He sent the Holy Spirit, who some think dwells in all of us, sinners and the righteous. "*But the Comforter, which is the Holy Ghost, whom the Father will send in my name, He shall teach you all things, and bring all things to your remembrance, whatsoever I have said unto you*" (John 14:26).

There is a theological construct called *prevenient* grace (Wikipedia, 2008). It means that there is just enough goodness in an individual to allow a nonbeliever the opportunity to recognize the Gospel and choose to be saved. Human nature has three separate parts. There is the natural, which addresses all human physical needs and desires. There is the soul, or the natural psychological being of men. It controls the emotional frailties of human nature. In fact, the Koin Greek word for soul is "psyche". However, the word for *spirit* is "pneumatos," which connotes God-blown breath or the Spirit of God. "*For the word of God is quick, and powerful, and sharper than any twoedged sword, piercing even to the dividing asunder of soul and spirit, and of the joints and marrow, and is a discerner of the thoughts and intents of the heart*" (Hebrews 4:12). This scripture explicitly says that God's Word will separate all three in an attempt to empower the believer in the attempt at Christ-like behavior. By conviction, the Bible will show a believer what is righteous and what is not. The end result is that believers have been given the spiritual right to communicate with God. Prayer and scripture combined comprise perfect Godly communication. The Holy Spirit hears our prayers, relaying them to Christ. Christ rubberstamps them and passes them on to God. God determines if what we are praying about is in our best interest. He then determines if He will answer, not answer, or answer with something different than what we have requested. That is how it works; that is how powerful and precious prayer is. Christ sacrificed His life so that all can have the right to talk to Him directly.

What, Who Is/Are the Trinity?

This is a most confusing question to even the most learned and seasoned Christians. If there are three deities, who is in charge? Is the Father in charge with the Son second and the Holy Ghost third? The Word says that all three were present at the beginning of time, but when was the beginning? These same questions have been asked a great number of times for a great number of years, by a great number of people. No one has come up with a definitive answer. My attempt is to explain the concept using generic Christian doctrine. Most Christian faiths believe that the Father, Son, and Holy Ghost are equal in Holiness. There are some religions, for example, the Jehovah Witness, who believe in subordination, a concept that ranks the three in order of importance. Moreover, Catholics and most Protestant denominations do not consider the Jehovah Witness faith Christian because it questions the complete divinity of Christ. There have also been controversial disputes engaged over who sent the Holy Spirit. Was it God and Jesus or was it God alone? The Western Church of Rome insisted that God and Jesus sent the Holy Spirit, while the Eastern Church, the Greek Orthodox, insisted that it was God alone. It was called the Filioque Controversy of 589 A.D. and ultimately was one of the deciding issues causing the split between the Western and Eastern Churches in 1054 A.D. (McGrath, 2001). Wars, torture, lying, cheating, stealing, and all types of despicable acts of sin were perpetuated because of trivial and ungodly attitudes. Who cares? The colorless man must be above the dangerous triviality of attitude.

Perhaps the following will make the Trinity clearer and clarify the role it serves in a believer's life. When I was a kid growing up in Philadelphia, there were these great hot pretzel vendors, who used to sell their pretzels on the street corners. You really didn't know what you were getting with your pretzel, but they sure were good, and the mustard killed the germs anyway. Picture the Trinity as a three-ring pretzel with three holes. The pretzel is a perfect metaphor. The Father, the Son, and the Holy Ghost are one, but separate. Like a hole, they are unseen and can only be identified by their surrounding substance. The Trinity's surrounding substance is love. We cannot see the three, because they are Spirits, but we know they are there. God is a Spirit, Jesus is no longer in His *hypostatic union* and is a Spirit, and the Holy Spirit was always a Spirit. *"God is a Spirit: and they that worship Him must worship Him in spirit and truth"* (John 4:24). A pretzel can be turned any way you wish, depending on what side one wishes to bite. If you need God and want a bite of Him, turn it one way. If you need a bite of Jesus, turn it another way. If you need a bite of the Holy Ghost, turn it to the third side. The Trinity is designed to satisfy all of a believer's needs. The ultimate reality is that all the world needs is God. Who came first and who sent who has nothing to do with God.

Unfortunately, religion still remains hocked by these trivialities. Almost every world religion has infighting. There are three prime examples. In Christianity, the Roman Catholics are at odds with the Greek Orthodox Catholics, and both Catholics have problems with Protestants. Protestants also snub their noses at each other. The "high class" Presbyterians and Methodists have a pejorative attitude concerning the Baptists, while all three look down on the Pentecostal, Apostolic, and Church of God in Christ assemblies. Church as we know it today is a religious culture and has forgotten the Gospel of Jesus Christ. It appears that we are too busy looking holy instead of trying to be holy. Too busy talking holy instead of acting holy. All of this affects the effectiveness of our prayers, because many of our prayers are associated with the trivialities mentioned above. Christ wants a Church united under His headship, not a group of scattered, envious fragments arguing over who is the most holy. When one prays, the prayers should be for the uplifting of God, Christ, His Church, and the righteousness of all mankind. That is what a colorless man does.

What Type of Prayers Should We Pray? ▬▬▬▬▬

Often, believers are confused on how to pray or what to pray. Please remember, any sincere, humble, and honest petition God will hear. Before we ask, the Father already knows what we want, but more important, what we need. Consciously asking Him is merely a respectful formality and a humble gesture of contrition.

According to 1 Timothy 2:1-2, there are four basic types of prayer. *"I exhort therefore that, first of all, supplication, prayers, intercessions, and giving of thanks, be made for all men; For kings, and for all that are in authority; that we may lead a quiet and peaceable life in all godliness and honesty."* The four types are prayers, which are: Prayers of Supplication unto God, Prayers of Worship unto God, Prayers of Intercession unto God, and Prayers of Thanksgiving unto God. The perfect example is the Paternoster, or "Our Father." If most were asked to repeat The Lord's Prayer, most would repeat Matthew 6:9 or Luke 11:2. *"And He said unto them, 'When ye pray, say, Our Father which art in heaven, Hallowed be thy name. Thy kingdom come. Thy will be done in earth, as it is in heaven. Give us this day our daily bread. And forgive us our debts, as we forgive our debtors. And lead us not into temptation; but deliver us from evil. For thine is the kingdom, and the power, and the glory, for ever, Amen'"* (Matthew 6:11-13). The above is the Paternoster or "Our Father," not The Lord's Prayer. Jesus taught this prayer to the disciples when they asked Him how to pray. It is accurately known as The Disciple's Prayer. The entire chapter of John 17 is The Lord's Prayer, which will be discussed later in this chapter. The Paternoster contains all of the necessary parts of an effective prayer. It begins with recognizing the holiness and sovereignty of God, and that he alone deserves worship and praise. Supplication and adoration is an attitude acknowledging submissiveness unto God and thirst for His divinity and wisdom. *A psalm of David. "The earth is the Lord's and the fullness thereof; the world, and they that dwell therein. For He hath founded it upon the seas, and established it upon the floods. Who shall ascend into the hill of the Lord? Or who shall stand in His holy Place...?" (Psalm 24)*. Please read Psalm 24 and 95 in their entirety. Thanksgiving is the grateful acknowledgement for the provision of our daily needs. It is given with the understanding that just because they are consistent and daily, they are not perfunctory. *"Give thanks in all circumstances; for this is the will of God in Christ Jesus for you" (1 Thessalonians 5:18)*.

Petition and intercessory prayer can be tricky. God loves it when we pray for each other. *"Confess your faults one to another, and pray one for another, that ye may be healed. The effectual fervent prayer of a righteous man availeth much" (James 5:16)*. However, intercessory prayer can become deadly when dealing with evil. Demons are not to be taken lightly. Ask Sceva and his seven sons. *"And there were seven sons of one Sceva, a Jew, and chief of the priests, which did so, And the evil spirit answered and said, Jesus I know, and Paul I know; but who are ye? And the man in whom the evil spirit was leaped on them, and overcame them, and prevailed against them, so that they fled out of that house naked and wounded" (Acts 19:14)*. Before you intercede in any demonic situation, be certain demonic intercession is your gift. My wife calls it "ghost busting." One must be certain of the gift. Pray for the protection of the Holy Spirit before confrontation. In addition, make certain that someone is praying for you while you are addressing the demon. If you deal with evil regularly, pray before you leave the sanctity of your home. There is no *Traducian* theory involved here. Just because a parent or relative may have the "ghost busting" gift does not mean you also have it.

There is another interesting part to intercession. The Holy Spirit can make intercession for us. In Acts, "speaking in tongues" is correctly defined in reference to the communication the disciples performed during Peter's sermon. The multitude of 3,000 understood through divine translation what was being said, and were delivered. Please understand, Paul is explicit when he charges that those who speak in tongues must have an interpreter. *"If any man speaks in an unknown tongue, let it be by two, or at the most by three, and that by course; and let one interpret"* (1 Corinthians 14:27). This is exactly what happened. The multitude to which Peter was preaching was an inter-clan, international conglomeration of Hebrews with several different languages all assembled in Jerusalem for the Passover celebration. The clans/nations were separated *homogeneously,* and the disciples were distributed among the mass of people one or more to every nation. The Holy Spirit empowered the disciples to speak to each individual nation and clan in their native language, even though the disciples were not versed in that particular language. *"And they were all amazed and marveled, saying one to another, Behold, are not all these which speak Galileans? And how hear we every man in our own tongue, wherein we were born?"* (Acts 2:12-13). This is truly speaking in tongues. It is not unintelligible utterances from a believer in the Spirit. However, those sounds are Holy. They are called Holy language. *"with sighs too deep for words the Holy spirit helps us in our weakness; for we do not know how to pray as we ought, but the Spirit Himself intercedes for us with sighs too deep for words"* (Romans 8:26). The above scripture is Holy language, not speaking in tongues as many believers incorrectly assume.

The Disciple's Prayer ends with praise and worship. We are to always give God praise and vocally show our worship of His divinity. God appreciates our appreciation, and showing it is a privilege and obligation. *"O come, let us sing unto the Lord: let us make a joyful noise to the rock of our salvation. Let us come before His presence with thanksgiving, and make a joyful noise unto Him with psalms"* (Psalm 95:1-2). Further discussion concerning the Paternoster or Disciple's Prayer will be explored in the section on intercessory prayer.

"Spress Yourself"

Back in the early '70s there was a rhythm and blues group called

Charles Wright and the Watts 103rd Street Rhythm Band. The name of one of their biggest hits was "Express Yourself," but Charles used to say "Spress Yourself." It is time for believers to "Spress Ourselves." There are three expressions of prayer: vocal prayer, Christian meditation, and contemplative prayer. Vocal prayer is exactly what it implies. The four forms of prayer are applied to audibly understandable language usually required in congregative settings. The prayer may be any of the four types mentioned above or an amalgamation of all.

The operative word in Christian meditation is "Christian." There are several types of meditation, but we are expressly speaking of spending silent time with the God of Abraham, Isaac, and Jacob. It is when the believer settles into his or her prayer closet. A prayer closet does not have to be a small confined room. It has nothing to do with immediate surroundings, but simply removing yourself spiritually and emotionally from environmental distractions. Your prayer closet can be at your desk at work, in the park, or at the gym while you work out. The prayer closet is specific to one's personal needs and comfort.

Contemplative prayer is prayer shared with God as your friend. It is a discussion with God in an effort to hash out, through questions and answers, perplexing natural or spiritual dilemmas. Contemplative prayer is a give and take conversation with God. Oftentimes there is no conclusive result; however, the spiritual wrestling itself brings one peace. Contrary to what some theologians consider, music can be prayer. David was a musician and penned several harmonic prayers. Read Psalms; most of them are poetic prayers set to music and rhythm.

The Lord's Prayer

As mentioned earlier, what some believers consider The Lord's Prayer actually is not. It is the Paternoster or Our Father, accurately known as the Disciple's Prayer. The Lord's Prayer is the entire Chapter 17 of the Gospel of John. It is the culminating pre-crucifixion prayer offered to God by Jesus, which was intended for all disciples to hear. Jesus, by way of the Last Supper, has already prepared the disciples for His death and resurrection. Chapters thirteen, fourteen, fifteen, and sixteen prepare them for His physical absence by assuring them of the spiritual power and love of God. Christ also warned of the eminent trials and persecution that await them in the future, and not to be discouraged. He prepared His disciples for the coming of the Holy Spirit and foretold great things that they would do for the building of God's kingdom. The most important comfort He left was the realization that He and the Father are one. "And I will pray the Father, and He shall give you another Comforter, that He may abide with you for ever" (John 14:16). The word for Comforter in this scripture is (Gk. paracleton, para-cle-ton), which denotatively means exhort, encourage, comfort, or help. Connotatively, "paracleton" means "legal advocate, or justifier."

The Lord's Prayer, John 17, is so powerful and moving that many theologians refer to it as the New Testament Holy of Holies. We must understand that Jesus was perfectly aware of what He was about to endure. Remember, Jesus prayed this prayer a few minutes before He left the Upper Room, and prior to He and the disciples trekking through the valley of Kidron and across to the Mount of Olives. In the darkness, He finally found His way to the Garden of Gethsemane where Christ prayed His passionate prayer. The prayer was so intense that He experienced *hemohydrosis*, and the bloody sweat dripped from His forehead as he prayed. Jesus naturally did not want to suffer the excruciating humiliation of crucifixion, but His greater fear was spiritual separation from His Father. The cup of sin was exceedingly more frightening for Him than the physical agony of death, for this would be the only time He would ever be separated from God. The glory of Christ shines after this purging. His attitude blossomed into that of anticipation, and almost joy, at the expectation of fulfilling His divine calling.

Aside from taking nails through our wrist and feet and a wound in one's side, God expects us to endure hardship. Hardship is what purges believers of sin. The result is a closer relationship to Christ and a spiritual promotion. *"For promotion cometh neither from the east, nor from the west, nor from the south, but God is the judge; He putteth down one, and setteth up another" (Psalms 75:6).* Jesus understands and appreciates that first He must be glorified that He may glorify the father. *"Father, the hour is come; glorify thy Son, that thy Son also may glorify thee" (John 17:1:1).* God has trusted Jesus with His disciples and Christ has prepared them well. *"I have glorified thee on the earth: I have finished the work which thou gavest me to do." (John 17: 4).* *"For I have given unto them the words which thou gavest me; and they have received them" (John 17:8).* Jesus trusts the disciples with the world, because He has trained them well. Jesus prays that God continue to bless the disciples and future believers from evil and empower then to continue building God's kingdom. Christ is asking God to equip the disciples and all believers to be duplicates of Him. *"Go ye therefore, and teach all nations, baptizing them in the name of the Father, and of the Son and of the Holy Ghost: Teaching them to observe all things whatsoever I have commanded you: and, lo, I am with you, always, even unto the end of the world" (Matthew 28:19-20).* Believers are "reasonable facsimiles" of Christ. We are to do what He did; a huge charge, but we have been given the power to complete the task. Remember, *"......For unto whomsoever much is given, of him shall be much required: and to whom men have committed much, of him they will ask the more" (Luke 12:48).* Jesus wants the disciples to be ready. God will require much of them and so will man. If a man gives you $5.00, he will want $10.00 in return! Jesus accomplished this unbalanced expectation as God's incarnate, and He is asking God to bless His people with the power to do the same. Jesus completes The Lord's Prayer with a request for God to protect, empower, and equip not only the disciples but also all that will believe in Him and the Gospel. *"Neither pray I for these alone, but for them also which shall believe on me through their (Gospel) Word" (John 17:20).* Christ incorporates all forms of prayer in John 17, and it is a perfect example of Holy discourse, and a divine example of spiritual relationship and theoanthropology. *"Pray as if* everything depended on God, and work as if everything depended on man" (Francis Cardinal Spellman, *God's Little...*,1994).

And They "Spin" Themselves Silly ───────────────

The spin masters are at it again, and the Obama saga continues. In an effort to gain further knowledge of mid-eastern and international affairs, Senator Obama has recently embarked on an international junket with the intent of gathering additional knowledge in specific reference to the Levant community and its present and potential impact on global as well as U.S. interest. He made strategic stops in Iraq, where he had discussions with Iraqi President Nuri Kamal al-Maliki. He made stops in Israel where he had meetings with Israeli Prime Minister Ehud Olmert and Israeli President Shimon Peres. The 85-year-old Peres, an Israeli political fixture who perhaps has seen it all, remarked, "My greatest wish is for a great president of the United States. That is the greatest promise for us and the rest of the world." This man has suffered through World War II, the Holocaust, all of the Israeli/Palestinian Wars, all of the Israeli presidents and generals plus several American presidents. His statement in essence says, "I have seen it all and you may be The One." Why were the political pundits reluctant to publicize this? Senator Obama had audiences with Palestinian President Ehaud Olmert, and several of the locals. Wael Hamad, a mechanic, who has kept abreast of the U. S. campaign, said he expected Senator Obama to be more understanding of the Palestinian plight because of the racial situation of blacks in the United States. This is a prime example of the international mirror of hypocrisy that the United States stares into and refuses to recognize. The people of the world want a new American face, an America they can trust. They want a face that looks like theirs!

McCain is crying foul. He's getting more attention than me, Boo Hoo, Boo Hoo, and the spin masters are whipping his tears. The irony is that subsequent to senator McCain securing his nomination, he did exactly the same thing. He met the same people and made speeches in Canada, Mexico, and Columbia, yet he accuses Obama of acting presidential and assuming a premature victory lap. Nobody said that about McCain, probably because his personality doesn't generate much interest. McCain actually suggested that Senator Obama make the trip; however, he never thought it would be this successful. The crushing blow suffered by the McCain campaign was the statement by the Prime Minister of Iraq, Nuri Kamal al-Maliki, who is in agreement with Senator Obama's sixteen-month timetable for the removal of American troops. The war in Iraq is the primary focal point of Senator McCain's political attack on Senator Obama. McCain's rallying point challenges his opponent's lack of military and international affairs. The Prime Minister's statement is in direct contrast to Senator McCain's weakening attitude of indefinite occupation, and entangles Senator McCain in a quandary. An earlier statement by Senator McCain indicated that he would abide by any timetable the Iraqi leadership thought proper for the systematic removal of American troops from Iraq. Maliki's agreement with Obama tacitly obligates McCain to defer to the Obama and Maliki plan, which also weakens his argument in regard to Senator Obama's international ineffectiveness. Mr. McCain made a severe miscalculation in regard to the media impact and political effectiveness of the Obama trip. The trip was an international success for Obama and improved the tarnished image of the United States. It garnered a huge amount of media attention and deflected all attention from the McCain campaign.

As a counter attack, Senator McCain criticized Senator Obama for his high-profile posture, accusing him of taking a premature victory lap and acting presumptuously presidential. It seems that perhaps Senator McCain should focus more on the economic doldrums of this country, health care, the budget deficit, the national debt, gas prices, and issues sensitive to the troubled hearts of Americans. Obama is.

Please do not misinterpret my next statements. Senator McCain is a great man, a great and sincere American with an outstanding war record. Although my political positions are *antithetical* to his, my respect for him as a man of character is undaunted. The problem is that Senator McCain does not have the charisma of Senator Obama, and he never will. Senator Obama is vastly more presidential in appearance than Senator McCain, and unfortunately for Senator McCain, Senator Obama is an overwhelmingly better orator. In addition, Mr. Obama is six-feet two inches tall, forty-six years old, and athletic. Mr. McCain, in addition to the animatronics of his demeanor, is a seventy-two year old, short, and relatively unattractive man. The contrast seems to be shades of the 1960 Kennedy vs. Nixon campaign. Couple this to the contrast in excitement of each political campaign, and one can see why Senator Obama garners more media attention. Obama's story is much more exciting. To counteract the contrast, McCain is deriding his opponent by attacking him with sophomoric negative campaign ads, with the intent of subverting Senator Obama's message of political change. It did not work this past week. It actually backfired. The public, even the media, is beginning to see the shallowness of McCain's message. In terms of Senator Obama garnering the lion's share of the publicity this week, what did McCain expect? He suggested that he go, and his challenge returned to bite him. You know where. One must always remember. Regardless of political preference, America "is all about the Benjamins." The media is much more concerned with its ratings than McCain's popularity, especially when Obama's trip was so successful. Senator Obama flat out knocked them dead! As they say on the street, "Baby boy had the juice." Pray for the colorless man.

The Colors of Prayer

The beauty of prayer is a kaleidoscope of loving colors: red, orange, yellow, blue, green, indigo, and violet. Although light has no color, Sir Isaac Newton was the first to demonstrate that white light was comprised of all the colors of the rainbow. The colors of light can only be seen through a prism like a rainbow. A rainbow is the combination of microwave waves ranging in length from 4,000 (violet) to 7,700 (red), which in combination is uniquely visible to the eye and brings the ease of sight and growth to all living creatures. Light is the glorious change from darkness into physical and spiritual revelation.

Everything on earth is either one of the seven colors or a combination of two or more. Jesus is the light of the world and is a holy amalgamation of all that is beautifully colorful in prayer. Christ is the colorless man, for he is the brightness of light and reflects all the colors of life. *"Again therefore Jesus spoke unto them, saying I am the light of the world: he that followeth me shall not walk in the darkness, but shall have the light of life."*

The colorless man's spirituality includes all of the praying gifts. However, there are three areas that predominate in his or her prayer life. Please understand, as a leader the colorless man's actions are spiritually motivated by his concern for God, mankind, and nature. Clearly, this campaign has one candidate who is forthright concerning his devotion to God and one candidate who is very ambiguous concerning his spiritualism. The overtly spiritual candidate is vociferous and clear concerning the nation's welfare in regard to America's social, economic, and security issues. The position of the ostensibly less spiritual candidate seems to be primarily focused on national security, war, and imperialism, which is tantamount to the "baby" Bush style of leadership. Katrina is a clear example of the callous brand of Republican leadership. America needs a leader with the Godly love of Christ. "A good thing to remember. It is a better thing to do work with the construction gang, not the wrecking crew." (Unknown, *God's Little...*,1994)

There are three *salient* prayer characteristics of a colorless theoanthropologic leader. The first is The Prayer of Petition, the second The Prayer of Intercession, and the third The Prayer of Healing. However, if one studies The Disciple's Prayer, the Paternoster, the reader will notice the word "give" precedes the requests of forgiveness and deliverance. "Give" must be addressed first. The prayer says, *"Give us this day our daily Bread"* (Matthew 6:11). Most understand "bread" to mean our daily staples, or what we need for survival. What about our spiritual staples? Jesus also says, *"I am the Bread of life" (John 6: 48)*. The identical word is used in both passages. Bread (Gk. artos) has a denotative and connotative meaning. It simply means that a colorless man requires physical and spiritual nourishing. The physical is obvious, but the spiritual bread is scripture. Christ in text is the Word of God, the Bible. Without spiritual nourishment, believers are totally powerless to effect fervent powerful prayer. Giving is reciprocal. God gives His Word to believers so believers can give it to others. The "others" will repeat the cycle. God's perfect Plan. Always give first. He did.

Giving empowers the believer to ask for forgiveness for self and others. *"Forgive us our debts, as we forgive our debtors" (Matthew 6:11)*. The charge is that we are forgiven as we forgive. "As" is said *temporally* and in reference to intensity. "As" means we are forgiven as we forgive and to the same degree as we forgive. *"For if you forgive men their trespasses, your heavenly Father will also forgive you: But if ye forgive not men their trespasses, neither will your Father forgive your trespasses" (Matthew 6:14-15)*.

We probably need to expand a little on forgiveness, because if you're like me, that is the most difficult prayer to pray. The most difficult prayer to pray is for someone whose chest you want to stomp a mud hole in. One can only say, "Help, Holy Ghost." Scripture says that Peter asked, *"Lord how oft shall my brother sin against me, and I forgive him? til seven times? Jesus saith unto him, I say not unto thee, until seven times: but, until seventy times seven" (Matthew 18:21-22)*. Gang, that is 490 times for the same trespass! Can you hang, "homies"? I can't. It is God's Word, so it has got to be righteous. Moreover, 490 is divisible by seven, and all numbers divisible by seven are holy numbers of completion. That tacitly means that all believers are charged to forgive each brother or sister 490 times for each trespass, before you have God's permission to bang them in the eye. Is that clear?

Seriously, there is some relief. Forgive does not mean forget. God does give us a modicum of common sense. The old aphorism says, "If you do me wrong the first time, it is your fault. If you do me wrong the second time it is my fault." Keep yourself out of compromising positions. Pray for spiritual discernment. The Holy Spirit will tell you who to trust and who not to trust. Also, don't confuse forgiveness for dislike. One can forgive another and still dislike what he or she does. As a personal example, there is a person that I thought I couldn't forgive. Every time I was in his presence, there was a literal emotion of violence that arose in me. However, forgiveness was not the issue. The specific incident had completely left my mind. My anger was toward what he continued to do to other people. My prayer for forgiveness was answered. My prayer, now, becomes one of anger management. "Anger is a stone thrown at a wasp's nest" (Unknown, *God's Little...*, 1994). God will provide.

Tools of the Spiritual Leader Are Petition, Intercession, and Healing

At this point, the critical importance of giving and forgiveness have been addressed, we can now turn to deliverance. God delivers through prayers of petition, intercession, and healing. As defined by Richard Foster in his book *Prayer, Finding the Heart's True Home*, prayers of petition are personal requests of God. God is excited about petitionary prayer, because it shows our dependence on His love. The Greek word is *deomai* (deomai), which has the righteous sense of beseeching Christ or God. Deomai is used in the New Testament on twenty-two separate occasions, and has a general English meaning of "I beg you."

Whether we accept it or not, asking is the rule of God's Kingdom. *"Ask, and it shall be given you; seek, and ye shall find; knock, and it shall be opened unto you; For every one that asketh receiveth; and he that seeketh findeth; and to him that knocketh it shall be opened"* (Matthew 7:7-8). Frankly, believers should continuously ask of God. Regardless of our personal salvation, believers are never independently good enough, sufficiently ethical, or have adequate righteousness to please Him. He is the adult. We are the children, and we honor Him when we admit to reliance on His parenthood. God's actualized plan allows all who repent, believe, and confess to gloriously engage as members of His family. *"That if thou shall confess with thy mouth the Lord Jesus, and shalt believe in thine heart that God hath raised Him from the dead, thou shalt be saved. For with the heart man believeth unto righteousness; and with the mouth confession is made unto salvation" (Romans 10: 9-10).*

Pray and be careful. Do not get entangled in false self-righteousness and false humility. The proverbial, "I don't want to bother God with my trivialities." Be real! God knows you're a liar. God is omniscient, omnipresent, immutable, ubiquitous, and infinite. He already knows what you want and need, and He has already promised to provide. When believers stumble into the trap of false humility or the attitude that God has blessed *me* especially to handle my special situations, it saddens the Father's heart. Our reluctance to ask prohibits God from giving. Remember, He wants to give to you so that you can generously share with others. When God answers our prayers of petition, it allows one to publicly celebrate and praise God's goodness, which bolsters one's personal faith and the faith of others. Faith is reciprocal. The more you give, the more you get. The more one receives, the more one can share. The colorless woman and man spiritually understand the reciprocity of faith.

Are All Prayers Answered?

No. All prayers are not answered. There is no definitive reason. Let us exercise a modicum of conjecture concerning this issue. It may give some explanation. In the Old Testament, Isaiah 38, the prophet told Hezekiah that he was going to die. In his distress Hezekiah turned his face to the wall, and in tears began to petition God to allow him to live. God honored his prayer of petition and extended his life fifteen years. "In those days was Hezekiah sick unto death. And Isaiah the prophet the son of Amoz came unto him, and said unto him, Thus saith the Lord, Set thine house in order: for thou shalt die, and not live. Then Hezekiah turned his face toward the wall, and prayed unto the Lord, And said, Remember now O Lord, I Beseech thee, how I have walked before thee in truth and with a perfect heart, and have done that which is good in thy spirit, And Hezekiah wept sore. Then came the Word of the Lord to Isaiah, saying, Go, and say to Hezekiah, Thus saith the Lord, the God of David thy father, I have heard thy prayer, I have seen thy tears: behold, I will add unto thy days fifteen years" (Isaiah 38:1-4). That is a perfect example of a petitionary prayer. However, sometime during that fifteen years King Hezekiah made a crucial mistake. During their visit, he allowed the Babylonians to see the riches of the temple and the kingdom. The error largely contributed to Nebuchadnezzar's taxing of the nation and finally the capturing of Jerusalem. Perhaps, if God had not granted Hezekiah the extra fifteen years, Nebuchadnezzar might not have been so apt to destroy Jerusalem. So how does that relate to unanswered prayer? As mentioned earlier, God lives in "kiros" time, which allows God to operate at the beginning whenever that was, and at the end, whenever that is. He knows how all prayers will affect the future. He knows which prayers will be beneficial and which prayers will be detrimental to the well-being of man, the world, and the universe. Obviously, God will make the perfect choice. If your prayer does not conflict with God's perfect future, perhaps He will grant your prayer request. Moreover, since God operates in eternal time, perhaps if one can develop the relationship that Hezekiah had with God, God might alter the sequence of future events for you. Apparently, that is what He did for Hezekiah. Please understand, God answers prayers with the perfect universe in mind. He arranges things with the perfection and righteousness of eternity in His infinite mind. P. T. Forsyth, a Scottish theologian, has a great quote regarding this quandary. He says, "We shall come one day to a heaven where we shall gratefully know that God's great refusals were sometimes the true answers to our truest prayer" (Forsyth, 1915, p. 63).

At the risk of sounding like a self-righteous holy rolling, fire-breathing, scripture-spouting, black suit, black tie-wearing preacher, sin can cause unanswered prayer. Please do not be misled. God does answer the prayers of sinners. If He didn't, this writer would be in deep trouble. However, the very condition of sin, its nature, and its spiritual substance separates one from God. God cannot abide where there is sin. Sin negates a close relationship with Christ and God, or theoanthropology. Once one becomes His child, God is obligated by Himself to provide what the believer needs. Pray for yourself; it will empower you to pray for others.

God Requires It, So Do It!

James says, "Confess your faults one to another, and pray one for another, that ye may be healed. The effectual and fervent prayer of a righteous man avaleth much" (James 5:16). Intercessory prayer is required of God. "Moreover as for me, God forbid that I should sin against the Lord in ceasing to pray for you: but I will teach you the good and the right way" (I Samuel 12:23). Interestingly in James 5:16, there are two different meanings for pray in this scripture passage. The initial use of pray (Gk. euchesthe), "and pray for one another," means vow. The second, "fervent prayer," (Gk. deesis), means a cry for help. The more accurate translation of the passage reads, "Confess your faults one to another and vow to and for another that ye may be healed. The cries for help of a righteous man avails much" (James 3:16). The passage says that if you want help from Me, make a spiritual confession, and cry to Me for help for your sisters and brothers. When one understands God's Word in the original languages, the language often becomes much more powerful and profound. "Study to show thyself approved unto God, a workman that needeth not to be ashamed, rightly dividing the Word of truth" (II Timothy 2:15).

One must also understand that intercessory prayer is not reserved for the fellowship's identified leadership. The veil of the temple has been rent. Now, with the power of the Holy Spirit, prayers of intercession can be made directly to the Throne of Christ. Intercession is the quintessential expression of the love. Love is the ultimate manifestation of intercession, and the propitious work of Jesus on the cross was the ultimate intercession. It was perfect in every way. Please remember, Christ doesn't expect us to be perfect.

As believers spiritually grow, He expects us to strive to be increasingly reasonable facsimiles. That pleases God.

Watch the "Knock Offs" ━━━━━━━━━━━━━

In contemporary industry and business, when someone invents a good product and it becomes popular, there is always someone ready to create a cheaper, less valuable copy. In Acts 8: 17-18, Simon Magnus tries to buy the special gifts of intercession and healing, which the Holy Spirit had anointed Peter and the other apostles. *"And when Simon saw that through laying on of the apostles' hands the Holy Ghost was given, he offered them money, Saying, Give me also this power, that on whomsoever I lay hands, he may receive the Holy Ghost. But Peter said unto him, Thy money perish with thee, because thou hast thought that the gift of God may be purchased with money"* (Acts 8:18-20). All that appears holy is not. *"Having a form of godliness, but denying the power thereof; from such turn away"* (II Timothy 3:5). Just because someone prays a long articulate prayer with expressive oratorical acumen, does not mean that they have a relationship with God. Just because they run around the church and speak in what they call tongues, does not mean you should allow them to intercede to God in prayer for you. There are plenty of the enemy's lieutenants who know scripture. It is my opinion that if one is aware of evil and you let evil pray and lay hands on you, God will chastise you for being foolish. Also, believers should be careful whom they pray for and touch. Often it is spiritually dangerous to pray in some situations. Use your spiritual discernment. Very often God will give you the spirit of flight. Often we find ourselves faced with evil for which we are not spiritually prepared. Run! *"Lay hands suddenly on no man, neither be partaker of other men's sins: keep thyself pure"* (I Timothy 5:22).

To Heal Is Real

Sometimes it is contrary to all empirical evidence, is antithetical to all heuristic procedure, contradicts scientific observation, disregards cause/effect rational, and gleefully confounds the most cerebral of physicians. The gift of healing is exactly what God says it is, a spiritual gift. *"To another faith by the same (Holy) Spirit; to another the gifts of healing by the same Spirit"* (I Corinthians: 12:7). The acceptance of the spiritual healing power of the Holy Spirit, through the gifting of men and women, has become so prevalent that ambivalent physicians, some previously atheist and agnostic, have accepted the healing power of faith in their practices. Doctors have aggressively sought out gifted Christians as medical consultants to assist in their treatment regimes for all illnesses. Several doctors have accepted Christ as their personal Savior and accepted the call to preach His healing power of love. An assortment of empirical studies has suggested that faith is a major and often critical component of the healing process. Prayer works.

However, let us not negate the contribution of medical advancement and effectiveness. Physicians are a critical extension of God's miracles and mercies. Always remember, God often works his wonders through the common hands of man. *"But God hath chosen the foolish things of the world to confound the wise; and God hath chosen the weak things of the world to confound the things which are mighty; And base things of the world, and things which are despised, hath God chosen, yea, and things which are not, to bring to naught things that are"* (I Corinthians 1:27-28). Conversely, while the vilification of faith healing has subsided in the medical profession, the spiritual realm should not malign, negate, or underappreciate the effectiveness of medicine and medical technology. To do so would be spiritually prideful and spiritually pompous. Dr. Ben Carson, the world-renowned neurosurgeon, is a devout believer and acknowledges his great successes to the power of God, Christ, and the Holy Spirit, whichever one happens to hit his mouth first. If you have the opportunity, please read his book *Gifted*

Hands. The previous scripture directly applies to him.

There is always the question, "Why does God heal some and not others?" The answer is congruent with why God answers some prayers and not others that we addressed in the previous section. However, my true answer minus conjecture is, I do not know. That will be one of the first questions I will ask when I get to glory. It will be directly after "Who cleaned out the bottom of Noah's Ark?"

There is a part to healing that is spiritually scary. My wife calls it "ghost busting." There may be a degree of levity in the name, but "ghost busting" is serious spiritual business. You can "pull up" on those demons unprepared if you like, but you may end-up screaming, bloody, and wounded like Sceva's sons *(Acts 19:14-16)*. Please believe me; demons are dangerous. If one is not spiritually prepared with prayer and scripture, you may find yourself rolling on the ground trying to slice your wrists and spitting nasty foam. One must sincerely ask for the anointing and protection of the Holy Spirit before confronting demons.

When teaching demonology at seminary, that particular year of instruction is always challenging for me. Evil attacks continuously until the academic year has concluded. Experience has convinced me that demons become considerably more active when you attack them. Preparing believers to challenge evil with prayer and the Word of Christ is a direct and unequivocal frontal attack. When teaching demonology, the instructor quickly learns to appreciate prayer and the protective power of Holy Spirit. Fortunately, at my seminary the course is offered every other academic year.

Please understand, "ghost busting" is a special gift. Not all can, and not all should, engage a known and active demon. May I suggest *Pigs in the Parlor* by Frank and Ida Hammond for those who wish to learn more about confronting demons. This book will educate you concerning when to engage, how to engage, and what prayers and scriptures to use in engagement. Read it. Theoanthropology will *inherently* sensitize one to evil. The sensitivity will become a *visceral* component of your spiritual and physical nature. Please always remember, *"There hath no temptation taken you but such as is common to man: but God is faithful, who will not suffer you to be tempted above that ye are able; but will with the temptation also make a way to escape, that ye be able to bear it"* (I Corinthians 10:13). Prayer in itself requires considerably more study than we can accomplish in this chapter. If one wishes to delve further into its study, the book recommended is *Prayer, finding the Heart's True Home* by Richard Foster.

The Race Card? Is Johnny Back?

The latest in the Obama Campaign symphony is the accusation that Senator Obama played the race card. The accusation came from the McCain camp, challenging a statement that Senator Obama made in reference to *phenotypically* specific dissimilarities to himself and the United States Presidents on U.S. currency. Why should McCain be upset? Obama does look distinctly different from all of the United States Presidents. The following is the Obama statement: *"They are going to try to make you afraid of me. They are going to say, "You know what? He's young and inexperienced and he's got a funny name. Did I mention that he's black?"* Did Mr. Obama tell a lie? Is it a lie? Please do not succumb to the McCain innocence façade. McCain responded, "I'm insulted you would think such a thing of me. . Mr. McCain is insulted about the playing of the race card? The race card was the first card played, and McCain played it in 1983 when he voted against the Martin Luther King Holiday. He let all of America know where he stands on diversity.

There is a word in the English language that defines the truncations of several meanings into one word. The word is *synecdoche*. For example, the Bible often refers to a meal as "sitting at meat." "Meat" synonymously identifies meat, fish, lamb, ribs, chitterlings, collard greens, sweet potatoes, rice, kale, corn, shrimp, lobster, Maryland crabs, Kool Aid, cake, and a few beers. Senator McCain uses the adjective "inexperienced" to describe Senator Obama's preparedness to assume effective presidency of the United States. In the McCain campaign vernacular, that means, "Has there ever been a black president? Perhaps there is a reason for that? What makes you think that a black person can identify with what white people need in this country? Does he drink 'Bud' and 'Jack Black' like you? I'm scared. Aren't you?" That is what the word "inexperienced" *connotatively* means to bigoted white folks. "Crackers"—please remember my definition of "cracker." "Crackers" are comfortable when they perceive themselves in a dominant position. However, let that perception of subordination of minority races erode, and they may become violently frightened. Perhaps one may recall lynching? For equal opportunity sake, my word for a "black cracker" is "wheat thin." There are African American racists also, perhaps a larger percentage per capita than white folks. Black folks contribute as much to racial tension in America as white folks.

Here is an interesting "Did You Know?" "Cracker," when referred to white people, has nothing to do with color. It identifies the sound of the whip the brutal white or sometimes black overseers used when intimidating and whipping the slaves. The cracking sound is the result of the whip's end breaking the sound barrier. Imagine a leather lash popping your skin at 761 miles per hour.

To continue with the campaign issues, Senator McCain uses the synonym "inexperienced" not only to reflect Senator Obama's alleged inexperience in foreign affairs and international conflict, but also to infer inherent racial incapability. There are others that have identified the collateral racial inference of Senator McCain. "To say that Mr. McCain is not playing the race card is tantamount to ignoring the elephant in the room," as senior CNN political analysts David Gergen and Jack Cafferty note. The elephant has been in the campaign room from the beginning, and we are standing knee-deep in elephant guano. Elephant feces stinks, and everyone in the room except Senator Obama is pretending to be anosmic.

The response from Mr. Darue, Senator McCain's campaign spokesperson was, "Barack Obama has played the race card, and he played it from the bottom of the deck. It is divisive, negative, shameful, and wrong." Is the truth divisive, shameful, and wrong?

In terms of getting cards from the bottom of the deck, every minority in this country has routinely received cards from the political, educational, economic, and social bottom of the white Anglo-Saxon deck. African Americans have been receiving marked cards in excess of 450 years. Please be advised, this is a continued divisive ploy of passive aggression, one that is cloaked in the facade of racial diversity. Some "crackers" continue to try to trick Americans into feeling guilty for exposing decades of murders, lynchings, rapes, incest, treachery, and deceit perpetrated by their seniors. They continue to benefit from institutional racism, manifested in excruciatingly high unemployment for all minorities, and struggle to maintain the attitude of privilege and subordination of the underclass. This attitude is coupled with bigoted, xenophobic, and jingoistic attitudes in all areas of society. The bamboozle slips by because African Americans and other minorities remain impressed with white culture, and are blinded by acculturation and assimilation. Malcolm was right African Americans continue to hold blinding scales tightly over their eyes for fear of taking responsible action that enlightenment requires.

Considering Senator McCain's alleged diversity, it is shocking to witness the senator's petty reaction to Senator Obama's statements. If he truly championed the plight of minorities, he would be in agreement, and would have a plank in his platform for minority relief. As it stands, there is a trapdoor where that plank should be. Watch out! With McCain you get more of the same!

His behavior seems to be contrary to what one would expect from a tortured war hero. Instead of his $500 Feragomo shoes, it sounds like he should be wearing pink pumps with laced bobby socks. When McCain says that America shouldn't trust its leadership to Senator Obama, he is tacitly saying do not trust America to a "niggra." Senator McCain's inexperience mantra is a political soft shoe designed to appeal to the "cracker" mentalities of this country. Mr. Darue's position and the position of his candidate points America back in the direction of "Jim Crow."

A "Ludacris" Defense ━━━━━━━━━━━━

If he can't back 'em up, I will. That's what you do for your boy. Ludacris is one of the "good guy" rappers. His music is generally focused on the uplifting of society and the addressing and alleviation of its ills. Senator Obama acknowledged the efforts of Ludacris and his music in a positive way by expressing his appreciation. It is natural that Luda, an intelligent, articulate, creative, vociferous, high-profile, and courageous artist, would recognize the stench of hypocrisy and bigotry and come to the aid of his friend. Senator Obama wisely discredited his song; however, every black American and some white folks understand that Luda said what Barack wanted to. Oh God! I just had a thought. I hope they don't ask Michelle about Luda's rap!

The lyrics are:

I'm back on it like I just signed my record deal
Yeah the best is here, the Bentley Coup paint is dripping wet
appeal
Never should have hated
You never should've doubted him
With a slot in the president's iPod Obama shattered 'em

Said I handled his biz and I'm one of his favorite rappers
Well give Luda a special pardon if I'm ever in the slammer
Better yet put him in office, make me your vice president
Hillary hated on you, so that bitch is irrelevant

Jesse talking slick and apologizing for what?
If you said it then you mean it how you want it have a gut!
And all your other politicians trying to hate on my man,
Watch us win a majority vote in every state on my man

You can't stop what's 'bout to happen, we 'bout to make history
The first black president is destined and it's meant to be

The threats ain't fazing us, the nooses or the jokes
So get off your ass, black people, it's time to get out and vote

Paint the White House black and I'm sure that's got 'em terrified
McCain don't belong in any chair unless he's paralyzed
Yeah I said it 'cause Bush is mentally handicapped

Ball up all of his speeches and I throw 'em like candy wrap
'cause what you talking I hear nothing even relevant
And you the worst of all 43 presidents

Get out and vote or the end will be near
The world is ready for change because Obama is here
'cause Obama is here
The world is ready for change because Obama is here

Artistic freedom in this country is great even if on occasion it becomes extreme. That is what we all should be willing to fight and die for. The text on paralysis may be a little risqué, but Ludacris is a rapper, not a politically correct socialite. Reflectively, if *The New York Times* can use satire with its depiction of both Michelle Obama as an armed Angela Davis and Barack as a caricature of bin Laden to make its point, why is it in poor taste for Luda to use artistic license in his music. Perhaps the song will motivate Senator McCain to secure wheelchairs for some of the disabled vets with whom he fought. Many of them certainly need help.

America is at a spiritual divide. The election of an African American president will do much to unite the nation. It may also divide it. America could develop a fundamental breach as socially profound and violent as the Yankees vs. the Rebs. Today's date is August 4, 2008, and "it's on." The gloves are coming off, and it's going to get funky. I pray that Senator Obama remains above the negative pull of political entrainment, and glows like the positive light of change we all pray for him to become. Pray for the colorless man and the nation. We need divine direction. "A half truth is usually half of that" (Bern Williams, *God's Little…*, 1994).

For Further Discussion ━━━━━━━━━━━━━━━━━━━

1. How does theoanthropology relate to prayer?

2. What is the difference between religious prayer and spiritually relational prayer?

3. Who are the Trinity? Can you explain? Is so, please do.

4. What is the Hypostatic Union?

5. What type of prayer do you use the most and why?

6. What is your opinion of spiritual healing of physical maladies?

Glossary ━━━━━━━━━━━━━━━━━━━━━━━━━━━━

Antithetical - in opposition

Anthropocentric - man centered

Conjecture - a formation of an opinion using some hypothetic reasoning

Connotation - a meaning in addition to or apart from the thing explicitly (dictionary meaning) named or described

Bombastic - pompous, pretentious, or extravagant language

Hemohydrosis - sweating blood

Homogeneity - of the same or a similar kind

Hypostatic Union - the accepted belief of the perfect union of Man and God in Jesus Christ

Hypostatic - means an unverifiable but accepted truth

Inherent - established as an essential part of something

Levant - the mid-eastern area of the world, i.e., Palestine and surrounding areas

Loquacious - talkative

Magniloquent - flowery speech

Ostentatious - showy, pretentious

Phenotypical - physical characteristics of a person, usually facial

Pontificate - pompously dogmatic

Preternatural - supernatural

Prevenient Grace - a small amount of grace given to everyone which allows one to accept the Gospel of Jesus Christ

Propitious - to reconcile

Progenitor - parent, usually father

Publican - a hated Jewish tax collector; puppet of the Roman Empire

Synecdoche - one word substituting for the meaning of many or several words substituting for the meaning of one

Salient - prominent, standing out, conspicuous

Salvific - saving grace

Temporal - having to do with time

Theopocentric - God-centered beliefs

Traducian Theory - the fallacious theory that the children are saved by the Gospel because their parents are saved

Visceral - a bodily function

References

Bible, King James Version.

Forsyth, P.T. *Soul of Prayer.*

Foster, Richard (1992). *Prayer: Finding the Heart's True Home.* HarpersCollins Publishers, 10 East 53rd Street, New York, NY 10022.

God's Little Instruction Book. Honor Books, Inc. Tulsa Oklahoma 74155.

Hammond, Frank & Mae (1973). *Pigs in the Parlor.* Impact Books, Inc. 332 Leffingwell, Suite 101, Kirkwood, Mo. 63122.

McGrath, Alister (2001). *Christian Theology: an Introduction.* Blackwell Publishers Ltd. 350 Main Street Malden, MA 02148 USA.

Stedman, Ray (2008). *The True Lord's Prayer.* The Ray Stedman Library RayStedman.org http://www.raystedman.org/jprayer/0064.html

Wikipedia, *Prevenient grace.* http://en.wikipedia.org/wiki/Prevenient_Grace

"Be ye angry, and sin not: let not the sun go down upon your wrath." (Ephesians 4:26)

"Anger is a stone thrown at a wasp's nest."
Unknown

The scriptural heading of this chapter is easier said than done. Anger is perhaps the single personality characteristic that most negatively affects an individual's behavior. Even for the most sanctified of believers, controlling one's anger is difficult. Difficult, in that anger is an emotion and can flare at any time. An analogy is gasoline accidentally coming in contact with a flame. The key to managing the damaging fires of anger is keeping the gasoline and flame separated.

At this point, gasoline is an extremely valuable commodity, which today's $4.00 plus gas prices are indicative. It has myriad uses, the more notable of which are: to power automobiles, boats, airplanes, and in emergencies, to power generators for hospitals, nursing homes, and other critically important facilities. Flames are useful also. Their heat provides warmth, light, cooking facility, even healing properties. Separately, they are invaluable. Carelessly combined, they can cause irreversible destruction. Metaphorically speaking, the uniting of the gasoline of our carnal nature and the uncontrolled contact with life's volatile situations will undoubtedly flare into destructive conflagrations. A spiritual buffer is required, and the buffer is prayer and God's written Word.

To understand the importance of scripture, it is vitally important to carefully look at what the Bible says. It is permissible to be angry. There are several biblical examples of each member of the Trinity becoming angry. Anger is not the issue. It is its resulting effects. *"Be ye angry, and sin not: let not the sun go down upon your wrath"* (Ephesians 4:26). The operative word is "wrath." In the original language it means "bitterness" or "hard feelings." That makes obeying this scriptural passage considerably more difficult than one initially may understand. Whatever is personally annoying you about a brother or sister, fix it before you "nod" off. Admittedly, my violations of this specific spiritual directive are too numerous to count! Regardless of how one feels, believers are required to make immediate conciliation. Perhaps personal emotions may not change for several days, months, or even years, but required obedience remains. God says make preparation to reconcile before the sun goes down. If it is evening, fix it before nightfall the next day. That is an insurmountable objective for anyone to satisfy. It is only achieved with prayer and humility.

Before we address anger, the difference between anger and forgiveness must be defined. Anger is the extreme and passionate displeasure with someone or something (*Webster's New World Dictionary*). It is often, but not necessarily, manifested in one's behavior, but may remain a seething degenerative astigmatism that will distort one's general spiritual vision. Anger then becomes an amalgamation of several entangled negative feelings. Anger may mutate into envy, jealousy, mistrust, covetousness, and several other distasteful emotions.

Forgiveness is the emotional erasure of all negative feelings toward the perpetrator for a specific trespass. Each trespass must be individually forgiven! Please do not fret. God does not expect us to suffer through repeated injury. Jesus expects us to forgive 490 times, but He also expects us to use common sense and remove ourselves from the offensive situation.

Moreover, we must differentiate between the sin and the sinner. Believers are to hate the sin and not the sinner. *"Ye that love the*

Lord, hate evil: he that preserveth the souls of His saints; he deliverth them out of the hand of the wicked" (Psalms 97:10). That is what is meant by *"be angry and sin not"* (Ephesians 4:26). Be angry at the sin, but do not hate your brother for his weakness. Anger is permissible. Some call it righteous indignation. It is how anger is applied that makes it righteous or not. Please remember that anger is almost always a result of a relationship gone sour. Anger is hurt! Relational expectations not realized result in one or both persons being hurt and wounded.

Does Size Matter?

It may be small, but the most lethal weapon of man is his tongue. It can be the deadly sword of the heart. When the heart is inflamed with anger, the tongue may become lethal. *"But the tongue can no man tame; it is an unruly evil, full of deadly poison"* (James 3:7). A brief thoughtless statement said in uncontrolled anger can permanently damage one for life. *"He that is slow to anger is better than the mighty; and he that ruleth his spirit, than he that taketh a city"* (Proverbs 16: 32). A person that controls his or her temper is a hero. They are more powerful that a warrior who captures a city, because the ruling of the tongue will ultimately save more lives. Metaphorically, the gasoline is one's anger and the alleged offense is the flame. Notice the reference is "alleged offense." Often, carnal nature reacts to *specious*, inadequate, or inaccurate information. The validity of the statement is inconsequential. What we see as mortals is often not the actual situation. Only the infinite omniscience of God understands the completeness of the events contributing to human behavior. Galatians 6:1 speaks specifically to this issue: *"Brethren, if a man be overtaken in a fault, ye which are spiritual, restore such an one in spirit of meekness; considering thyself, lest thou also be tempted."* As sinners saved by grace, no man has the right to judge another.

Anger Is Stress and Stress Will Kill ━━━━━━━━━

For those of us who do not completely comprehend the negating effects of anger, let us consider the damage it may do to the human body. Anger has a negative physiological effect. The negative emotional effect of anger is tantamount to the systematic corrosion of your internal organs. Not only does it directly attack vital organs, but it compromises the immune system and the body's entire genome.

Anger attacks the nervous system. Our bodies have what is called an *Autonomic Nervous System.* This system is divided into two parts, the *Sympathetic Nervous System* (SNS) and the *Parasympathetic Nervous System* (PNS). The Sympathetic Nervous System enables the body to react to fear by activating the flight or fight response. In short, the SNS increases the heart rate, blood pressure, and cardiac output. It diverts blood from skin to the skeletal muscles, increases pupil size, bronchiolar dilation, and digestive functions. Its purpose is to prepare the body for survival.

In contrast, the Parasympathetic Nervous System (PNS) is primarily charged with conservation of energy and the constant systematic supply of blood and nutrients to major organs and body parts. The PNS facilitates the slowing of the heart rate, reduction in blood pressure, absorption of nutrients, and the resultant elimination of waste. In addition, the PNS has the overall responsibility of establishing homeostasis. This equilibrium is essential in the body's process of rejuvenating damaged cells and growth, especially in young children. As a "Did You Know?", children who are faced with consistent critical stress/anger are often afflicted with what physicians and psychologists call *Psychological Dwarfism.* The malady drastically affects their growth and often these children are drastically smaller and less able than children of comparable age. The blessing is that once they are removed from the stressful environment, the children often compensate with rapid and full growth, and they generally reach their intellectual and psychological potential. It is a wonderful process to witness. It's one of God's little miracles.

Continuing with the physiological effects of anger, it is devastating to the human immune system. The human genome, the amalgamation of all our individual genes and chromosomes, is primary to the human systems of fighting disease and aging. Each chromosome is ended by telomeres, which are like the little plastic endings on shoestrings. Uncontrolled stress frays them. When this occurs, the individual genes may become damaged. This results in disease: cancers, diabetes, heart disease, kidney failure, and an assortment of ailments. The good news is that once the stress/anger is eliminated, the telomeres begin to rejuvenate and the susceptibility to disease is lessened. Contemporarily, this is pretty common knowledge. Dr. Oz has even discussed it on the Oprah show; there is an assortment of validating information on the Web. Understanding the above, one should easily realize the *physiological* gravity of unaddressed anger. Anger may not affect adults as profoundly as children; however, it will put you in your grave prematurely.

Angry Enough to Kill?

If you said no, then you are either the second coming of Christ or you have not lived long enough. Frankly, this holy and sanctified, saved, righteously indignant, Bible-toting, fire-breathing, Gospel-preaching ordained preacher has wanted to put bullets in several people on several different occasions. It is totally by the grace of God that this writer is not doing life in prison. Remember, it is O.K. to be angry. The issue is how you react. Please read the following. David was really "pissed off."

Psalm 109: 1-21

Hold not thy peace, O God of my praise;

For the mouth of the wicked and the mouth of deceit
have they opened against me; they
have spoken unto me with a lying tongue.

They have compassed me about with words of hatred,
And fought against me without a cause.

For my love they are my adversaries: But I give myself
unto prayer.

And they have rewarded me evil for good, And hatred for my love

Set thou a wicked man over him; And let an adversary stand
at his right hand.

When he is judged, let him come forth guilty;
And let his prayer be turned into sin.

Let his days be few; And let another take his office.

Let his children be vagabonds, and beg;
And let them seek their bread out
of their desolate places

Let the extortioner catch all that he hath;
And let strangers make spoil of his labor.

Let there be none to extend kindness unto him;
Neither let there be any to have pity on
his fatherless children.

Let the iniquity of his fathers be remembered with Jehovah;
And let not the sin of his mother be blotted out.

Let them be before Jehovah continually, That he may cut off the
memory of them from the earth.

Because he remembered not to show kindness, But persecuted the poor
and needy man, And the broken in heart, to slay them.

Yea, he loved cursing, and it came into his inward parts like water,
and like oil into his bones.

He clothed himself also with cursing as with his garments, And
It came into his inward parts like water, And like oil into his bones

Let it be unto him as the raiment wherewith he covereth himself,
And for the girdle wherewith he is girded continually

This is the reward of mine adversaries from Jehovah,
And of them that speaketh evil against my soul.

But deal with me, O Jehovah the Lord, for thy name's sake:
Because thy lovingkindness is good, deliver thou me.

Knowing David's reputation, it was really dangerous being in his presence when he was this aggravated. If an unsuspecting slave had wandered innocently into his presence, he might have paid the ultimate price. Remember, David didn't have a problem "taking you out" if you said or did something stupid. Do you remember the story of Saul's death? Saul's demise is recorded in I Samuel 31:4. He was mortally wounded in battle and because of the gravity of his wounds, he took his own life, as did his "armourbearer." *"Then said Saul unto his armourbearer, Draw thy sword, and thrust me through therewith; lest these uncircumcised come and thrust me through, and abuse me. But his armourbearer would not; for he was sore afraid. Therefore Saul took a sword, and fell upon it"* (I Samuel 31:4). The Amalekite who brought the information to David was uneducated and it cost him his life. Apparently, the Amalekite did not know the customs of the Israelites and to whom he was talking. During ancient times, it was forbidden by civil and religious law for a non-royal to kill an Israelite king. Saul's armourbearer wouldn't do it, and he was one of the few allowed by custom. This Amalekite did a stupid thing, and then admitted it stupidly to one of the fiercest men in history. The Amalekite summarily and irreverently was killed because of David's hurt and anger. Uncontrolled anger is deadly.

In my prison ministry, there are two saved inmates, who previous to their arrest and conviction, had had no criminal records. Their anger flash points led to their conviction of double and triple murder and life sentences. These particular gentlemen are good men, but their carnal reactions of angry rage led to the destruction of seven lives. Most of us, to a greater or lesser degree, have been pushed to or near that extreme. As a personal testimony, I was moved to murder, but by divine intervention, the person that was destined for demise departed through a different door. Alliteration and levity aside, uncontrolled anger will kill physically and emotionally. Pray for Christ-like self-control.

If God is Good, Why Doesn't Prayer Eliminate Evil?

One might ask the question, "Why pray if bad things are still going to happen, especially to good people?" There is no definitive response. The theologians call the question a "demergeological" dilemma. The question is unanswerable. Brilliant minds have been trying to answer that question for centuries. Bad things happening to good people is one of the questions I'm going to ask Jesus as soon as he tells me who cleaned out the bottom of the ark. Noah had his boys do it, I bet. Money says Shem, Ham, and Japheth and their wives shoveled all that guano. Noah probably used the "I'm too old, my back's bad" trick. The two other brothers probably dogged Japheth since he was the only white boy on the boat. Can't wait to get the story from the Lord. It has to be hilarious; brothers know how to tell a story.

One also may ask, why are title waves, hurricanes, forest fires, plagues, and earthquakes called natural disasters? There is nothing natural about a natural disaster. "Natural disasters" are *preternatural*. The definition of the noun *disaster*, both denotative and connotative, indicates that *disaster* is not natural. If it were natural, it would not be called disaster. Natural disasters are supernatural. When is a succession of forty-foot waves natural? When are 400,000 acres of burned forest natural? Is AIDS natural? When are earthquakes that register 8.5 on the Richter scale natural?

Time out! Time for a "Did You Know?" Charles F. Richter, an American seismologist, invented the Richter scale in 1935. The scale measures earthquakes on a scale from 1-10, although a quake of 10 has never been recorded. The interesting thing about the Richter scale is that it measures logarithmically. The measurements are exponential. For example, an earthquake that measures 4.0 is ten times less powerful than an earthquake that measures 5.0. An earthquake that measures 8.0 is 40 times more powerful than an earthquake that measures 4.0. Moreover, every whole number increase on the Richter scale equates to 31.6 times more energy release. Multiply the difference between a 4.0 and an 8.0 earthquake, and it is easy to determine the potential damage of a major quake. Add water to that equation and we have a tsunami. An earthquake with water is unimaginable. Tsunamis are unique, because they are a succession of tidal waves. The subsequent waves are often larger and more devastating than the first. Additionally, every working seismograph in the world will detect an earthquake of 4.6 or larger. It does not matter where it is located, which makes an earthquake a world event. Considering the above, earthquakes do not sound "natural." Please do not be confused. Do not call natural disasters supernatural and supernatural disasters natural. The Alaskan Valdes oil spill is a natural disaster. Three Mile Island is a natural disaster. They were caused by a natural series of controllable human events. Earthquakes, tsunamis, and hurricanes are not.

Harry Houdini was obsessed with exposing illegitimate *paranormal* behavior. Houdini disputed all who professed to have supernatural powers, the ability to foresee future events, and fortunetellers. He knew that these so called *paranormals*, *clairvoyants*, and *prognosticators* were counterfeit. Houdini excelled at exposing several charlatans, because he was a master magician and knew the difference between the natural and the preternatural. Houdini also knew the master of the supernatural. Houdini was aware that disaster is supernatural; therefore, God is involved.

As another note of conjecture, natural man must realize that supernatural disasters are "God's heads-up" and part of a divine purging process. God is not going to allow evil to run rampant. Recall the *antediluvian* crisis. God was so disappointed in the decadent lives of His human creations that He saw no redeeming qualities in mankind. He directed Noah to give the world the "heads-up" concerning the coming judgment, but the world was too deeply entrenched in sin to listen. One must admit it was an unusual scenario.

In the middle of the desert Noah was building a huge "something" 150 yards long, three stories high, and 25 yards wide. Nobody knew it was a boat. What was an ark? What was rain? Nobody had ever seen either. They only knew that a 500-year-old man and his three sons were building an alien structure to save them from rain and a flood, neither of which they had ever seen. Imagine the ridicule that Noah and his sons endured, until "drip, drip, drip, drip, drip." What a difference a day makes. Time proves the prophet. Biblical history may be repeating itself. Please look at where these disasters are happening. There are continuous forest fires in California, the most promiscuous city in America next to New York. New Orleans, second only to Haiti as Voodoo capital of the world, was almost blown off of the map by hurricane Katrina. The tsunami devastated the Far East, where the religions are largely non-Christian. Remember, God purged the Earth with water the first time, and He will use fire the second time. Heads-up, hint, hint: forest fires, hurricanes, tsunamis? God hates sin. *"God judgeth the righteous, and God is angry with the wicked every day"* (Psalm 7:11). Sin makes God angry and wrathful. Pleasant things will not follow. Even though He hates to, God is bound by His righteousness to judge sin. *"For the Lord shall rise up as in mount Perazim, He shall be wroth as in the valley of Gibeon, that He may do His work, His strange work; and bring to pass His act, his strange act"* (Isaiah 28:21). What God is referring to in this scripture is David's great and devastating victory over the Philistines. *"And David came to Baal-Perazim, and David smote them there, and said, The Lord hath broken me, as the breach of waters. Therefore He called the name of that place Baal-Perazim" (II Samuel 5:20).* Baal was the Philistine God. Perazim means breach. That is where David breached the walled city, and mightily overran the Philistine army. In the valley of Gibeon, Joshua asked the Lord to still the sun so the Israelite army could secure the victory over the Amorites. *"And the sun stood still, and the moon stayed, until the people had avenged themselves upon their enemies...So the sun stood still in the midst of heaven, and hasted not to go down about a whole day" (Joshua 10:13).* These are the types of amazing retributive judgments that God will bring to the sinful. "Strange work" refers to reluctant divine judgments that are beyond natural comprehension. God brings the kinds of devastation that human intellect cannot explain. Can anyone say earthquake? Can anyone say flood? Can anyone say fire? Can anyone say tsunami? Can anyone say AIDS? Can anyone say biblical history repeats itself? Can anyone say Help Holy Ghost?

Without theoanthropological insight, one will not recognize the "heads-ups."

The second part of the question asks, "Why do bad things happen to good people?" You tell me. Perhaps they did their time on this carnally corrupt planet, and it is their appointed time to go home? Like prison, they're short timers. Those who commit fewer and less severe crimes go home early. Sin more, live longer? Try preaching that!

Just recently two of my friends passed. Ben Eaton, a fellow I played football with in college, and a man of tremendous character. He was a leader of men, and former high-school football coach at Dunbar High in Baltimore, Maryland. He won three state championships, and died from an embolism while working out after a minor operation. Perhaps he was the most respected man in Baltimore, especially in the African American community. Unfair? God doesn't care about fair. God never uses the word "fair." The Bible refers to "fair" as meaning physically attractive. God only acknowledges righteous vs. unrighteous, or good vs. bad. God keeps it simple and uncomplicated. There is a theory called Ockham's razor, which is the belief that God and nature are *parsimonious*, meaning the simplest method possible. God is always uncomplicated.

My other friend, Ruby McNair, died after a long battle with breast cancer. She was perhaps the sweetest person I will ever know. She never complained about her condition or pain. Unfair? It would appear so, as mortals understand the definition of fair. Why do some good people live short lives, and the less than honorable folks get to stay around? Not fair? That may make you angry, but pray for a peaceful spirit, because one's anger can flare at any moment. After the death of these two friends I just wanted to find two nasty people I know, one in particular, and punch them in the face for just being alive. Tell the truth and shame the devil. Salvation does not end spiritual wrestling; prayer is your only effective weapon against rage. One must remember the dual responsibilities of anger. They are control personal anger, while being careful not to anger God. Consistently pray for control and obedience. Remember what Pascal said: "God allows man to participate in the honor of the execution of His will, God's institution of prayer lends to His creatures the dignity of causality" (Blaise Pascal). The operative word is "allows." God is sovereign and can set limits on man's participation in His sovereignty. Also, do not forget P.T. Forsyth's quote, "We shall come one day to heaven where we shall gratefully know that God's great refusals were sometimes the true answers to our truest prayer." God loves a colorless man.

For Further Discussion

1. If you have an anger problem and intend to control it, please explain how you will accomplish your goal. If you do not have an uncontrolled anger problem, how will you help friends or family do that?

2. Can anger be a positive emotion? If you think so, please explain.

3. Can you explain the physiological effect of stress?

4. How does prayer help uncontrolled anger?

Glossary ━━━━━━━━━━━━━━━━━━━━━━━

Antediluvian - before the biblical flood

Autonomic Nervous System - visceral bodily system that regulates organ function and homeostasis (balancing of the human system)

Holy Bible - King James Version

Clairvoyant - being able to see things in the future

Conflagration - a very big fire

Demerge- the justification of God allowing evil

Genome - the amalgamation of all the genes of an individual human being

Paranormal - beyond the scope of normal objective investigation or explanation

Parsimony - less complicated, stingy; shortest distance between two points

Parasympathetic Nervous System - Without external environmental stimulation, this system retains the body's chemical balance and promotes rejuvenation of damaged cells, healing and growth.

Preternatural - supernatural

Prognosticator - foretell, foresee, prophesy

Psychological Dwarfism - stunted growth and development due to environmental stress

Physiological - having to with bodily functions

Specious - plausible but wrong; appears to be correct but misleading; used as a sophistic tactic

Sympathetic Nervous System - enables the body to prepare for the fight or flight; is a reactionary but relatively intentional

Synecdoche – one word that represents many

References

Hough, Susan (2007). *Measure of an Earthquake, Measure of a Man*.

Kalush, William & Soloman, Larry (2006). *The Secret Life of Houdini: The Making of America's First Sup...* Atria Books, 1230 Avenue of the Americas, New York, N.Y. 10020.

Reference Results For: "Richter Scale." http://plus.aol.com/aol/reference/Richtrsc/Richter_scale?flv

Webster's New World Dictionary (1968). The Southwestern Company. Nashville, Tennessee.

"Be ready always to give an answer to every man that asketh you a reason of the hope that is in you." (II Peter 3:15)

In the writer's opinion, prayer is the most important tool of the colorless man. However, scripture, the immutable Word of God, is equally important at second place. It is of lesser importance only because the enlightenment of the Holy Spirit is necessary to spiritually comprehend God's Word, and prayer is necessary for that enlightenment. Although many secular scholars and some theologians question the Bible's inerrancy, careful study and meticulous interpretation reveal its accuracy.

As we continue our study, we will discover that the Bible is not a mythical amalgamation of unverifiable fairytales, but a perfectly valid record of *historicity* and empirically substantiated evidence. We will find that contrary to what many scientists, philosophers, and secular historians espouse, modern technology validates many of the previously questioned biblical stories as historically accurate.

God reveals Himself to man through His Word, and substantiates His Word through prayer. In terms of hermeneutics, this study will not address the many non-biblical traditions of the church, or investigate allegorical interpretation. God's Word needs no interpretive "spicing up." Even Revelation, if one thinks through ancient eyes to contemporary times, is literally understandable.

We also must remember that the Bible is post-apostolic preaching. The Scriptures had been preached for several years, and decades, before they were written, and centuries before they were mass duplicated. God used men to first preach and then write His blueprint for human existence. Not until Gutenberg invented the printing press, circa 1440, did the Bible become available to the masses.

It Takes More Faith Not to Believe

Hebrews 11:1: "Now faith is the substance of things hoped for, the evidence of things not seen." The Bible requires faith to believe; however, as we will see after empirical comparison, the Bible requires much less faith than the "religion of science."

One of the many classes I teach at seminary is Christian Apologetics. Apologetics is not an apology for Christianity, but an explanation of the Christian faith. There are several books addressing the subject. However, most commonly, scholars focus on theological concepts like pantheism, panenthisn, theodicy, realism, and religious traditions. Myriad theologians foster what are in some cases abstract secular philosophies and convoluted religious doctrine, which have little relevance to theoanthropology. All are interesting to some, but most have very little to do with the validation of the Bible, or the explanation or validation of Christianity. *"Beware lest any man spoil you through philosophy and vain deceit, after the traditions of men, after the rudiments of the world, and not after Christ"* (Colossians 2:8).

The Bible speaks of Christ from Genesis 1 to Revelation 22. Christianity is the Bible. The Bible is Christianity. This chapter specifically addresses portions of the Bible that are routinely challenged by Bible critics. It uses contemporary empirical evidence and recent archeological, DNA, and contemporary investigative technology to validate Scripture. The reader will also see the speciousness of the negative attacks, and the often silly assumptions Bible critics make.

Archeology, the Great "Validator"

After 200 years of archeological discoveries, carbon dating, and DNA investigation, pertinent information has been unearthed, tested, and accurately chronicled in regard to biblical accuracy. This information substantiates what is formally challenged by Bible critics as myth, folk tales, and rampant imaginative folly.

Unquestionably, this attempt is not to exhaust the historicity and empirical validation of every scripture challenged by philosophy and academia, but to select a few of the most familiar for discussion. At this point, we are aware of the improbability of the random occurrence of the cosmos. Cosmos itself means "organized beauty," inferring that it was purposely created. Again, the mere anthropic environmental condition of the earth is evidence enough to the mastery of God's flawless creative ability.

Previously discussed is the now scientifically accepted "Big Boom" theory, which is congruent with God speaking the world and cosmos into existence. Let us now consider one of the most critically challenged stories in scripture, the Universal Flood.

In every corner of the world in almost every civilization, there are variations of the story of the great flood. The Oceanic peoples believe the god Tawhaki stubbed his toe and opened a hole in heaven's floor and flooded the earth. The Tolecs of Central America believe that a boxlike chest made of cypress wood protected the survivors of the flood. The Tupi Indians of Brazil believe in the flood, and every major Native American tribe has a parallel recounting of Noah's flood (Caesar, 1994).

Moreover, each variation has a name for its hero, Noah (Caesar, 1994). Even the Efe Pygmies of Central America have a story regarding "The Great Flood." You guessed it. The pygmies' name for Noah is Ffe (Caesar, 1994). The following may be of interest. According to the Persians:

"The hero Yima, was warned by Ahuramazda (god) that the world was about to be destroyed by water. He was ordered to construct

an enclosure, and to store in it seed, animals, plants and men. When the Flood came everything was annihilated except for Yima's garden, from which the world restocked" (Hitching, F., 1978, p. 165).

The Hindus of ancient India believed:

"The hero Manu came across a tiny fish in his washing water, which announced that it would save him from a "purification of the worlds" which was about to occur. Manu reared the fish, first in a jar, then in a pond, until it was fully-grown. He then released it into the Ganges, and the fish rewarded Manu for his kindness by instructing him to prepare a ship and stores. When the flood came everyone was destroyed except Manu and seven Rishis he had taken with him. For many years the fish guided their boat until they reached a mountaintop where it revealed itself as Prajapati Brahman, the supreme God. With His help Manu recreated all living beings" (Hitching, Francis, 1978, p. 165).

The Maoris of New Zealand believe:

"Mankind once became so disrespectful of the great god Tane who had created them that there were only two prophets left who preached the truth. Insulted by men, they built a house on a large raft, stocked it with food and dogs, and brought down heavy rains by incantations to demonstrate the power of Tane. The waters rose and the prophets embarked with a few others. After six months the Flood began to subside and they settled on dry land, to discover that the whole world and its inhabitants had been destroyed" (Hitching, Francis, 1978, p.165).

The Lake Tyers Aborigines of Australia even have a flood legend:

"Once all of the waters of the world swallowed by a gigantic frog, *and all other animals were deprived of drink. They decided the best way to release the waters was to make the frog laugh, but the ridiculous contortions of an eel made the frog laugh so much that the whole world was flooded. Many people were drowned, and mankind would have been completely destroyed had not the pelican gone about in his canoe picking up survivors"* (Hitching, Francis, 1978, p.165).

The Chingpaws, a Southeast Asian tribe, tell this story:

"There was once a great deluge from which only two people were saved, Pawpaw Nan-choung and his sister Chang-hko. They escaped in a large boat with nine cocks and nine needles, which they daily threw into the water to see if they were subsiding. On the ninth day the last cock crew and the last needle was heard to strike a rock. They took refuge in a cave with two elves, and Chang-hko eventually bore a child. The female elf, a witch, tore it to pieces at a nine fold crossroads and curried its parts. The unfortunate Chang-hko ate the curry, discovered the crime and invoked the Great Spirit to avenge her. He named her the mother of all the nations and caused the races of the world to spring up from the nine roads" (Hitching, Francis, 1978, p. 165).

The stories and legends border on the ridiculous; however, their frequency is innumerable and the similarity unquestionable. The mythical recounts of the Flood are global, which validates its universality, and the age-old aphorism, "Water, water everywhere and not a drop to drink."

Fossils, an Enormous Testimony to the Biblical Flood

Anthropology and the formation of fossils also give credence to the historical authenticity of the biblical flood. A global flood would deposit huge masses of organic material at the bottoms of newly formed water depositories. These newly formed lakes and ponds would serve as graves for freshly drowned animals of all types that would settle to the bottom of these watery *sarcophagi*. The graves were almost instantaneously covered with massive amounts of sediment consisting of mud and silt, which would form an airtight casting. Understanding that the world is covered by 75% sediment, it stands to reason that a tremendous amount of water was required to attain that high a percentage. In addition, based on the depth of the remains, ad-stratum allows archeologists to assign a relatively accurate epoch to the fossils.

Fossils require special physical conditions. Dead or dying material must quickly be covered with watery sediment. The material must be firm or hard such as bone, teeth, shells, or wood. The mud silt must make an airtight cocoon surrounding the material, which provides minimal decomposition and permanent preservation. As the water subsides, the earth surrounding the material becomes firm, often rock, and the material becomes fossilized (Morris, Henry, 1980).

There is archeological evidence from all over the world documenting mounds of fossil discoveries of animals heaped in bunches in mountainous caves and the bottoms of dry lakebeds. It appears that these animals seeking safety in higher ground eventually succumbed to the heightening water. All indications point to a catastrophic natural event, i.e., a tsunami, earthquake, or ocean overflow. All have been dated to circa 11,000 to 12,000 years ago, which is congruent with the time of the Universal Flood. The evidence of these *hecatombs* indicates that something of massive proportions eliminated total species of fauna and flora resultant of an almost immediate environmental change (Caesar, 1994).

There are remnants of drowned animals in caverns and caves all over the world, where in a desperate attempt animals congregated in an attempt to survive. Dr. J. Mason Valentine, a paleontologist and zoologist, has visited several of these sites and has written about several of these bone yards of 11,000 years ago:

"In Wales Devonshire and various places in Southern England we find, filling crevasses in the hills, massive deposits of splintered

bones of hyenas, hippopotami, elephants, Artic bears and a host of more familiar animals, a phenomenon repeated in a number of sites in Western Europe. In rock crevasses on Mount Genay in France were wedged the bones of rhinoceros, elephants, lions, and wild oxen; in the Swiss Alps, crocodiles, giant ostriches, and polar bears. In the Dakota bone yards the pushed together bones of camels and horses along with other animals difficult to identify have consolidated through pressure into huge bone blocks. In Nebraska the bone yards include rhinoceros and giant pigs. In the LaBrea pits of California there are giant sloths, camels, lions, horses, peacocks, and prehistoric buffaloes.

In a sinkhole in the Florida Everglades a huge curved tusk protruding out of the mud was to be connected to a skeleton of a giant mastodon dead at least eleven thousand years. Around it were crowded camels, horses, tigers and sloths with an incalculable number of other species under the muck.

In the hills of Montreal and New Hampshire and Michigan five and six hundred feet above sea level, bones of whales have been found. In many places on earth on all continents, bones of sea animals and polar land animals and tropical animals have been found in great melees; so also in the Cumberland Cove in Maryland, in the Chou Kou Tien fissure in China, and also in Germany and Denmark. Hippopotami and ostriches were found together with seals and reindeer...from the Artic to the Antarctic... in the high mountains and in deep seas, we find innumerable signs of great upheavals" (Berlitz, Charles, 1987).

It is interesting that some of the fossilized animals that Dr. J. Mason Valentine identifies are no longer indigenous to Europe or America. It makes their discoveries more unique and tacitly validates the Flood. It simply gives credence to the notion that only an exterminating catastrophe could permanently eliminate a species from its environment. Contrary to the Bible critics, there is undisputable evidence related to a worldwide catastrophic event. Analogous worldwide bone yards have been synonymously dated at 11,000-12,000 B.C., and are harmonious with the Bible's recounting of the Great Flood.

Are We Still Babbling?

It appears that every religion has its separate deity, legends, mores, doctrines, and rituals. Considering the many different languages, how is it that they all have fairly similar beliefs in a supreme God and similar ethical foundations? Scholars and theologians have promoted the theory of the independent development of world religions; however, when investigated, the theory may be specious. There are several similarities between religions, not only in the major religions, but also in the minor, more pagan tribal beliefs. Polytheistic worship is considered pagan by civilized societies, and as a result, European religion has misinterpreted many worldly religious beliefs.

For example, the African spiritual connection to God is not restricted to a supreme deity. Worship in most African religions is appreciated in how God provides a spiritual connection to the earth, family, ancestry, and even the flora and fauna of the immediate environment. To indigenous Africans, theoanthropology is the communication with the Supreme Being through all earthly facilities. Hillary Clinton's skeletal interpretation of "it takes a village to raise a child" falls short of the connotative African meaning. To Africans, even the dust of the land has a profound influence on their relationship to God. The lesser gods in African worship and other religious orders is often not polytheism. It is called "diffused monotheism," which assigns lesser divinity to spiritual beings (Dick, K. A., 1984). The irony to this spiritual criticism by mainstream theologians is that there is a striking similarity to the reverence the Roman Catholics attribute to angels and dead saints. "Our Lady of the Highway" is certainly no more of a deity that Asse Yaa, the spiritual earth goddess of the Akan tribe who serves as a *mediatrix* to the one and true God. Asse

Yaa is similar to the Roman Catholic Virgin Mary, who Catholics believe is a *mediatrix* for Christianity. Although oxymoronic, religions are glaringly similar in their dissimilarities.

This obvious similarity of dissimilarity gives validity to an original *proto-religion*. This first religion was dismantled because of sin. *"And the Lord said, Behold, the people is one, and they have all one language; and this they begin to do: and now nothing will be restrained from them, which they have imagined. Go to, let us go down, and there confound their language, that they may not understand one another's speech. So the Lord scattered them abroad from thence upon the face of all the earth: and they left off to build the city. Therefore is the name of it called Babel; because the Lord did there confound the language of all the earth: and from thence did the Lord scatter them upon the face of all the earth"* (Genesis 11: 7-9). Believing that man, in his finiteness, could build his way to God was the sin. Notice the scriptural passage identifies "let us" go down, which also infers the divinity of the Holy Trinity. The *ziggurat* was an offense to God; therefore, he scattered the culprits and confounded their language. The word *proto* means "initial and universal." Consequently, proto-religion explicitly refers to the first and universal belief system. The babble clearly explains the many morphed religions of the world. God confused man, because he was "full" of himself, which resulted in the poly-religious state of the world. It seems counterproductive, understanding that God seems to require loyalty and worship. However, perhaps it's tantamount to keeping blinders on a horse. The horse becomes controllable, because the blinders will keep him less distracted by his surroundings.

Contrary to Baptist religious doctrine, perhaps God is satisfied with man worshiping a supreme being "in spirit and truth" regardless of how it may deviate from man's perceived idea of perfection. *"But the hour cometh, and now is, when the true worshippers shall worship the Father in spirit and in truth: for the Father seeketh such to worship Him"* (John 4:23). Consider this. Why would God punish a person for loving Him? Is there a correct or incorrect way of loving? "Spirit"

(Greek connotation) is a participle, or better defined, an action adjective. Spirit and Truth means actively loving and submitting to God, whoever one's god is. If one's god is not an idol, for God hates manmade objects of worship to supplant Him, perhaps He is lenient and accepts non-Christian worship? Not suggesting that this be preached from the pulpit, but it certainly is a matter worth pondering. The colorless man, as a result of his theoanthropological relationship, strives to be understanding and tolerant of other beliefs, and if he is a Christian, will offer the nonbeliever the *salvific* love of Christ.

Continuing the Obama Drama

The Obama drama continues with the choice of Delaware senator Joe Biden as his vice presidential running mate. As usual, one can always expect critical evaluation by the "knowledgeable" political pundits and a distorted media "spin" by what one may assume is the liberal press. The criticism rings, why would a candidate who is promoting change choose as his running mate a thirty-five-year senior senatorial veteran? If one thinks logically, it is the perfect choice, if that senior senator is also dedicated to change. A thirty-five-year veteran knows exactly what changes need to be made and why. Moreover, a thirty-five-year veteran is seasoned and should be completely versed in the most expedient and effective ways of realizing change. Change in government is not turning a calibrated dial; change in government is by the use of established trusted relationships. Obama has the vision and Biden has the facility. Very seldom are any significant accomplishments realized through the front door. In politics, changes are accomplished through back and side doors. To get that done, one has to know where the doors are. After thirty-five years of seasoning, Senator Biden knows each door, and more important, the doorkeepers. In order to realize change in time to make a significant difference for the American populace, it's going to require immediate efficient decisions and action. Joe Biden can facilitate that.

Senator Biden's choice has led to an interesting National Democratic Convention. The convention's opening address was masterfully delivered by Michelle Obama. She addressed and corrected several issues, personal and political, which were distorted by the media. She revealed the personal side of the Obamas. The misleading information of alleged privilege and affluence were dispelled, and the meager beginnings of both Michelle and Barack were made clear. Their financial success was not realized by privileged inheritance, but by conscious academic preparation and hard, dedicated effort. Their success is not defined by elitism but "achievism." She spoke with soft comforting femininity, but with an edge of competence and assurance encased in the articulation of a profoundly spiritual and worldly-wise person. The colorless woman *"[w]ill go forth as sheep in the midst of wolves: be ye therefore wise as serpents and harmless as doves" (Matthew 10:16).*

Tuesday night was Hillary's night, and she was magnificent. There was no hedging on her support for Obama, and she forcefully encouraged her supporters to honor the Democratic Party's choice. There was one black eye on the entire evening. Ann Price Mills, a delegate from Washington, D.C., who obviously is well acquainted with the democratic process, made an egregiously thoughtless statement. Mills was interviewed by CNN commentator Suzanne Malveaux and deservedly gave Hillary Clinton accolades for her speech and campaign. This African American delegate rightfully celebrated Mrs. Clinton for not totally breaking the glass ceiling of gender bias, but putting 18,000,000 cracks in it. She attempted to disguise her undisciplined emotional disappointment at Obama's nomination by attacking his experience a la the Republicans. Disgustingly, she said that she would not vote for McCain, but indicated that she was uncertain if she would vote at all! Please understand, this is a national delegate, an African American woman on national television, CNN. She unthinkingly said that she would rather not vote at all than vote for Barack Obama because of his inexperience? This is a black woman! Surely there is someone in her immediate family who has been called "nigger," lost an employment opportunity because of color, doesn't have health insurance, or is on food stamps. Surely she has relatives who have children of college age, or are suffering from other social, racial, and economic ills. Has this woman forgotten the price of the African American vote? Unfortunately, the nation saw this buffoon and her embarrassing diatribe. This was not an innocuous blunder. This could influence thousands of potentially Democratic votes in November. In my opinion, the National Democratic committee should have pulled her credentials. Moreover, as a Hillary supporter, and obviously a feminist, attitudes and statements like these support erroneous stereotypes of women being too emotional to make disciplined decisions. Perhaps this sounds like a reactionary stretch; however, thousands of people have been influenced by less.

Fortunately the embarrassing blunder was softened by a demonstrative gesture of unity on Wednesday evening at 6:55 p.m., when the delegate role call was being conducted and it was New York's opportunity to cast its vote. Mrs. Clinton proposed that the role call be terminated and suggested that Barack Obama be nominated by acclamation. It was an historic occasion and a magnanimous gesture on the part of Mrs. Clinton. Mr. Obama's acclimatized nomination was a coronation for black folks. It was something that every racially aware African American had been waiting for, but surprised to experience in their lifetimes.

Tuesday night was an anxious evening for the Democratic Party. Bill Clinton was going to speak, and as per usual his unpredictability had most people on edge, except James Carville. Most were wondering if Bill would energetically support Barack Obama as his wife did, or incase his support in a perfunctory address that would be respectful but anti-energizing. Carville was right. Bill Clinton brought it! Bill Clinton set aside the harsh acrimony of the primaries, and as only Bill Clinton can, unleashed the mastery of his oratorical acumen. He surgically attacked the faults of the Bush administration and allegorically and metaphorically super-glued them to the platform of John McCain. He simultaneously negated the specious attacks of the McCain campaign, and celebrated the myriad presidential qualities of Barack. Former President Clinton was direct and emphatic about his confidence in Barack Obama's readiness to be president of the United States. After the primaries, I was disappointed in the Clintons' campaign character; however, in my eyes they have redeemed themselves. The support of the Clintons will be invaluable for the remainder of the campaign, and more significant after Obama's victory. Bill Clinton's behavior during the primary elections really pissed me off, but admittedly, he is one "bad boy!"

Joe Biden did a great job. Very few speakers are as gifted as the Clintons, and being sandwiched between the two of them was obviously precarious. To exacerbate the situation, his son, Beau, delivered a wonderful introductory speech. Some criticized daddy Joe's content and delivery. However, the majority of the seemingly unbiased critics was pleased with his barebones delivery and acknowledged that his persona directly identified with middle-class America. Often it takes more creativity to dress down and achieve sartorial splendor than to dress up and attain the same attractiveness. At this point Joe Biden is "Dapper Dan."

He Was Magnificent

History was made Thursday evening August 28, 2008, at Denver, Colorado, with the acceptance speech of Barack Obama as the national Democratic candidate for president of the United States. His acceptance speech was extraordinary. Not only did he delineate each one of his proposals for change, Senator Obama categorically addressed each one of the ideological challenges that McCain uses as critical ammunition against his campaign. He was clear, decisive, and his oratorical skills are without parity. The question of his ability to fight was completely dispelled by this classily delivered, in-your-face challenge to Senator McCain. With respectful grace and character, Senator Obama offered a "bring it on challenge."

Often people misinterpret meekness for weakness. Meekness is not the inability to be aggressive. It is the ability to control one's aggression until the appropriate time. Often it is more productive to exercise disciplined restraint, and orchestrate strategic strikes rather than behave in thoughtless reaction.

Contrary to the submissive and benign meaning that most people believe, Matthew 5:39 is a challenge to an aggressor. *"But I say unto you, That ye resist not evil: but whosoever shall smite thee on thy right cheek, turn to him the other also"* (Matthew 5:39). Correct exegesis and proper hermeneutics reveal the proper meaning of this scripture. The scripture says that if someone hits you on the right cheek, you should turn your left cheek to him for a subsequent blow. The question is why would Jesus suggest that one suffer a second blow? As it is today, most people are right-handed. In order for a man to hit another man on the right cheek, he would have to "back hand" him with what in the "hood" we called a pimp slap. It is the blow that a pimp would use to hit a whore, a significantly emasculating blow for a man. The victim turns his left cheek not as a gesture of submission, but as a challenge to the aggressor. When the victim turns the left cheek, he physically implies "hit me like a man" if you have the courage. Please note, Christ doesn't suggest that one absorb more that two blows. Jesus also said, *"And he said unto them, but now, he that hath a purse, let him take it, and likewise his script; and he that hath no sword, let him sell his garment, and buy one. For I say unto you, that this that is written must be accomplished in me, and he was reckoned among the transgressors: for that things concerning me have an end"* (Luke 22:36). Succinctly, Jesus is telling the disciples to buy a sword to protect yourself, because I need you guys to spread the Gospel. Because he or she is sensitive to divine direction, the theoanthropological man knows when to exercise restraint and when to be assertive.

In college one of my sports was track, competing as a sprinter. The classic sprint is the 400 meters. The world-class runner begins the race quickly and builds a significant head of speed around the first and second turns. The trek down the straightaway is controlled, during which time the better runners maintain world-class speed. As the runners approach the third turn, they begin to strategically position themselves as they build toward a strong fast finish. Between the third turn and fourth turn, the runners shift into overdrive. This is where the real race begins. The previous portion of the race was merely jockeying for position. That is what Senator Obama has done. He was maintaining position until after the convention, and shifted gears with arguably the most spectacular and successful national political convention ever.

Discipline, character, talent, vision, intellect, communicative skills, wisdom, courage, humility, and most of all a pastor's heart are all characteristics of the colorless man. The pastor's heart is tantamount to what this writer calls psychological stigmata. *Stigmata* is the unexplained and spontaneous bleeding from the wrists, feet, and side by an anointed Christian believer. Stigmata was first experienced by St Francis of Assisi in 1224. There is a perceived sense of hurt that Obama feels for his country, contrary to a sense of power hunger that emanates from Senator McCain.

The Panderer Pimps the People

Is this desperation or a calculated gamble? Senator McCain chose Alaskan governor Sara Palin, a complete surprise to most of the nation, as his running mate. There is an enormous amount of conjecture attached to this decision. In her initial press conference, she immediately referenced the 18 million cracks in the glass ceiling that Hillary Clinton referenced in her speech at the Democratic National Convention. It was an obvious inference that she expected to attract a portion of the Democratic female vote that was dissatisfied with the Democratic vice-presidential pick. What makes the McCain camp think that a "pro-lifer" and staunch supporter of the National Rifle Association will attract female Democratic voters? This is a tacit assumption that women, in feministic flavor, will succumb to emotion rather than objective decision making. That is exactly the pandering deception that pimps use to confuse young girls and boys. "Your parents don't love you. Look at how they treat you. Let me take care of you. I'll love you, and give you what you need." Naiveté plunges the children into a spiraling life of prostitution, drugs, disease, and death. Politically, that is exactly what will happen to this nation if the rouse is realized. McCain has complained about the playing the "race card," but he is playing the "gender card!" McCain has given the voters a glaring revelation into his character and integrity; it is wanting. The question is, will the American electorate succumb to the deceit?

The next few weeks will be interesting. Already, CNN politicos like Jack Cafferty are receiving thousands of e-mails expressing outrage at the assumption that women would mindlessly support McCain because of gender. The hypocritical irony of the selection is that Governor Palin has less experience than Obama. She has been governor for two years, has no international experience, and before she was elected governor, she was mayor of a town with less that 5,000 people. Senator McCain said that his pick for vice-president would be ready to run the country if he were no longer available. Perhaps I'm confused, but do you think that a hockey mom with two years of experience as governor and experience managing an Alaskan town of 5,000 is qualified to be president of the United States? McCain's camp constantly publicized his preference for personal familiarity in selecting his inner circle. Governor Palin is a major portion of the circumference of the McCain inner circle. He only met with Palin once before his choice, which is obviously contradictory to Senator McCain's pattern.

The Republican "spin" is that Palin as an experienced executive is profoundly more experienced that Obama, and her renegade persona makes her a comfortable fit for Senator McCain. Senator McCain has contradicted his major criticism of his opponent by selecting a running mate who barely has more administrative experience than a senior high school principal.

If one looks at the events chronology, Senator McCain didn't choose his running mate until after the Democratic Convention. It appears that the success of the Democratic Convention prompted a reactionary response by the McCain camp. It also appears that it caused them to take a calculated gamble in their selection of a running mate, which could be an indication of desperation. Irrespective of the specifics of this week's events, this week has given us important insight into the character of John McCain.

There is a political aphorism that says, "The first executive decision a presidential candidate makes is his choice of a vice-president." It appears that Senator McCain's choice was made in deference to winning the election rather than thinking of the social, military, and economic security of the nation. In contrast, Senator Obama's choice of Senator Joe Biden was obviously a decision with the best interest of the American people. What did John McCain say about the senator's patriotism? He said that "Barack Obama would rather lose a war than lose an election." McCain's choice of an inexperienced running mate sacrifices the nation's security for a potential election victory. Whom should you trust? One of the divine characteristics of God is immutability. *"Wherein God, willing more abundantly to shew unto the heirs of promise the immutability of His counsel, confirmed it by an oath; That by two immutable things, in which it was impossible for God to lie, we might have a strong encouragement, who have fled for refuge to lay hold of the hope set before us. Which hope we have as an anchor of the soul, both sure and steadfast, and which entereth into that within the veil; whither the forerunner is for us entered, even Jesus, made an high priest for ever after the order of Melchisedec"* (Hebrews 6:17-20). In summary, the previous scripture is saying that God is joyfully eager to show us his perfect consistency and His inability to lie. The Koin Greek word for immutability is (ametatheton, a-meta-the-ton). It is in the second aorist tense, which means, "I was unchangeable, I am unchangeable, and I always will be unchangeable, and my council is perfect." God is explicit about His inability to lie, which is His first promise. God's second promise is that Jesus, with His perfect work on the Cross and resurrection, has secured direct access to Himself through Christ the perfect intercessor. In the weakness of humanity, we are unable to reach His perfection; fortunately, God doesn't expect us to. However, He does want us to try through the power of the Holy Spirit. The theoanthropological colorless man understands this, and knowing his imperfections strives to reach the divineness of his perfect example, Christ. America needs a leader without deception and political guile. Considering what you know and have seen thus far, whom do you prefer? Pray for the colorless man.

He Came, Ministered, Died, and Was Resurrected. ━━━━━ What More Do You Want?

It is useless to try to validate scripture. If the acts, teachings, and miracles of Christ are not sufficient, then perhaps there is nothing that will suffice. The Word says that we are saved by faith in the Lord Jesus Christ. *"For God so loved the world, that he gave His only begotten Son, so that whosoever believeth in Him should not perish, but have everlasting life. For God sent not His Son into the world to condemn the world; but that the world through Him might be saved"* (John 3:16-17). God purposefully withholds "scientific" cause and effect and empirical validation to test our belief and trust in Him. For us to be saved requires total dependence on the belief that Christ has made the way. Scripture defines faith as *"Now faith is the substance of things hoped for, the evidence of things not seen"* (Hebrews: 11- 1). Initially, faith in God seems illogical. However, most children hold their parents, even bad parents, as all knowing and all-powerful. God expects us to reverence Him in the same way. *"But Jesus said, Suffer little children, and forbid them not, to come unto me: for such is the kingdom of heaven"* (Matthew 19:14). Christ simply meant if one wishes to attain everlasting life, he/she must come to God as humble as children. Humility requires faith. Faith is the belief in something with little or no substantiation.

God did not intend His Word, the Bible, to be doubtless. To be so would not require faith and a choice. Faith and choice are essential to salvation as John 3:16 emphasizes. What we can most hope for is to show that faith and choice in God are far superior to man's explanation of our existence and worth.

To begin, please read what is theologically known as Pascal's wager. Pascal was a seventeenth-century French mathematician who formulated his pragmatic argument for the belief in God. One must understand, scholars at that time were truly scholars, and were accomplished in several different academic and spiritual disciplines. Being touched by the Holy Spirit was an emotionally profound epiphany for Pascal, which led him to the insatiable study of scriptures. Pascal, during the latter part of his life after trying to validate God's Word empirically and mathematically, simply resigned to faith. His famous aphorism follows:

"If you erroneously believe in God, you lose nothing (assuming that death is the absolute end), whereas if you correctly believe in God, you can gain everything (eternal bliss). But if you correctly disbelieve in God, you gain nothing (death ends all), whereas if you erroneously disbelieve in God, you lose everything" (eternal damnation).

In terms of logic, the above clearly outlines the benefit of taking a chance and believing. If you disbelieve and are correct, one loses nothing. If you believe and are correct, one gain's everything. If one doesn't believe and is incorrect, then you lose everything. If one doesn't believe and is correct, then one loses nothing. Pascal's wager seems like a safe and costless bet on God's promise of eternal bliss.

The above is a rudimentary explanation for believing; however, rudiments will not suffice the skepticism of academic and scientific non-believers. Science has one major, primary, and foundational *axiom*. It is "cause and effect." All *empirical* observation and analysis is grounded in "cause and effect." The question is, what is the cause and what is the effect, and which precedes the other? Is there a direct cause of the effect, or is it mitigated by a lesser or disguised variable? Empiricism is the god of scientists and science tends to be the god of the man. In reference to God and cause and effect, academics and philosophers have been grappling with this *conundrum* for centuries. Greater minds than ours have come up empty when trying to justify the puzzling question of cause and effect in regard to God. Stay with me for a couple of pages; we will be wading in deep water, but I will make it plain with a few clarifying life preservers.

In order to understand, one must have a tertiary understanding of the theory of "cause and effect." As a visual, let us consider: BEGINNING Cause--→Effect, Cause--→Effect, Cause--→Effect, Cause--→Effect, Cause--→Effect, Cause--→Effect, Cause--→Effect, Cause--→Effect, Cause--→Effect, Cause--→Effect, Cause--→Effect, Cause--→Effect, Cause--→Effect, Cause--→Effect, Cause--→Effect, END. Let us assume that this chain begins at the beginning of time wherever and whenever that was, and ends at the end of time, wherever and whenever that is. As we backtrack through the infinity of "causes and effects," we will finally get to the initial cause. What is the initial cause? Was it God? If it was God, who or what caused God? If something or someone caused God, is He still God? If God was caused, doesn't that negate His sovereignty, which causes Him not to be God? To complicate matters, look at the reverse of cause and effect. The effect will dictate the cause. This is profoundly meaningful when we continue to define kronos time vs. kiros time.

To further explore cause and effect in regard to the validation of the Bible, we must understand the foundations of *epistemology*. The etymology of the word epistemology is (Gk. episteme) "knowledge" and (Gk. logs) "word." Together they mean knowledgeable word/ theory. It is an academic discipline addressing the theory, nature, and acquisition of knowledge. The next question is "what is knowledge?" How is knowledge acquired? When does one know, or does one ever really know or have knowledge? How do we know what we know? Epistemology is divided into two primary divisions. The first epistemological division is "knowing that." "Knowing that" knowledge understands that $2 + 2 = 4$. The next is "knowing how," which understands the process of addition. In order to completely understand "knowledge," one should strive to master both concepts. Michael Polanyi offers a descriptive example in his book *Personal Knowledge*, when he speaks of the ability to understand the theoretical knowledge of the balance required in riding a bicycle, and the more important practical knowledge of actually riding the bicycle.

Belief is another issue. There are also two designations. The belief that the Baltimore Raven football team will defeat the Pittsburg Steelers this Sunday, or the belief that if I toss a ball in the air, gravity will pull it back to the earth. The first belief is more akin to faith. The second is a terrestrial truth. Newton's first law: Every object in a state of uniform motion tends to remain in that state of motion unless an external force is applied to it. The next step is justifying one's belief. The Baltimore Ravens did not defeat the Pittsburg Steelers this past Sunday. It would be correct to say that I believed that the Ravens would be victors, but my belief obviously was flawed; consequently, my belief in the Ravens does not qualify as knowledge. In contrast, my belief that a ball tossed in the air will fall to the ground every time is a terrestrial truth, and qualifies as knowledge or truth. The Aristotelian definition of truth states: "To say something **is** that **is** really not, or to say something **is not** that really **is**, is false. However, to say something that actually **is**, or to say something **is not**, that actually **is** not, is truth." The overriding question is the verification of what **is** and what **is not.**

Returning to the theological apologetic point of view, Gordon Clark (August 31, 1902–April 9, 1985) was an American philosopher and Calvinist theologian. He was a champion of *presuppositional apologetics* and *propositional revelation* and defended them against all forms of empiricism and rationalism. Dr. Clark believed that all truth is propositional and adheres to the biblical laws of logic. What are the biblical laws of logic? Simply stated, it is accepting the historicity of the Bible, its historic accuracy, and the ethical and *didactic* foundations of scripture as inerrant (Clark, 1998).

Moreover, the definition of axiom is the principle on which all other precepts of a specific discipline rest. Returning to the previous linier graphic of Cause--➔ Effect, Gordon Clark explains that the initial cause of God can be resultant of three possibilities. The first is that God is caused. If that is true, God is not sovereign, and He therefore cannot be God. The second explanation is that God caused Himself. That is impossible, because God will not defy His physical laws. If one is not, then one cannot create himself or anyone or anything else. The third possibility is that God is uncreated, which is substantiated by Exodus 3:14.

"And God said unto Moses, I AM THAT I AM: and He said, Thus shalt thou say unto the children of Israel, I AM hath sent me unto you" (Exodus 3:14). God was not being flippant with Moses; He frankly couldn't explain His own sovereignty. God concluded with telling them that the "I AM" sent you. Based on *presuppositional* apologetics, *propositional* revelation, and scriptural inerrancy, Gordon's thesis makes the most sense (Clark, 1995). To clarify, presupposition means to accept scripture as true, because it is grounded in propositional axioms. Propositional axioms are the foundations of accepted truth. Example: Gravity (propositional axiom) exists; therefore, a ball thrown in the air will return to the earth (presupposition).

In support of Gordon Clark's critics, his argument resembles circular thought, which is generally considered contrary to logic. The *presuppositional* argument purposes that the Bible, as the revelation of God, is the cornerstone of truth. The presupposition becomes the propositional or axiom/truth. If one does not accept that presupposition, then the position is circular. It is not circular if one believes God is real because His Word says so (presupposition), and His Word as the source of all truth becomes one's proposition or axiom. *"Jesus/God saith unto him, I am the way, the truth, and the life"* (John 14:6). *"Even the Spirit of truth; (Holy Spirit) whom the world cannot receive, because it seeth him not, neither knoweth Him: but ye know Him; for He dwelleth with you, and shall be in you"* (John 14:17). Moreover, Gordon's thesis is grounded in fideism, which is faith in God and the Bible. The argument for *presuppositional* apologists, the belief that the Bible is inerrant, is that all other arguments associated with cause and effect are in themselves circular. For example: it would be more logical to believe that God spoke the cosmos into existence as the Bible says then to believe in the impossible exponential chance that the cosmos formed on its own. Creationism is actually more scientifically sound. Teleological rational dictates, if there is a cosmos there must be a cosmos maker. Moreover, one will find that proper exegesis, hermeneutics, and *philology* give support to the presupposed validation of the Bible. Seemingly, this is a question that can only be accurately answered in the next life. Of course to believe that one must believe in the presuppositions of salvation and the Bible. Now that you are totally confused. Try to understand the following.

Perhaps a view from a literary perspective may increase our understanding of the historical validity of the New Testament? There are four general forms of literary presentation. The first, the folk tale, is a form of literature that makes no attempt at accuracy. It simply tells an interesting story and often promotes a *didactic* lesson. The second, the legend, possesses a modicum of authenticity but the actual facts are several years removed and sometimes centuries. The lack of eyewitnesses allows for embellishments and profoundly vitiates its accuracy. The third is myth. Myths are grounded in "information" so far back in history that the imagination of the *raconteur* determines the message of the story. The developmental time period is a minimum of centuries, most likely millenniums. The third is history. History is the attempt to chronicle the story as accurately as possible, by several writers. Over the years, there are no significant factual changes in the recounting of the specific event/ events. When one considers the literary history of what this writer considers the major religions of the world, Hinduism, Buddhism, Judaism, Islam, and Christianity, only one is profoundly salient. That is Christianity. For more detailed information on these differences, please consult Dr. Subadh K. Pandit, *Come Search with Me, Let's Look for God* (Subadh, 2008, pp. 66-73).

The earliest written Christian documents are those written by Paul. Many biblical scholars believe that many of the suspected thirteen were written within ten years of the death of Christ. One must also remember that the Gospel was established earlier because of the oral tradition and that the written word of any kind was rarely available to the masses. Even the Gospels, which were written at later dates, are believed to have been written earlier than previously accepted. "We can already say emphatically that there is no longer any solid basis for dating any book of the New Testament after about A.D. 80" (Albright, 1955, p. 136). More interestingly, the New Testament should be classified as more valid than most secular ancient history. Dr. K. Pandit offers three sound reasons for thinking so. The following examples exemplify his point:

- Cesar's *Gallic Wars* was written circa 100 B.C.; however, the first known copy is dated circa 900 A.D.

- Herodotus' *History* is estimated to have been written circa 400 B.C., but the earliest copy is dated 1300 A.D.

- Tacitus's *Annals* was written in 100 A.D. and the earliest copy of it is dated 1100 A.D. All of the above writings are considered authoritative historical documents. He shows that there are major gaps of 1000 years in each of the above documents, and only 10-80 years between the death of Christ and the New Testament writings. Not to consider the New Testament valid history by secular historians is insultingly ridiculous.

Another indication substantiating the accuracy and authenticity of the historical documentation of the Bible is the number of back-up congruent copies. The fewer the number of copies, the greater the ability to alter each. The greater the number of copies, the greater the geographical spread, and the more difficult will be the task of making uniform alterations in the manuscripts. *The Gallic Wars* is backed by ten official manuscripts, Herodotus by eight, and Tacitus's *Annals* by twenty. Homer's *Iliad* is sound at six hundred and forty-three manuscripts. However, 5,664 congruent Greek manuscripts support the New Testament, far more than what is necessary for secular authenticity. "To be skeptical of the resultant text of the New Testament books is to allow all of classical antiquity to slip into obscurity, for no documents of the ancient period are as well-attested bibliographically as the New Testament" (Montgomery, 1976).

For Further Discussion

1. Did this chapter help in your personal belief in the validation of the holiness and inerrancy of the Bible?

2. Considering the narrative of the Tower of Babel and the diverse languages and religions resulting from God's actions, if one truly loves Him, do you think God cares about one's religion?

3. What does "to love God in Spirit and Truth" mean to you?

Glossary

Apologetics - In the Christian faith, apologetics is not the defending or making excuses for Christianity. The Greek word "apologeomai" means to defend or explain the Christian faith.

Axiom - the principle on which all other precepts of a specific discipline rest

Circular Thought - on a problem-solving continuum of A--------→Z; one's thought process moves from A toward Z, but stalls at M and returns toward A; the thought process never reaches conclusion; doing the same thing over again and expecting a different result

Conundrum - puzzle

Didactic - having a ethical or moral lesson

Empirical - based on observation or experiment

Epistemology - the study of knowledge and its cause

Hecatomb - tombs with an excess amount of corpses

Historicity - historical genuineness of an event

Mediatrix - a female intermediary; example: the Virgin Mary for Jesus Christ, a Roman Catholic doctrine

Presuppositional Apologetics - the assumed prior belief that all scripture is inerrant, and that the Bible is the foundation of all truth

Philology - the study of language

Propositional Revelation - that the assertions offered by the Bible (revelation) are logical when subjected to scrutiny

Proto-religion - first religion

Raconteur - storyteller

Salvific - the saving element of Jesus Christ

Sarcophagi - stone coffin

Stigmata - the physical bleeding from the wrists, feet/ankles, and side a la Christ; stigmata was first documented in 1224. St. Francis of Assisi was the first to experience this phenomenon

Terrestrial - of or on the earth

Ziggurat - rectangular stepped pyramidal tower in ancient Mesopotamia, surmounted by a temple

References

Albright, William (1955). Recent Discoveries in Bible Lands, 1955, p. 136.

Bible, King James Version.

Berlitz, Charles (1987). *The Lost Ship of Noah.* G.P. Putnam's Sons, New York, pp. 123-124).

Clark, Gordon. *A Christian View of Men and Things,* 3rd ed., Trinity Foundation, ISBN 1-8911777-01-7.

Clark, Gordon (1998). *Logic,* 3rd ed., The Trinity Foundation, pp. 115-121. ISBN 0-940931-81-8.

Clark, Gordon (1995). *Religion, Reason, and Revelation,* 3rd ed., Trinity Foundation, ISBN 0-940931-86-9.

Dick, K.A. (1984). *Theology in Africa.* Maryknoll, New York. Orbis Books.

Hitching, Francis (1978). *The Mysterious World: An Atlas of the Unexplained.* Rinehart & Winston, New York, p. 165.

Pandit, Subodh (2008). *Come Search With Me, Let's Look For God.* Xulon Press.

Morris, Henry (1980). *King of Creation.* C.L.P. Publishers, San Diego, p. 151.

Montgomery, John W. *History and Christianity.* InterVarsity Press, p. 29.

Project Constant Hope (1995). *How Can I Pray When I Am Angry?* American Bible Society, New York. N.Y. 10023.

"In the Beginning was the Word,
and the Word was with God, and the
Word was God."
(John 1:1)

"And the Word became flesh,
and dwelt among us and we beheld
His glory as of the only begotten from the
Father, full of grace and truth."
(John 1:14)

He Showed Us He Was God.

Jesus showed the world that He was God incarnate. He showed them physical, tangible, and natural experiential miracles that could only be done by a divine being. One could feel them, taste them, smell them, and see them with the natural eye. They still wouldn't admit that He was God. Moreover, we must realize that for every miracle recorded in the Gospels, conservatively, there were perhaps 50-100 identically wondrous preternatural non-recorded situations. As history records, Jesus used to simply walk past ailing people and heal them. In addition, because of the divinity of Christ, His mother, as some of the lost books of the Bible claim, possessed divine qualities (Lost Books, 1979). Considering the variety and number of supernatural examples, it seems mindless that the Pharisees and Sadducees didn't accept His divinity. "Then said Jesus unto him, Except ye see signs and wonders, ye will not believe" (John 4:48). They still didn't believe in Him. The Pharisees and Sadducees saw His miracles, how big a "knucklehead" can one be?

Christ's wonders should not be considered unusual. Additionally, the disciples/apostles, including Paul, were anointed with supernatural powers, as evidenced by Simon the sorcerer's request. *"Then Simon (the sorcerer) himself believed also: and when he was baptized,* he continued with Philip, and wondered, beholding the miracles and signs which were done" (Acts: 8:13). Simon, in his ignorance, offered the apostles money for a Holy Spirit's charismatic anointing. "Saying, Give me also this power, that on Whomsoever I lay hands, he may receive the Holy Ghost" (Acts 8: 17). Little did he know that God could not be purchased.

In addition to examining the Gospels, we will be referencing additional historical information offered by what scholars consider valid historical evidence. We will be considering the *Lost Books of the Bible*, Josephus, and other valid sources of biblical information. These special writings are called *hilesgechesnichete*, or "sacred history." Plainly, *hilesgechesnichete* is not quite as holy as scripture but more holy than secular history. The Gospels are the accepted truth of God. There are four Gospels, three of which are synoptic, meaning they describe identical events in a similar way. The fourth is the Gospel of John, the "eagle" Gospel connoting the kingship of Christ. Another historical account, the Protevangelion, which many scholars feel was written by James, the brother of Christ, gives a surprisingly similar and fuller accounting of His early childhood. Please remember the Protevangelion is not the Holy Word; however, it gives a surprisingly *congruent* account of the *salient* events of the Synoptic Gospels. All three Gospels give a similar account of the birth of Christ and subsequent events. The Protevangelion identifies the stable as a cave and the manger as a stone trough used for the feeding of livestock, which is perfectly accurate. In ancient times, stables were caves and feeding troughs were carved out of stone. The materials required to build wooden structures for animals were cost prohibitive for all except the very rich or royal.

The accounting of the wise men, Magi, coming from the east is also chronicled. Perhaps some may wonder why they came from the East. Prior to the dominance the Roman Empire, perhaps the most dominant nation in the Levant region was Babylon or Persia. A magus was a priest of ancient Babylonian, a holy man. The holiness of Babylon may sound peculiar without understanding the history of Persia, and the man who contributed to Babylon's holiness. In time, there were many Hebrew holy men in Babylon, thanks to Daniel. Studying scripture will reveal that Daniel was placed in charge of the entire assemblage of Babylonian "wise" men. Nebuchadnezzar assigned Daniel the designation because his wise men could not interpret his dream. *"And the king (Nebuchadnezzar) said unto them, (his holy men) I have dreamed a dream, and my spirit was troubled to know the dream"* (Daniel 2:3). *"The king answered and said to the Chaldeans, The thing is gone from me: if ye will not make known unto me the dream, with the interpretation thereof, ye shall be cut to pieces, and your houses shall be made a dunghill"* (Daniel 2:5). The inadequacy of the Babylonian wise men put every holy man in the nation at risk, including Daniel. As Scripture says, Daniel was summoned to the aid of the threatened spiritual sages. Nebuchadnezzar promised that the person who could tell him details of his dream and interpret it would receive gifts, rewards, and great honor. *"But if ye shew the dream, and the interpretation thereof, ye shall receive of me gifts and rewards and great honor"* (Daniel 2:6). Daniel accurately recounted the king's dream and gave Nebuchadnezzar the Godly interpretation. Daniel was summarily rewarded and placed in charge of the king's entire spiritual council. *"Then the king made Daniel a great man, and gave him many great gifts, and made him ruler over the whole province of Babylon, and chief of the governors over all the wise men of Babylon"* (Daniel 2:47). Daniel subsequently reeducated the entire Babylonian spiritual council in the Hebrew faith, and educated them in God's Holy Scriptures. The holy men of Babylon knew the Messiah was coming. They knew the spiritual signs, and became the accepted "king makers" of their time. There could be no Hebrew king without their anointing. They truly came from the East, and they were fully believers in the true God.

As an interesting side bar, King Herod, a nefarious king who feared his potential dethroning by the Messiah, Jesus, demanded that these same wise men reveal the location of the newly born Hebrew king. As scripture indicates, the Wise Men knew exactly where Jesus was, because the star was directly over the house where the family of Christ was now living. Being wise, they did not tell Herod. Herod reluctantly accepted their word, but charged them to search and find Jesus and return with word of His location. However, the Wise Men were spiritually discerning. They knew of Herod's evil plans and returned to Babylon using an alternate route. Herod, in his evil discernment, and in an effort not to miss his chance to eliminate the new king, ordered all of the newborn males of two years of age murdered. God's angel, probably Gabriel, warned Joseph to gather his family and flee to Egypt where Jesus was protectively blended into the population. *"And when they were departed, behold, the angel of the Lord appeareth to Joseph in a dream, saying, Arise, and take the young child and His mother, and flee into Egypt, and be thou there until I bring thee word: for Herod will seek the young child to destroy Him (Matthew: 2:16). Then Herod, when he saw he was mocked of the Wise Men, was exceeding wroth, and sent forth, and slew all the children that were in Bethlehem"* (Matthew 2:16). At God's appropriate time, Joseph was allowed to return from Egypt. There is an interesting " Did You Know." The family encountered two robbers on the highway. Their Greek names were Titus and Demakus. In Latin their names were Dismas and Gestas. Titus/Dismas was the repentant thief on the right of Jesus, who entered heaven with Jesus. They were a couple of the most notorious criminals of the land. Their intent was to rob and murder the entire family; however, Titus, in a moment of uncharacteristic favor, convinced his partner not to harm the family (Infancy, Chapter 8: 2-7, *Lost Books of the Bible*, 1979).

The interesting thing about *The Lost Books of the Bible* is that although they are not a part of the accepted 66 books of the Bible, they do fill in some of the gaps that the New Testament Gospels leave unexplained. If nothing else, the *Lost Books* clarify the mores and customs of the times. The Protevangelion and the Infancy (*Lost Books of the Bible*) are suspected to have been written by James, the older brother of Christ, and document events of the early childhood of Jesus.

The books are interesting; however, to some they may be mildly distressing. One of the more intriguing narratives chronicles the first meeting of Simon and Jesus, prior to the Roman soldiers *impressing* Simon into helping Jesus carry the cross to Calvary. Simon was actually brought back to life by Jesus when they both were children. Simon was playing in the woods with some of their mutual friends when a viper bit him. As his friends were carrying him home to his parents apparently dead, the boys who were playing with Jesus stopped them. They begged Jesus to bring their mutual friend back to life. Jesus had them return the seemingly dead Simon back to the hole from which the viper came. Jesus demanded that the snake come out, reinsert its fangs, and extract its poison. The action definitely seems supernatural, but similar to the lifesaving process practiced by us mere mortals. The miracle is that Jesus got the snake to cooperate.

Another interesting story in the Infancy reflects the creativity of Jesus and the uniqueness of His toys. He and His friends were making clay men, oxen, birds, and other figures out of dirt and sticks. To the glee of His buddies, Jesus brought the clay figures to life, and had them marching in rhythm, and playing with each other and His friends (Infancy 15: 2-5). That's one of the things I want Jesus to teach me when I get to heaven. Think about that. To be able to give your toys life!

One of the somber childhood confrontations of Christ was His first encounter with Judas. "Judas, who was possessed, came and sat down at the right hand of Jesus. "When Satan was acting upon him as usual, he went about to bite the Lord Jesus. And because he could not do it, he struck Jesus on the right side, so that he cried out. And in the same moment Satan went out of the boy, and ran away like a mad dog. This same boy betrayed Him to the Jews. And that same side, on which Judas struck Him, the Roman soldier pierced with a spear" (Infancy 16: 5-10).

In addition to being an interesting "Did You Know?", the previous has biblical validation. The operative words in the Infancy narrative are "When Satan was acting upon him as usual," which is prophetically similar to John 13:26. *"Jesus answered, he it is, to whom I shall give a sop, when I have dipped it. And when He had dipped the sop, he gave it to Judas Iscariot, the son of Simon. And after the sop Satan entered into him. Then said Jesus unto him, That thou doest, do quickly"* (John 13: 26-27). The text from *The Lost Books of the Bible* further validates and explains accepted scripture. Jesus apparently was aware that Judas was a toiler of Satan and a regular instrument of evil. Judas was well used by the Devil by the time Jesus chose him as a disciple. Perhaps, all of us who once questioned God's judgment in what we assumed was the intentional corrupting of Judas and his subsequent selection as a pawn in God's plan of salvation, now have enlightening clarity. God chose an already fully corrupted vessel. *The Lost Book of the Bible's* chapter, "Infancy," provides a logical explanation of Christ's choice of Judas as a disciple and God's ultimate plan of salvation.

Perhaps to some, the most sensitive narrative of young Jesus is His taking the lives of two young boys. "At length the son of Hanan coming to the fish-pool of Jesus to destroy it, the water vanished away, and the Lord Jesus said to him, In like manner as this water has vanished, so shall thy life vanish; and presently the boy died. "Another time, when the Lord Jesus was coming home in the evening with Joseph, He met a boy, who ran so hard against Him, that he threw Him down; To whom the Lord Jesus said, As you hast thrown me down, so shalt thou fall, nor ever rise. And that moment the boy fell down and died" (Infancy 16: 20-24). The operative words in the first text is "coming to the fish-pool of Jesus to destroy it, the water vanished away" (Infancy 16: 20-24). The son of Hanan purposely came to Jesus' fishpond to destroy it. Why would the boy think he would be successful? The revealing key is "the water vanished away." The son of Hanan thought he would be successful because he obviously had demonic supernatural powers and was confident as an instrument of Satan that he could make the water disappear. Water, as we theologians acknowledge, is a metaphor for spiritual cleansing. Jesus was protecting His spirituality by destroying the satanic demon. In a second instance, the Lord and Joseph were coming home and were attacked by an apparently ruthless boy who threw Jesus to the ground. Jesus was God incarnate. If Satan could enter Judas and have him attack Christ, obviously the enemy could influence other youths. What would one expect after attacking God? It seems fitting. To attack the Truth deserves death and Hell! Please understand, this is purely Greg Ogle's conjecture and speculation, but it could happen!

More Obama Drama

The gloves are off. It's on! It's getting nasty. It's September 10, 2008, and the polls have the candidates deadlocked. The Sara Palin nomination, although an obvious play for the female vote, was effective. The Republican spin with the surreptitious help of the news media has made this election tighter. The race has deteriorated embarrassingly into a silly name-calling fight, which is to the advantage of the Republicans and John McCain. The impact of the selection of Sara Palin emotionally knocked the Democrats off stride, and caused a clear advantageous shift in momentum to the McCain campaign. The Democratic focus suddenly switched from John McCain/Bush and the Republican political failures concerning their economic, social, and international record, to defending themselves against the emotional turbulence of the Palin phenomenon. It was a brilliant Republican tactic; however, it was less than honorable. Please allow me to reiterate. The American public is improving, but a large number of our population remains prone to "knee jerk" reactions. For all of our wealth, technology, and information dissemination, we are an incredibly ignorant and a dangerously credulous society. Unfortunately, and often to our political detriment, Americans react to social stimuli that is superficial rather than digging and examining its tertiary meaning and effect. The first response is usually emotional. An example is Palin's selection purely because of gender. As one digs to the second level of understanding, one realizes that the position/political views of Palin are antithetical to those of most female liberals. The third is to recognize the deprivation of character and the lack of ethical integrity required to pander to females.

Let us examine the Palin selection.. As mentioned earlier, her selection is an example of classic pandering. Pandering is nothing more than *PIMPING!* The very first statement of substance from Palin's mouth was her reference to the 18 million cracks in the glass ceiling, obviously referring to Hillary Clinton's quote and vie for the Democratic nomination. This behavior is exactly what pimps do to attract young girls. "Little girl, they didn't love you enough to pick Hillary. I love you and will take care of you, so pick me. We love you. Let us take care of you and everything will be fine." What is the difference? My mental image of McCain is that of a man reclined next to his stretch Cadillac with a full-length Chinchilla coat, platform shoes, diamonds, gold, and other extraneous "bling" recruiting sixteen-year-olds to prostitution. Please understand, John McCain should be celebrated for his war record. Many of us cannot imagine enduring what he did, and I sincerely admire his patriotism. John McCain sacrificed greatly for America. However, twenty-seven years in Congress can change the character of a man or women. Remember the definition of entrainment. My coach used to say, "It's not what you did for me, it's what you did for me lately." At this point in his political life and career, John McCain is a political pimp and Sara Palin is a political "ho."

The political pundits are correct. The Democrats were not prepared for the Palin phenomena, and have lost the direction needed to win the election. The Democrats were unprepared; they were totally knocked off stride by the Palin selection. One must admit that it was a nefariously brilliant move by the McCain camp. One may ask, "Is the McCain choice a reflection of the character of a president of the United States?" Our political process has become degraded to the point of allowing, almost celebrating, unethical and dishonest tactics, as evidenced by the vote thievery employed by the Bush camp and his brother in the 2000 national election. Is this what our nation has become? Perhaps Americans are infidels as the fanatical Whahbi Muslim terrorists proclaim.

The Supreme Court's decision allowed the larceny. To exacerbate the evil, and I paraphrase, the United States Supreme

Court led by Scalia and "Uncle Thomas" responded, "We don't care, and we are not going to ever care. To make sure you understand, we are going to make it unlawful for you to ever again ask us to care. Do you understand?" Perhaps in my credulousness and naiveté, I'm missing something? Is that the process our founding fathers had in mind? Would Washington, Jefferson, and Adams be proud? Is this worth the death of numerous African American heroes and heroines? Is this America? We need more colorless men. A colorless man will try at all costs to remain a Christ-like man of integrity. It is difficult. When the characterless are throwing excrement at you, it is extremely difficult not to reciprocate, but the colorless man will always try his or her best.

Obviously by now, it is not necessary for me to identify my political preference. However, this Obama supporter would rather he lose the election than to have Senator Obama succumb to the entrainment of the less than scrupulous establishment. One must shun evil even at the expense of perceived failure. George Bernard Shaw said, "All great truths begin as blasphemies." Christ was crucified as a failure, the profound blasphemy of His time, but He became the biggest truth ever recorded in history. It is greatly more peaceful to be righteous than to be a winner. God Bless the Colorless Man!

Roland Sees the Elephant and Smells the Guano

As mentioned throughout this book, one of the major issues in this election is the obvious, purposeful, strategically and calculated avoidance of the racial issue. The two other hot topics, age and gender, have been openly discussed and politically weighed. However, with the exception of the McCain camp accusing the Obama camp of playing the race card, and Senator Obama responding with his race speech, both political camps have avoided the race issue. There have been brief references in subdued forms from Roland Martin, Jack Cafferty, and David Gergan, all CNN political pundits, but nothing that approaches the sustained intensity of debate like the previous two.

From the beginning, the obvious white elephant in the room has been purposely avoided. In his speech, Senator Obama said, "Racial resentments aren't always expressed in polite company." Please understand this political election is not polite company, and the Obama assumption may have been a lethal mistake. As mentioned previously, the McCain camp uses the adjective of "inexperience" as a synonym for African American leadership, and the fear of what it may mean to "good" white people.

One must understand that there are always at least two meanings for words. There is the denotative meaning, which is the strict dictionary meaning, and the connotative meaning, which is the emotional meaning of a word. The English language is an analytical language that places its parts of speech in a relatively systematic sequence called syntax. Analytical syntax often diminishes the meaning of the sentence. In contrast, most languages are synthetic, which allows the use of specific declensions, augments, endings, and definite and indefinite articles. Their use increases the overall meaning of the sentence. Unlike English, most languages are not held to rules of word placement. Therefore, they are inherently more expressive in both denotative and connotative meaning. A good speechwriter understands syntax. A skillful author will purposely employ literary techniques to take advantage of this dynamic, hopefully to the benefit, but often to the detriment of the unaware public.

Subliminal messages may be communicated by syntax, and research supports that subliminal messages have an effect equal to or greater than cognitive messages, and may be easier to communicate surreptitiously (Barh et. al. (1996), Moore, T. (1992). It may sound paranoid; however, Woody Allen said, "Being paranoid is knowing the truth."

Finally, someone has bitten the bullet. I commend CNN for allowing Roland Martin to confront and host a program addressing the issues of gender, race, and age. The initial expose aired on September 13, 2008, and is entitled *CNN Special Investigation*. Mr. Martin attacked the issues from three different vantages. The beginning of the show featured three radio hosts, each having independent audiences. Martha Zoller is the hostess of station WDUM in Georgia, and a Republican who supports Senator McCain. Mr. Joe Madison is the radio host of XM Satellite Radio. He is a Democrat and supporter of Senator Obama. Finally, Mr. Joe Pagliarulo, a Republican supporter with a large audience in San Antonio and Houston, Texas. Gender was the first issue addressed. Ms. Zoller made the statement that gender is the new race, to which Joe Madison immediately responded. His counter was that gender is not the new race. It was his opinion that each issue should be addressed separately. With levity, he noted that if Senator McCain were an old black woman, then one could amalgamate the three. Joe Pagliarulo concurred; however, his comment was flippant, which indicated that he did not understand the gravity of the statement. In addition, he made a comment concerning Branch Ricky's signing of Jackie Robinson to the major league. His comment was that Senator Obama was not the exemplary man that Jackie Robinson was. In his forgivable ignorance, Joe Pagliarulo showed the "cracker" attitude referenced to earlier. He is affected by the dangerous *aphorism*, "Some of my best friends are colored," the unrealized attitude of a bigot. Had he had the opportunity, Pagliarulo would most certainly have made the same comparison of Joe Louis to Jackie Robinson. Pagliarulo was looking through racially tainted eyes as we all do. He, as did Ms. Zoller, failed to see the calculated diversion that the appointment of Sara Palin caused. First, the Republicans capitalized on the non-selection of Hillary Clinton by the Democrats, which was exacerbated by her to date less than vigorous participation in the Obama campaign. Second, discussing the gender issue is politically acceptable, unlike bigotry. Third, the McCain camp has negatively and completely fabricated the Democratic position concerning women. The McCain camp has cleverly and strategically capitalized on the sympathetic flavor of appalled sexism, while disarming the issue of racism by acting wounded by the "race card." Senator Obama's integrity ethically prohibits him from exploiting race, because he knows, win or lose, the "race card" will split the country.

Colorless men are ethically driven towards national unity. He knows that the "race card" will cripple the national oneness he seeks.

The next segment of the expose addressed Drew Weston, author of *Political Brain*. The discussion centered around his opinion that elections are won not on issues but emotions. As a result of his research he has concluded that regardless of the issues, the majority of people in this country are prone to cast their vote according to emotion rather than logic and issues. To emphasis his position, Mr. Martin played a tape from a sports event where a "gentleman" said on camera, "The only black man he has ever seen make change was holding a cup." Remember this is America. The question is, how many "good" Americans have similar bigoted attitudes, but do not have the nerve, as this man to say it on camera. Frankly, this man's honesty is refreshing.

Several voters called into the show to express their opinion, and several made interesting comments. Earlier in the show, Joe Pagliarulo made a statement concerning the voting preference of Michigan's blue-collar workers. At present he is hosting two radio shows in Texas. However, as a former Midwesterner, he seemed knowledgeable concerning the Midwest. It was his belief that under no circumstances would Michigan workers vote for Obama. Please remember, his market now is Texas, San Antonio, and Houston, not Michigan, Detroit, or Flint. Roland Martin fielded a call from Linda of Connecticut. She is a white, Catholic, blue-collar woman, who was insulted that McCain would assume that women of her ilk would opt to switch allegiance simply because of gender. Moreover, her brother is the president of a labor local in Michigan, and she indicated that her brother and 3,000 members of his local plan to vote for Obama, precisely because of the issues. Another taped responder indicated that voters say one thing in public, but in private they feel differently and are prone to vote for Senator Obama. In an attempt to remain chronologically consistent, my goal is to maintain the historic and timely order of events and statements of this campaign. However, I just couldn't resist the Nah, Nah, Nah, Nah rebuff of Joe "Pags" Pagliarulo's miscalculation of the Michigan voter. The date is November 2, 2008, two days before the historic election. Approximately three weeks after Pagliarulo's Michigan statement, Senator McCain stopped campaigning in Michigan. McCain acknowledged Michigan as an "un-winnable" state. To date, Joe Pagliarulo has not returned as a CNN political pundit. "Pags" was as wrong as two left shoes. Nah, Nah, Nah, Nah!

The third and final segment addressed the clergy's position. Again, there were three panel members, Rev. Dr. Susan Johnson Cook, representing Christians, Rabbi Shumuley Boteach, representing Judaism, and Isahd Manji, a female Muslim scholar. The question was, is bigotry a sin? Rabbi Boteach began the dialogue by unequivocally responding yes. His explanation was scripturally sound. He justified his position by noting that God created man in His image. *"So God created man in His own image, in the image of God created He him; male and female created He them" (Genesis 1:27).* In the second chapter, we genetically validated and emphasized the oneness of all men. Not acknowledging that all races have God as their common Father is particularly insidious, and obviously sinful.

Isahd Manji spiritually articulated the difference between bias and bigotry. In her opinion, bias is the simple preference of *one* over *two*. Bias becomes bigotry when it dehumanizes people. Bias is often grounded in *xenophobic* or *jingoistic* attitudes of fearful ignorance. Isahd Manji continued by emphasizing that everything that God creates is excellent. Therefore, by reducing the humanity of some people, you are disloyal and offending God.

Rev. Dr. Susan Johnson Cook supported the previous two. Moreover, Rev. Johnson Cook was able to speak from two perspectives. She has experienced racism and sexism. She cited, *"And thou shalt love the lord thy God with all thy heart, and with all thy soul, and with all thy mind, and with all thy strength this is the first commandment. And the second is like, namely this, Thou shalt love thy neighbor as thyself. There is none other commandment greater than these" (Mark 12:30-31).* Her major point was love. One must love God, first asking Him to empower us to love yourself and then others. Rev. Cook's statement was, "Hurt people, hurt people."

Scripture says, *"There is no fear in love; but perfect love casteth out fear: because fear hath torment He that feareth is not made perfect in love"* (1 John 4:18). One must understand that hate is not the opposite of love. Fear is the opposite of love. Fear leads to bigotry. The cause of racism is ignorance. Ignorance spawns fear, and moves human nature to control, subordinate, and ultimately destroy that which is fearfully different. Fear underpins bigotry and is counter to God's Word and the harmonious unity of humanity. Bigotry is a sin.

Manji concluded the session with a reference to the parable of the Good Samaritan. *"But a certain Samaritan, as he journeyed, came where he was: and when he saw him, he had compassion on him, And went to him, and bound up his wounds, pouring in oil and wine, and sent him on his beast, and brought him to an inn, and took care of him"* (Luke 10:33). To clarify, Samaritans and Hebrews did not get along. Samaritans were considered mongrels and half-breeds because of their *acculturation, assimilation,* and ultimate *miscegenation* with their former Assyrian captors. "In the ninth year of Hoshea the king of Assyria took Samaria, and carried Israel away into Assyria" (II Kings 17:6). Isahd Manji suggested that we abandon our tendencies toward our personal fears, search for truth, and understand that there is such a thing as "the common good."

If you lie down with Dogs, It's Hard not to get up with Flees ━━

The advanced technology of the media has exposed this presidential campaign's dirty laundry from both political camps. Neither side is without fault; however, the Republicans seem to have initiated the malice, with the Democrats retaliating with an ethically questionable defense. The fear of the phenomena entrainment, mentioned earlier, has disappointingly manifested itself. The ugly realities of politics cannot be suppressed, and the result is a manifestation less than each candidate's pristine vision for the direction of America. A synonym for *politics* should be *compromise,* and God hates lukewarm spiritualism. *"And to the angel of the church in Laodoicea write: These things saith the Amen, the faithful and true witness, the beginning of the creation of God: I know thy works, that thou art neither cold nor hot: I would thou wert cold or hot. So because thou art lukewarm, and neither hot nor cold, I will spew thee out of my mouth"* (Revelation 3: 14-16).

One must always strive to understand and forgive unrighteousness, but from it remain separate. Humanity will never be faultless. We can only strive to live a Christ-like life. It is tantamount to entering a dusty room and trying to remain dust free. Scripture dictates: *"Be not unequally yoked with unbelievers: for what fellowship have the righteous and iniquity? Or what communion hath light with darkness?"* (II Corinthians 6:13). Fortunately, God sent His Son for our salvation. *"For God so loved the world, that He gave His only begotten Son, that whosoever believeth in Him should not perish, but have everlasting life. For God sent not His Son into the world to condemn the world; but that the world through Him might be saved"* (John 3:16).

Michael Eric Dyson makes a poignant point by examining political ethics vs. personal ethics. In his book *April 4, 1968, Martin Luther King Jr.'s Death*, he called attention to how political judgment may expose an individual's personal ethics. In Dyson's opinion, the American public is more concerned with puritanical, provincial "bedroom" issues rather than other areas of character assessment. "In addressing moral failure, they pay little attention to how political judgments may reveal ethical poverty. "As long as a decision, say, to cut millions of the needy from welfare rolls is made by a politician without a sexual problem, the outrage it may cause is chalked up to ideology, not morality."

"On the other hand, liberals are infamous for underplaying the relation between personal and public life. When liberals justly defended Bill Clinton during the impeachment debacle, few remembered that the same president had demanded Surgeon General Joycelyn Elders's resignation after she suggested that masturbation should be openly discussed with young people" (Dyson, 2008, p.

198). To continue, Dr. Dyson defined hypocrisy. "Hypocrisy comes when leaders conjure moral standards that they refuse to apply to themselves and when they do not accept the same consequences they imagine for others who offend moral standards" (Dyson, 2008, p. 198). Leaders who are hypocrites do not understand Romans 8:1. *"There is therefore now no condemnation to them which are in Christ Jesus, who walk not after the flesh, but after the Spirit."* The theoanthropological man is flawed, as is everyone; however, his faith allows him to make prudent but courageous decisions in the face of overwhelming descent, even treachery.

There is one salient difference separating the McCain campaign and the Obama camp. It is intent. The McCain camp's goal is to strike fear. The Obama camp strives to foster hope. McCain's campaign *mantra*, "Obama's lack of experience," is anchored in the "fear card." The "fear card" plays to the established racial, xenophobic, and imperialistic attitudes of this country's past politics, and the unabashed arrogance of the present but soon to be past administration. Senator Obama understands America's need to reverse America's generally foul domestic and international policies, to a hopeful bipartisan goal of unity and increased national character. McCain, in contrast, is manipulating this election by using the perceived fear of immanent peril. He claims America may be dangerously exposed by electing an "inexperienced" president.

Contrary to the negative, Obama's mere candidacy is a reflection of the beginning of a national healing process. Some of us never thought we would see this day. There is much more at stake than the simple election of a president. Weighing in the balance is the soul of a nation. It is a classic protagonist vs. antagonist confrontation: classic good vs. evil. The healing of this nation is *The Audacity of Hope.* It is the hope that this country can reclaim the ethical honor it once had internationally, but most of all establish true domestic integrity without racial, economic, social, religious, or gender dilution. Although humanity is reflected imperfectly through the prism of life, the colorless man bleeds with the stigmata of emotional anguish for truth. Change in the raw reality of this election means far more than political change. It reflects positive growth in the ethical integrity of our nation. The theoanthropological man will continuously strain for integrity and truth. He will most times reach through the fire of pain and humiliation to grasp it. The best way to validate his authenticity is to look at the fruit on his/her tree. *"Ye shall know them by their fruits. Do men gather grapes of thorns, or figs of thistles?"* (Matthew 7:16). *"Even so every good tree bringeth forth good fruit; but a corrupt tree bringeth forth evil fruit"* (Matthew 7:17).

Integrity has no color. It can be encased in the *epicanthic fold* of an Asian's eyes, the sea-blue eyes and pale skin of a Nordic, the brown eyes of a European, or the deep brown eyes and skin of an African. The "heart" is the key to determining a good leader. *"A good man out of the good treasure of his heart bringeth forth that which is good; and an evil man out of the evil treasures of his heart bringeth forth that which is evil: for of the abundance of the heart his mouth speaketh"* (Luke 6:45). Which leader is preferable? From an undeniably biased point of view, perhaps it is the one who turned down several lucrative jobs to dedicate himself to the plight of the *marginalized*? Perhaps it is the candidate who wants to end an unjust war that is killing brave American youth? Is it the one who understands the economical plight of the middle class? Is it the one whose congressional votes and positions were 90% congruent with arguably the most incompetent American president of all time? Is it the one who "flip-flopped" on the issue of flying the confederate flag in South Carolina, and voted against the Martin Luther King national holiday? Do you think the candidate best suited to lead America has virtually ignored the African American and Latino communities, or the candidate who addresses the needs of the complete population of The United States of America? The operative word in United States of America is "United." Disunity is the destructive malady of America, but finally this nation has the opportunity to elect someone who views this nation as an ailing whole. Obama aches to attack the excruciating divisional pain of America and the world. Which person do you think is more ethical and has the character to lead a nation that leads the world?

The Obama Saga Continues ━━━━━━━━━━━

There is always one element persistent in the life of a theoanthropological woman or man. Without exception, when their lives seem to be distressed and confused, or continually face extreme peril, the saving blessing is that God will always show up to do His God thing. As usual, God stepped up. At the conclusion of the Republican convention, and solely because of the selection of Sara Palin as the Republican running mate, the McCain campaign realized a positive "bump" in the polls. Palin's selection was effective. The convention bloom persisted well past its expected duration and was significantly damaging to the Obama campaign.

According to the political pundits, Palin's selection severely crippled Obama's message. In the opinion of the political experts, the Democratic camp focused too much on addressing her hype while ignoring John McCain's liabilities. McCain actually surged from a five-point deficit to a two-point lead, a dead heat considering the three-point margin of error. It looked like Senator Obama was in deep "kaka," but on September 15, 2008, the stock market virtually crashed. Merrill-Lynch went belly up and was purchased by Bank of America. Leaman Brothers, a one hundred and fifty year old financial institution, closed its doors. On the same day AIG, perhaps the largest insurance company in the world, closed its doors and sent the majority of its one hundred and fifty thousand employees home.

There was a brief lull in the storm. On September 16, with the rumor of governmental "bail out," the economy recovered slightly. The "buy out/bail" out was a $700,000,000,000 loan, at the expense of the American taxpayer, to the "crashing" Wall Street financiers.

According to the economic experts, without the loan the nation and perhaps the world would crash and burn in a heap of cosmic bankruptcy. America thought the "buy out/bail out" would turn the economy around. It did not. The economy recovered slightly, but not enough to stabilize Wall Street.

The "crash" was a mixed blessing for Obama supporters. The country was "two inches" from bankruptcy, but the economic calamity gave clear example of the irresponsible economic mismanagement of the present Republican Administration. The "irregulation" of the banking industry is the virus that perpetuated the economic disease. The economic crisis immediately diverted the frivolous attention garnered by Sara Palin, and provided fuel for Senator Obama to attack the dangerous economic precepts of the Republican Party and John McCain. It was a huge Obama "I told you so!" "Do you want more of this?" was Obama's expletive. Unfortunately, the economically precarious position that the next president will be facing will undoubtedly hock his effectiveness as president. The irony is that the Republican Party, the deregulators and "trickle down folks," are forced to partner with the super liberal Democrats to potentially pass the most extreme example of big government and socialism this country has ever experienced. The proposal is a $700,000,000,000 buyout of our dollars, the taxpayer's dollars. The Secretary of the Treasury, Henry Paulson, basically came to this figure without statistical validation. The $700,000,000,000 figure may be sufficient, but leading economists estimate it will not suffice. Paulson and the remaining contingent of apparently pseudo-economic experts honestly have no clue. Led by Henry Paulson, the ironic evil paradox is that the same ravenous foxes that perpetuated the money meltdown are positioning themselves as caretakers of our 700,000,000,000 chickens!

Let us briefly discuss and understand Henry Paulson's pedigree. He was former chairman of the most successful Wall Street investment bank, Goldman and Sachs. He nationalized two mortgage giants, Fanny May and Freddy Mack, and he seized the largest insurance company in the world, AIG. Before he left Goldman-Sachs and took the Secretary of the Treasury position, he was worth $500,000,000. The questions are: is he one of us, and whose interests is he considering? Paulson talks about the best interests of the American people. To him, who are the American people, and what are "best interests" in his view? At this crucial point, America obviously needs governmental intervention, but is he the proper point man?

Moreover, Paulson submitted a five-page document requesting a governmental loan with no accountability and few regulatory restrictions. Perhaps in your life's experiences you may recall the deluge of paperwork you waded through when you applied for a credit card, or a line of credit at your neighborhood bank. Five pages of documentation, are you kidding? With all of the "0's" in $700,000,000,000, it may take three pages just to write the number. There should be at least 50 pages explaining each 0 in the seventy billion dollar number.

Perhaps I'm confused, but isn't the collateral for the congressional "bail out" billions of dollars worth of basically unaffordable housing? Who in America can buy a $500,000 house with no job, questionable credit, and the reluctance of American banks to give credit? In the month of September 2008 alone, America has lost 159,000 jobs in construction, manufacturing, and retail jobs. The housing industry underpins America's economy. The success of home sales, to coin a Republican aphorism, "trickles down" to directly affect business and tertiary industries.

In the last twelve months the unemployment census has increased by 2.2 million, an average of 183,333 *counted* persons per month. Please be advised that this number does not count the lupenproletariate, or the uncounted poor who exist under the statistical radar. From January 2008 to August 2008, America has lost conservatively an average of 63,222 jobs per month, a large portion of which may be unrecoverable. The potential employment atmosphere is bleak. Who does this "bail out?" Tacitly, Paulson is requesting a blank check, and asking the American taxpayer to make it good. The national debt at present is $11,000,000,000,000, a major portion spent on a war that, minus the Bush administration's imperialist motives, should have never been initiated. Moreover, rumor has it that the economic meltdown will require at least an additional $1,000,000,000,000 to $2,000,000,000,000 to maintain America's economic buoyancy. In plain language, this means the American taxpayer will suffer continued long-term tax liability in order to keep this nation's economic head above water. This debt will be generational. Our grandchildren and great-grandchildren will suffer the burden. What Baby Bush didn't waste on the Iraqi War, Paulson's pals stole. Yes, Paulson's pals. Please remember he was past CEO of Goldman-Sachs Investment Bank, perhaps the most powerful investment firm on Wall Street. Please let us not be delusional and think that Mr. Paulson hasn't had dinner with, or his children haven't gone to private school with, or his wife hasn't frequented the spa with, associates and family members of Wall Street colleagues. Although Mr. Paulson may not be one of the directly guilty scallywags, a rational person must question if his proposed irresponsible legislation was prompted by his camaraderie towards the "Golden Airborne." Giving Paulson and pals $700,000,000,000 is tantamount to capturing the largest, most hungry fox in the woods, driving Mr. Hungry Fox to Mr. Purdue's eastern shore chicken plantation, opening the gates, and placing Mr. Hungry Fox in charge of protecting the chickens. As Arsenio Hall used to say, "Ummmmmmmmmm." America's banks, savings and loans, Wall Street, and other financial *prestidigitators* have been using economic "mirrors" to legally steal money for years. Now the mirrors are beginning to crack, and all that may be left is a pile of broken worthless scraps of processed sand. The potential "bail out" is the largest socialistic action America has ever proposed.

The Republican Party took the lead in the passing of legislation to remove mortgage regulations, which ultimately precipitated the mortgage meltdown. However, President Clinton, perhaps in a moment of mindless Monica ecstasy, signed the bill. The Democrats are not faultless. They supported the travesty, but are desperately trying to deflect responsibility. Unfortunately, without the ethics of spiritual intervention, *cupidity* becomes a *virulent* human anathema that affects all.

In the face of an economic meltdown, it appears that the Republicans are coerced into accepting legislation that forces them into total violation of their political ethics. Because of the mysterious "trickle down" theory, and obvious cupidity, the Republicans have found themselves hemmed into a socialistic political polity that their party caustically opposes. Considering the stench of this economic *carrion*, and the potential collapse of our financial system, there will be an acrimoniously "bloody" battle in the legislature. Will President Bush, in his lame duck position, have enough "juice" to sufficiently consolidate the votes needed to past the $7,000,000,000 loan?

In My "Hood," They Call It Being a Little Bitch ━━━━━━━

The latest Republican nonsense is John McCain's request that the first presidential debate be postponed so he can help congress "fix" the financial crisis. Stevie Wonder can see that this is a disgustingly dishonorable campaign ploy. His action is consistent with the previous "Bush/Karl Rove" 2000 and 2004 campaign bags of dirty tricks. This attitude and behavior, the win-at-all-cost position, is a Republican campaign staple, previously employed by the Bush camp and now the "McCain gang." Can you say Florida and Al Gore?

One must acknowledge John McCain's military contribution. The abuse he endured in a Vietcong prison camp, and the denial of an easy ticket home because of his father, is truly the stuff of heroes. Unfortunately, character, integrity, and honor can change over thirty-six years. Ostensibly, this appears to be the case, judging from Senator's McCain's most recent behavior in his vie for the presidency of the United States.

Now that America's focus has changed from national security, for which Senator McCain is well prepared, to a potential crumbling of our economy and an economically focused debate, Senator McCain's advantages in the upcoming debate have decreased substantially. He obviously is requesting a postponement to provide additional preparation time. Letting the economic panic subside is to McCain's advantage, and to the disadvantage of Senator Obama.

Philadelphia is my original home. At the risk of sounding *misogynistic* and with no attempt to insult human femininity, in my old neighborhood, we would call McCain a scared little "bitch." *God's Little Instruction Book* quotes, "Character is not made in crisis, it is only exhibited." The sheep's clothing is coming off the wolf. Whom would you trust, or at this reading, whom did you trust to lead America? Pray for the colorless man.

For Further Discussion

1. Have you read *The Lost Books of the Bible?* If so, what is your opinion of their value in interpreting the validity of the 66 books of the Holy Bible?

2. If you have not read them, do you intend to, and why?

3. At this point, the presidential election should have been concluded. Were your opinions of Barack Obama, Hillary Clinton, John McCain, and the chronicling and tenor of the election process similar to those of the author?

Please explain.

Glossary

Acculturate - to assume the culture of another race or ethnicity

Aphorism - a short saying stating a general truth

Assimilate - to become one with another culture to where no difference is detected

Carrion - rotting flesh

Congruent - agreeing when superimposed; not out of alignment

Cupidity - greed

Epicanthic Fold - the physical characteristic that distinguishes the Asian's eyes

Hilesgeschesnichete - holy history; not as holy as Scripture, but more holy than secular history

Impress - In ancient times, the Roman soldiers could require a non-citizen do whatever the soldier required.

Jingoistic - extreme chauvinism or nationalism

Mantra - a mystical chant, or a speaking point/theme

Marginalized - at extreme risk or disadvantage

Miscegenation - intermarriage between two races

Misogynistic - a woman hater

Prestidigitation - magician or slight of hand

Salient - to stand out; conspicuous or obvious

Virulent - highly infectious

Whahbi Muslims - the Extremist Muslim sect that is responsible for the majority of terrorism; bin Laden's group. They were founded by Wahibi in the late 1700 and eventually with the assistance of king Al Saud formed the nation of Saudi Arabia.

Xenophobic - fear or hatred of foreigners or what is strange or foreign

References

Bargh. J.A., Burrows, L, and Chen, M. (1996). Automaticity of Social Behavior: Direct Effects of Trait Construction and Sterotype Activation on Action. *Journal of Personality and social Psychology*. Vol.71, No. 2 230-244

Dyson, Michael Eric (2008). *April 4, 1968 Martin Luther King,*

Jr.'s Death. Basic CivitasBooks, 387 Park Avenue South, New York, NY 10016-8810.

God's Little Instruction Book. Honor Books, Inc., P.O. Box 55388 Tulsa, Oklahoma 74155.

Moore, T. (1982). Subliminal Advertising: What You See is What You Get. *Journal of Marketing.* Vol. 46 (Spring 1982), p. 38-47

Obama, Barack (2006). *The Audacity of Hope.* Crown Publishing Group, a division of Random House, Inc., New York.

"For though I be free from all men, yet have
I made myself servant unto all, that
I might gain the more." (I Corinthians 9:19)

Perhaps the most powerful feature of divinity is sovereignty, which means God is a living entity unto himself, who is omniscient, omnipresent, immutable, and omnipotent. Moreover, God's sovereignty permits and supernaturally empowers Him to be all things to all people at all times. As Homo sapiens, our human frailties are absent of divine attributes. The frailty of the flesh will not allow humanity to perfectly duplicate God and be all things to all people. However, with the anointing of the Holy Spirit, God expects believers to be Christ-like, living and ministering with the Holy Spirit's divine equipping and empowerment. God knows occasionally we will fail, but He accepts our feeble attempts and anoints them into effectiveness. Paul said it best. *"For though I be free from all men, yet have I made myself unto all, that I might gain more"* (I Corinthians 9:19). A spiritual leader attempts to do what Christ did. He goes to where the need is, and physically and spiritually empathizes with the needy and the hurt. Please understand that there is a huge difference between sympathy and empathy. Sympathy is the simple concern and cognitive understanding of the pain or need of an individual. Empathy is the emotional involvement in an individual's distress. Empathy is emotional and physiological stigmata. One actually feels the pain and often manifests the emotional wounds. Christ felt the pain of the woman at the well, and John wrote, *"And he must needs go through Samaria" (John 4: 4).* Christ used her fallen situation to lead her to God and her village. Please remember, the Samaritan woman had five "husbands," and the man she was with was not hers.

Although Zacchaeus was a hated publican, Christ purposely made His way to Jericho to save him and his family. Ultimately, Zacchaeus witnessed to the loving salvation of Christ, and his salvific message spread exponentially. *"And behold, a man called by name Zacchaeus; and he was a chief publican, and he was rich. And he sought to see Jesus who He was; and could not for the crowd, because he was little of stature. And he ran on before, and climbed up into a sycamore tree to see Him: for He was to pass that way. And when Jesus came to the place, He looked up, and said unto him, Zacchaeus, make haste, and come down; for today I must abide at thy house. And he made haste, and came down, and received Him joyfully. And when they saw it, they all murmured, saying, He is gone in to lodge with a man that is a sinner. And Zacchaeus stood, and said unto the Lord, Behold, Lord, the half of my goods I give to the poor; and if I have wrongfully exacted aught of any man, I restore fourfold. And Jesus said unto him, today is salvation come to this house, forasmuch as he also is a son of Abraham" (Luke 19:2-9).*

Jesus went to a man who was blind from birth. *"When He had thus spoken, he spat on the ground, and made clay of the spittle, and He anointed the eyes of the blind man with the clay" (John 9:4).* Christ found His way to the blind man and healed him both spiritually and physically. Listen to the response of the blind man and his parents when confronted with the jealous Pharisees. The blind man was asked who opened his eyes for him. The blind man's response was, *"A man that is called Jesus made clay, and anointed mine eyes, and said unto me, go to the pool of Siloam, and wash: and I went and washed, and I received sight" (John 9:11).* The Pharisees asked the blind man's parents: *"And they asked them, saying, Is this your son, who ye say was born blind? How then doth he now see? His parents answered them and said, We know that this is our son, and that he was born blind: But by what means he now seeth, we know not; or who hath opened his eyes, we know not: he is of age; ask him: he shall speak for himself"* (John 9:21). People do not care who you are, what you do or did, just as long as you bring them the truth. The blind man was told to keep his blessing to himself and he did. The blind man was loyal; he only admitted to information the Pharisees had already been privy. The blind man's parents were also tight-lipped. Often that is one of God's blessings that He gives His soldiers. Theoanthropologic women and men occasionally receive loyalty from other believers, often in the face of extreme pain. A man becomes a man, and a woman becomes a woman, when we realize that often loyalty supersedes security. Be prepared! You will be tested.

Small blessings are usually just enough to keep the colorless woman or man spiritually motivated and dedicated to God's ultimate victory. To colorless folks, what may be minor wins in the secular world are major victories in God's kingdom building.

Theoanthropology and the resulting anointed metamorphosis ostensibly change the worldly weak into the spiritually mighty. *"But God hath chosen the foolish things of the world to confound the wise; and God hath chosen the weak things of the world to confound the things which are mighty: And base things of the world, and things which are despised, hath God chosen, yea, and things which are not, to bring to naught things that are"* (I Corinthians 1:27-28).

Winning at All Costs, Costs Too Much.

Winning may often cost you the victory. Often we are mesmerized with what we think is right without understanding what is righteous. Correctness is often crippling. "Being right" often leads one into neglectful arrogance and errors in integrity and character. Often one gets erroneously trapped into valuing the end result more than the means and method of getting there. Even if the cause may appear "right," win at all cost is dangerously sinful. "Win at all costs" is fueled by corruptive pride. The colorless man understands that winning at all costs, costs too much. Often winning, with the most innocent intent, may cause severe damage to the defeated. What may be innocuous to one may be injurious to another. Paul says, *"Howbeit there is not in every man that knowledge: for some with conscience of the idol unto this hour eat it as a thing offered unto an idol; and their conscience being weak defiled. But meat commendeth us not to God: for neither, if we eat, are we the better; neither, if we eat not, are we the worse. But take heed lest by any means this liberty of yours become a stumbling block to them that are weak. For if any man see thee which hast knowledge sit at meat in the idol's temple, shall not the conscience of him which is weak be embolden to eat those things which are offered to idols; And through thy knowledge shall the weak brother perish, for whom Christ died. But when ye sin so against the brethren, and wound their weak conscience, ye sin against Christ"* (I Corinthians 7:12). What Paul is saying is that eating meat sacrificed to an idol is not a sin. However, if eating the meat leads another weaker brother or sister into sin, and the stronger is aware of the danger, and does not adjust, the act becomes a sin counted to the stronger person. Leadership will require sacrifices in excess of the obvious. The appearance of impropriety is as injurious as actual impropriety. A spiritual leader must remain in prayer not only for the strength not to sin, but also the avoidance of all appearance of misbehavior. Moreover, the spiritual leader must be willing to seek God's forgiveness. Often, open repentance is required, but be careful. Seek the Holy Spirit's direction. The Holy Spirit may cover your sin. Please remember, the sins of a leader may be more damaging to the congregation if exposed. If one is sincere in the desire for forgiveness, God will cover one's transgressions and "cast them in the sea of forgiveness." Hidden garbage usually tends to fester; however, with God's forgiveness one's sin will result in a blessing for all of God's children.

The McCain, Obama Trauma Drama Continues

Today is September 28, 2008, approximately thirty-six hours after the first presidential debate between Senator Obama and Senator McCain. Despite the transparent gamesmanship of threatening not to post for the first presidential debate and shutting down his campaign because of America's financial meltdown, McCain and the GOP continue to spin this political ploy as an act of unselfish patriotism. To exacerbate the crisis, and prior to the debate, President Bush, in his "infinite wisdom," summoned both candidates to the White House for what was defined as a "high-level economic strategy" meeting. Senator Obama was opposed to returning to Washington for fear of politically influencing the tentative and highly volatile negotiation in Congress regarding their economic "bail out" of the Wall Street banditos. When the candidate's planes were in the air, word came that Congress had reached an agreement and was prepared to sign documentation and send it to the president.

Perhaps it was a coincidence, but as soon as the candidates touched down and Congress was aware of the candidates' presence in Washington, the deal fell through. To add insult to injury, the "high-level" discussions at the White House became caustic and broke without resolution. In a tongue-in-cheek gesture, Frank Paulson, the Treasury Secretary, went on bended knee to the House Speaker, Nancy Pelosi, and with a degree of levity begged her not to speak to the press concerning the White House debacle. Obama was correct: their arrival in Washington at the request of President Bush derailed the talks. The process became completely politicized as Obama anticipated.

The first debate, despite the partisan evaluations of both sides, was good. In my biased opinion, Senator Obama was strong on the economic issues and Senator McCain was strong and aggressive in his area of expertise, national defense. What I didn't like was Senator McCain's condescending, patronizing attitude. His constant mantra, "Senator Obama just doesn't understand," prior to his answers gave the effect that Senator Obama was a "young 'un" and did not understand the complexities of international negotiations. Obama, however, did confront him finally with a face-to-face confrontation about the Iraq War. McCain was a formidable opponent; however, if

I were to give an objective evaluation, and considering the economic catastrophe, my pick is Obama. The next time the Obama camp should factor in and prepare for the "I know best, little boy" tenor that McCain may bring to the debate.

One must understand that because Obama is a colorless man, his visceral instincts are to meet a bloodless compromise. His instincts are to acknowledge truth whenever he sees it, as evidenced by his agreement with McCain of certain issues. Unfortunately, the political experts criticized Obama for his candidness. One would think that the search and acknowledgement of truth would be an attractive character advantage for a leader. Unfortunately, history supports that Americans give lip celebration to honesty, integrity, and good character, while often rewarding the fraud of the victorious. It's all about getting the "W." The perfect national example is the sub-prime mortgage rates and the predatory lending practices that corrupted our financial institutions.

The country's greed is international in scope. Our predatory instincts and imperialist attitudes are disguised in what this country promotes as defending democracy. When in reality the motivating force is monetary greed.

Our national character and ethic is strength without compromise. The media and the "Right" consistently deride negotiations without preconditions. Preconditions are set with the intent of gaining an advantage. America's attitude is, "We won't talk to you unless you give us what we want first." America used to be able to get by with that imperialist attitude. Now, the world is no longer intimidated by American threats. America is rapidly becoming a toothless tiger. The nations that we used to bully have internationally maneuvered their way into a position of economic dominance or tactical military advantage, and America is losing its "juice." The critical problem is that we are still trying to hold on like an old washed up boxer.

Do you remember the Ali vs. Larry Holmes fight? America at this point in history is spiraling downward into oblivion. Obama understands this and so does the remainder of what we call the "third world." To coin an entertainment aphorism, Russia, Iran,

Afghanistan, Pakistan, Sudan, North Korea, China, and several other countries are on their way to the top with a "bullet."

If elected, Obama's personality and inclination to compromise will do more to restore America to prominence than McCain's "take no prisoners, shoot from the hip" volatile philosophy. The John "Waynian" profile is a dangerous international philosophy. McCain will get us shot down just like he admittedly got himself over Hanoi with his ill-advised "cowboy" attitude. "People who *fly* into a rage often make a bad landing" (Will Rogers, *God's Little...*, 1994). John Wayne is dead, and when he was alive, it was only a movie. God is hopefully resting his soul.

It is no time for America to be mired in destructive nationalism. Nationalistic bravado has gotten us into trouble, and if continued will keep us in trouble, especially considering the volatile climate of the world. America is rapidly becoming a fading bully. In school, do you remember what happened when the bully met his match? The bully went down, he went down hard. Most times he or she was shown to be weak and empty, a paper tiger. Now, there are other kids in the international schoolyard almost as big as we are, and they have most of the oil. America has to learn that "you can build a throne with bayonets, but you can't sit on it long" (Boris Yeltsin, *God's Little...*, 1994).

News Flash, No Cash!

On June 27, 2008, in Raleigh, North Carolina, my friend, Mr. John Melvin Beacon, a mortgage and economic consultant for the Progressive Action Community Development Corporation, gave a speech at a housing expo concerning the critical housing and mortgage situation in America. Mr. Beacon's audience was moderate to low-income earners interested in first-time home ownership, or present homeowners experiencing contemporary mortgage dilemmas. Consumer education is Mr. Beacon's area of expertise. As a consultant, he prepares predominantly African Americans living in the southeast area of Raleigh for home ownership. He and his colleagues meticulously educate potential homeowners in the areas of credit analysis, credit restoration, maintenance of their property, legal liabilities, homeowner's insurance, and personalized environmental requirements for family domiciles. Each client is required to attend and complete ten classes of instruction in financial management.

His prophetic thirty-minute caveat was a chilling look into the future. The future is now. On September 29, 2008, as a result of Congress's rejection of the national "buy out" legislation for the tacit criminal actions of Wall Street, the Dow Jones has fallen to –777 points, the lowest in history. Not just the American economy, but the world's financial stability has been sabotaged. The sky may truly be falling and there appears to be no shelter. Today, September 29, 2008, we are halfway to national bankruptcy and the most crippling American financial crisis since the Great Depression and Stock Market Collapse of 1929.

In June the prophet Beacon forespoke exactly what has come to fruition today. In what periodically was a caustic tone, he warned, chided, and derided the mortgage industry for knowingly placing America in peril. His *diatribe* was forceful but weighted with the vicarious pain of the many victims and potential victims of predatory mortgage loans.

Perhaps you saw the September 28, 2008 edition of *60 Minutes*. Scott Pelley asked Henry Paulson's opinion of the following e-mails written by analysts for two credit-rating agencies. Both agencies were under federal investigation at the time. The first read, "It could be structured by cows and we would still rate it." The second read, "Let's hope we are all wealthy and retired by the time this house of cards falters." Paulson's paraphrased response was, "We are in the mess now and if we don't clean it up immediately, the American house of cards will crumble." Again, who is "we?" Is Paulson referring to 95% of Americans who just want the staples of life satisfied? Is Paulson referring to the vast number of Americans who simply want to retire with dignity? Is Paulson speaking to Americans who are satisfied with a less than an extravagant vacation, or is he speaking to people who are not satisfied unless they have their own private island? Is Paulson talking about Americans who simply want the means to send their children to college so they may mature to be Barack and Michelle "Obamas?" Is Paulson speaking to the folks with an income that exceeds $10,000,000 per year, own nine houses and twelve cars, or the man with one house, two cars, children, and an income that he earned through academic diligence, brutally hard work, or entrepreneurial ingenuity? In 2008, what is the American dream? Is it the same as Paulson and his pals? The ex-chairperson for Goldman & Sachs is estimated to be worth $500,000,000. It seems that his dream is about $450,000,000 larger than the average American. What do the Paulsons and McCains of America do when the "economic feces hits the fan?" They launch their yachts, float to their islands, and turn their backs on those of us who are left behind to kill our dinners with a stick. Today, September 29, 2008, the once American dream of owning a house, educating one's children, comfortably paying bills, and retiring in dignity has exploded into an "illusionary," delusional *conflagration*. Today, America is a tinderbox of burning fagots perishing in the belief of false security. "The happiness of every country depends upon the character of its people, rather than the form of its government" (Thomas Chandler Haliburnton, *God's Little…*, 1994). Will we be happy again?

Don't lose faith. God is about to do his God thing. *"For His anger endureth but a moment; in his favour is life: weeping may endure for a night, but joy cometh in the morning"* (Psalms 30:5). Don't fret. God always leaves a remnant to rebuild his kingdom. However, if believers refuse to return to His love, the blessing of the remnant will be lifted. God hates judgment. His promise is, *"If my people, which are called by my name, shall humble themselves, and pray, and seek my face, and turn from their wicked ways; then will I hear from heaven, and will forgive their sin, and will heal their land"* (II Chronicles 7:14). This election is America's chance. It may be America's last chance.

The operative words are *"If my people shall humble themselves."* It is my spiritual conviction that Senator Obama is God's chosen to lead America back to spiritual civility. Civility, because government is an inanimate entity and cannot be personally saved. America can only be brought to adherence to God by the spiritual nature of its citizens. We need a Godly example. God bless the Barack Obamas and John Melvin Bacons of the world, who sacrificially commit themselves to the betterment of humanity. We need more colorless men and women. Pray for the colorless man.

The Tongue, a Double-Edged Sword

The tongue is a greater healer than the most effective "super" drug. In contrast, the tongue is also more deadly than the most poisonous elixir. *"Death and life are in the power of the tongue: and they that love it shall eat the fruit thereof"* (Proverbs 18: 21). *"He that keepeth his mouth keepeth his life: but he that openeth wide his lips shall have destruction"* (Proverbs 13:6). Let us recall what happened to the young man who apparently thought he was doing a service by completing Saul's attempted suicide. When he reported it to King David, David slew the self-fashioned hero for having the nerve to kill God's anointed. *"David called one of the young men, (David's Warrior) and said, Go near and fall upon him. And he smote him that he died. And David said unto him, Thy blood upon thy head; for thy mouth hath testified against thee, saying I have slain the Lord's anointed"* (II Samuel 1:1-15). "One reason the dog has so many friends: he wags his tail instead of his tongue" (Unknown, *God's Little...*, 1994). My parents would periodically share a well-used African American aphorism, "Don't let your mouth write a check your butt can't keep." Oftentimes we metaphorically kill ourselves with our mouths. My mom always says, "Give a fool enough rope and he'll hang himself." Often the ropes are our tongues. The theoanthropological man strives to keep a reign on this tongue and use it to build, not tear down. Always remember the tongue can be *"... a fire, a world of iniquity: so is the tougue among our members, that it defileth the whole body, and setteth on fire the course of nature; and it is set on fire of hell"* (James 3:5).

It appears that John McCain's barrage of negative untruthful and semi-truthful television ads is beginning to backfire. Americans are presently terrified of the potential nation-destroying financial condition, and Americans have finally reached annoyance with the miasmic stench of McCain's petty and untrue character attacks. Although Obama has reacted to the negativity, his ads have been for the most part defensive. Even Jesus warns us to protect ourselves. *"And He said unto them, But now, he that hath a purse, let him take it, and likewise a wallet; and he that hath none, let him sell his cloak, and buy a sword. For I say unto you, that this which is written must be fulfilled in me, And he was reckoned with transgressors; for that which concerneth me hath fulfillment"* (Luke 22:36-37). To paraphrase, Jesus is saying, "Soon I will be gone and unable to protect you. Now you must protect yourself, because you are my emissaries of the 'Good News.'" It must be spread throughout the world.

The American public is beginning to recognize the underlying negative foundation of McCain's attacks, especially after his latest *faux pas* during the second debate. Earlier I identified the labeling of Senator Obama as "inexperienced" by Senator McCain as synoptically saying, "The black man doesn't know what he is doing. A black man cannot possibly lead this nation." Recently, it has been brought to the attention of the nation by CNN that a euphemistic nominative for characterizing a black man, Senator Obama, is Muslim. It appears to be politically acceptable for bigots to disguise their prejudice by insisting that their reluctance to vote for Senator Obama is his tie to Islam, which every intelligent American knows is untrue. American bigotry is riddled with code words. Hint. Please remember, Senator McCain "flip-flopped" on the South Carolina Confederate Flag issue, and voted against the Martin Luther King holiday. Is the picture a little clearer? This is exacerbated by the inflammatory statements of Sara Palin, as evidenced by the racial epithets and violent threats targeted towards Senator Obama from the McCain and Palin supporters at Republican rallies.

Subsequent to the primaries, McCain has totally abandoned his sham of trying to appeal to the African American and Latino voter, and *mendaciously* accused Senator Obama of "playing the race card." The accusation prompted Senator Obama's eloquent "race speech." Additionally, Senator Obama's quote that "it's often not proper to discuss race in polite company" gracefully and tactfully dismantled McCain's awkward "race card" attack.

The latest racial blunder by Senator McCain clearly illuminates his *pejorative* attitude toward black people. What did "that one" mean?! Senator McCain, when referencing a congressional bill that Senator Obama voted for and he did not, referred to Senator Obama as "that one." Most people with a modicum of psychological training could clearly see that the statement was a conscious or subconscious attempt to dehumanize Senator Obama. The statement "that one" was an attempt to emasculate and dehumanize, as degrading as referencing African American men as boy, coon, and "nigger." One must remember Luke 6: 45: *"A good man out of the good treasure of his heart bringeth forth that which is good; and an evil man out of the evil treasures of his heart bringeth forth that which is evil: for of the abundance of the heart the mouth speaketh."* "The heart has no secret which our conduct does not reveal" (Unknown, *God's Little...*, 1994). At this point even the Republican pundits are abandoning McCain and Palin. Some have changed their rhetoric because they honestly have come to see McCain's character flaws, but most I assume don't want to be associated with a loser. Remember the American mantra: "Win at all costs."

There is an interesting feature of language. What is said often is not as important as what is not said. Senator McCain continually derides Senator Obama for the mere consideration of negotiations without preconditions. As discussed earlier, McCain's definition of international preconditions, when dealing with a hostile nation, is forcing the sovereign nation to comply with America's object demands prior to the beginning of earnest negotiations. That is not negotiation. That is, "Do what we say, and then we will tell you if you complied, why you should have complied, and if you did it correctly," ostensibly a strong-arm tactic. America's arms are no longer that strong. The infamous "they countries" have wrenched and secured control of the oil and more recently most of the world's financial resources. Muscle in this contemporary world is money and oil, and America is rapidly becoming depleted of both. The methods of negotiations must be adjusted. The president of the United States must learn how to speak in tongues. Not the "tongues" that the Pentecostal denomination espouses, but the tongue of global cooperation and mutual peaceful existence.

To reiterate, speaking "in tongues" as described in Acts 2 is not the accepted tongue speaking to which most religious denominations refer. It was the custom of Hebrews to remain in Jerusalem after the Passover holiday to celebrate the Feast of Weeks. For this reason, there were several thousand Hebrews available to hear Peter's inaugural sermon to the newly birthed church. The Christian name for this special day is the day of Pentecost. The name "Pentecost" means fiftieth day. It was exactly 50 days after Christ's crucifixion and ten days after his final ascension. As was the tradition, the Jewish holiday drew several nations together with a diversity of languages. When Peter began to preach, the Holy Spirit empowered several spiritual men to directly address each nationality in their native language, even though the men speaking were not familiar with the languages emanating from their mouths. This is consistent with what Paul says in *I Corinthians 14: 27*, *"If any man speak in an unknown tongue, let it be by two, or at the most by three, and that by course; and let one interpret. But if there be no interpreter, let him keep silence in the church; and let him speak to himself, and to God."* My suggestion is that the entire chapter of Acts 2 be studied.

The above is consistent with the Biblical definition of speaking in tongues. However, there is a difference between holy language and speaking in tongues. Speaking in tongues should always have an interpreter. When experienced firsthand, one has truly witnessed a miracle. During a class that I was teaching at Family Bible Seminary, we had two guests in attendance from different countries. Neither student knew each other. One of our guests was from Nigeria. The other was from Cameroon where French is spoken and several other regional dialects. Her accent was wonderfully beautiful. However, as I was teaching, the multilingual guest, anointed with the power of the Holy Spirit, began to prophesize in Hausa, a language endemic to Nigeria. She expounded on my text, and spoke English and Hausa, skillfully alternating languages while remaining under the anointing of the Holy Spirit. We were all astounded and blessed. To date I cannot remember what the text was, and this was the only time this author has experienced the actual speaking in tongues as explained by the apostle Paul in scripture.

What many commonly mistake for speaking in tongues is speaking in Holy Language. Holy Language is the communicative intercession that the Holy Spirit provides for the believer. To the natural ear, it may seem like unintelligible moans, groans, and babble, but it is the unbridled spiritual language of a believer to God. The conduit is the Holy Ghost, who acts like a *metergemean*, or translator/ interpreter. *"Likewise the Spirit also helpeth our infirmities: for we know not what we should pray for as we ought: but the Spirit itself maketh intercession for us with groanings which cannot be uttered"* (Romans 8:26). Please understand that Romans 10: 9-10 is explicit concerning salvation. *"That if thou shalt confess with thy mouth the Lord Jesus, and shalt believe in thine heart that God hath raised Him from the dead, thou shalt be saved. For with the heart man believeth unto righteousness; and with the mouth confession is made unto salvation."* The preceding scripture says nothing concerning speaking in tongues, or being filled with the Holy Ghost, or dancing with snakes. The Scripture says *"That if thou shalt confess with thy mouth the Lord Jesus, and shalt believe in thine heart that God hath raised Him from the dead, thou shalt be saved."* No equivocation!

Nineteen Days Out

America is nineteen days from selecting a new president. It's October 13, 2008, and anything can happen. The polls have Obama ten points ahead. However, by this point the reader already knows the outcome of the election. Whoever was the victor needs our prayers, because he will be critically challenged. For America to reestablish our ideological mantra "The land of the free and the home of the brave," a colorless man must lead. America's president must be colorless as Christ directed. America does not need a man tangled in the religious rhetoric that Bill Maher caustically describes, but a leader with the spirit of theoanthropology. He must have a living relationship with Christ.

To be successfully effective, America's president must become a man that can speak in the tongues of the world. He must be understood by the world and not just America. The colorless man has a monumental burden. The next American president is responsible to the world. He must remember that the position of the man is more important than the man himself. Even if you're displeased with America's choice, please pray for him. As Americans, we must continue to provide the true Christian light of the world. As best as we can, Americans must accept the responsibility for modeling what is righteous, not what society or the world accepts as right. Pray for the calming influence of our nation on the world, and the spiritual empowerment of America's president, whoever he might be. "The price of greatness is responsibility" (Winston Churchill, God's Little..., 1994).

The Unconsciousness of Racism

The more one thinks he is not a bigot, the more likely he is a bigot. Everyone in America six months of age and older is a racist. The fundamental underpinnings of this nation dictate this to be so. Once we all realize this truth, the nation can truly begin to heal. Americans are trained from infancy to be race conscious. The media, family relationships, subliminal messages, Barbie dolls, toys, television, magazine ads, billboards, and myriad other influences continually distort one's ethnocentrism. In America, this phenomenon is manifested in the classic attitude of entitlement by the dominant race towards minorities. No nation will be totally *homogeneous*. There will always be differences no matter how slight. Ethnic, clan, and racial differences are healthy and positive if *symbiotic*. Moreover, evaluating one's ethnicity as it relates to another is not inherently destructive. The construct is called ethnocentrism; it becomes racism when one ethnicity believes it is entitled to and attempts to subordinate another. At present, unaddressed racism is what we have in America. The problem is that Americans would rather be politically correct than lance the racial boil on America's societal butt. A butt bump will get bigger until you "bust" it, remove the core, and clean, and cauterize the wound.

At present my favorite author is Michael Eric Dyson. In one of his interviews or books, he cited Stewart Hall. Dr. Hall refers to contemporary racism in America as inferential racism. Inferential racism is a subliminal influence that devalues others and one's self through subtle *inculcated* stereotypes by using words, media, pseudoscience, acculturation, assimilation, fear, and sporadic brutality. In addition, inferential racism is not overt. It is often "politically correct" and benignly disguised in attractive rhetoric, rendering it exponentially more dangerous. Inferential racism is anchored in presupposition, offensive metaphors analogies, and moral and ethical decline. It is a socially surreptitious sickness, and the infestation has seeped into America's economic and social systems. Unfortunately, economics and social status have become the new racisms. America is an economic *oligarchy*. The irony is that "Joe Six-Pack and Joe the Plummer" have become the "new American niggers" and don't know it. Mr. "Six-Pack" and his wrench-wielding buddy think that the conservative Republican faction of the America's political machine is going to provide the vehicle for them to attain the American dream of economic affluence. It's a trick of the privileged ruling class. Government is in their pockets. Both the Democrats and Republicans are guilty. Geppetto is pulling Pinocchio's political and economic strings, and the manipulation has been devastating to the American people. Everyone is financially vulnerable except the "boys" who walked away with the half billion dollar parachutes.

Please remember, according to George Stephanopoulos, the

middle class has an income ranging from $90,000 to $250,000. According to these standards and Senator Obama's statistics, 95% of Americans are broke, ergo the need for change from the crippling economic policies of the previous eight years of Republican leadership and Democratic compliance. Who wouldn't be angry? According to these statistics, I'm destitute.

Dangerously, some Americans are drowning in *obscurantism*, and until the recent economic "bust," refused to see the result of this nation's economic manipulation. "Joe Six-Packs" will remain fiscally numb until the Joes find it difficult to buy their Budweiser. History has shown that when nations experience economic distress, it will also decline into racial and religious strife, i.e., Nazi Germany. America is in the midst of economic trauma. America's president, much greater than an economic plan, must become sensitive to a potentially corruptive racial confrontation that may develop in the United States. He must preempt a national racial/socioeconomic divide that may inflame America's political and spiritual health. America is positioned to become a tragic white-hot ember of social, economic, religious, and gender *conflagration*. The next president will unequivocally have to address a racial backlash from both sides of the divide that could destroy America. More than ever, America needs a colorless man.

Presupposition Determines Position

It is unquestionably divine how the masterful understanding of one concept can lead to the enlightenment of another. This semester at seminary, one of my classes is the study of exegesis and hermeneutics. Exegesis is the critical research and explanation of biblical texts, and hermeneutics is the interpretation and potential application of the researched information. During this class, we were discussing presupposition, metaphor, and analogy. We were also interested in how these communication skills apply to the *didactic* and ethical preaching of the Gospel of Jesus the Christ.

Presupposition is the "pre-supposing" or assumption that

a situation is factual and deduced or induced from personal experience, perception, or environmental influence. Presupposition is often formed from specious information. For all of us, there is a bounty of half-truths that subconsciously distorts our decisions and ultimately our lives. What may appear to be fact is often fiction. The class discussed parts of speech that effectively communicate presuppositions. The students settled on two specific similes, metaphors and analogies. A metaphor is a figure of speech that implies a close relationship between two seemingly unrelated things. For example, Peter is a rock. We also defined an analogy. The difference between a metaphor and an analogy is that analogies form a reference or a likeness between two or more things. Using the previous example, "Peter and John are like rocks" is an analogy. "He was as hot as a branding iron, and as mean as a rattlesnake" is another. The verbiage "like a thing or as a thing" is usually found in analogies. Presuppositions, many of which are assumptive half-truths, often have several decades of *inculcation*. This generational brainwashing directly affects speech and ultimately behavior.

Metaphors can be both verbal and visual, similar to the one used when a McCain supporter put an Obama hat on a toy monkey, inferring and using the racial *epithet* that black people are akin to apes. Let us consider the not-so-disguised analogy of Sara Palin referencing Senator Obama as "palling around with terrorists." Everyone is familiar with the aphorism "Birds of a feather flock together." Again, Stevie Wonder can see what she was saying. Please consider the previous reference to Stewart Hall's definition of inferential racism. We must be vigilant in our spiritual and political alertness. An experience *sophist* can disguise half-truths in a cacophony of colorful oration and text that will confuse the most experienced and intelligent.

To continue with the third part of the puzzle, we may now relate presuppositions, metaphors, and analogies with didactic and ethical understanding. As one teaches, both verbally and with behavior, the above become increasingly critical. If the presuppositions, metaphors, and analogies are faulty or specious, the maladies become ingrained in the student and ultimately accepted into the moral fiber of society. Please remember that ethics in this country are grounded in Judeo-Christian Scripture. Moral adherence is what society presently or contemporarily accepts as proper behavior and attitude. Morals will change as public opinion changes. Ethics will not.

It is totally politically unacceptable for the above McCain supporter to call Senator Obama and his supporters monkeys. However, the racial effigy was thought to be subtle, so the offender thought. However, it was a perfect example of inferential racism. Sara Palin would never say that Senator Obama was a terrorist. Her inference was more effective. Instead of being called a liar, she becomes an enlightened patriot. This is an example of a double-edged cut. The perpetrator employs inferential racism while engendering herself to the constituency. This is classic *demagoguery*.

The final two presidential debates were relatively insignificant. With one exception, the third debate did directly address some of the pressing issues. Despite the irritating distraction of the "Joe the Plummer" buffoonery, the salient difference between the two candidates finally became glaringly apparent to me. Their presuppositions are different. Remembering Senator McCain's position on South Carolina and the confederate flag and his refusal to vote in favor of the Martin Luther King Holiday, I realized that the above, combined with his age, distort his worldview and are profoundly different from Senator Obama's. Please remember that John McCain was 22 years old in 1958. He matured in the world of Donna Reed, *Leave It to Beaver*, and *Mayberry MFP*. He was a mature American adult when children and Negroes were to be seen and not heard. He lived through the years when African Americans were cemented in subordinate social and economic positions. No wonder he bristles at the thought of losing to whom he considers a subordinate. Please recall Senator McCain's condescending "how dare you" attitude during the debates. Even Bill Clinton is still festering in regard to Senator Obama's usurping his wife's privileged and entitled position as Democratic nominee. Recall the synoptic metaphors of inexperienced, risky, and dangerous that Senator McCain used in describing Senator Obama. They were euphemisms for "reckless black man." Inferential racism? Senator McCain's presuppositions poisoned his metaphors, analogies, and subsequently his ethics and temperament. His less than presidential persona was evidenced by his surly and condescending attitudes during all three of the debates. Senator McCain sees through a 50-year-old stigmatism. My biggest question is, what does he know about "Joe the plumber"? Senator McCain's grandfather was an admiral, his father was an admiral, and his wife owns a lucrative Budweiser distributorship. Do plumbers socialize in these circles? One must realize that admirals entertain presidents and heads of states in their homes.

Please give this some thought. McCain, admittedly an average at best high school student, party man, and maverick, was accepted into The Naval Academy? Please understand that the American military academies are the premiere undergraduate institutions of the world. They are more prestigious than Harvard, Yale, Princeton, Oxford, or the Sorbonne. Can you say *consanguinity*? Moreover, how does one graduate fifth from the bottom of your class at the Naval Academy and become a fighter pilot? Perhaps I'm misinformed, but isn't the pilot program supposed to accept only the best? Can you say *consanguinity*? Senator McCain accused Barack Obama of being elite. When has John McCain ever not been elite? The only period in McCain's life when he was not elite, privileged, or entitled was the five years he spent in a Hanoi prison. Is his political base so blinded that they cannot see past the magician's mirrors, or is America basically stupid like Bill Maher says?

Barack Obama's presuppositions are antithetical. He understands that for 95% of white America and perhaps upward of 97% of American ethnicities realizes that the American dream is a nightmare. His presuppositions are different. Senator Obama understands the critical need for adequate health because he watched his mother die for lack thereof. Do you think Senator Obama's presuppositions are different because his single mom and white grandparents raised him? Perhaps his early racial confusion and conflict matured into ethnic understanding and racial tolerance? Do you think that Senator Obama's presuppositions are different because he spent a portion of his formative years in Malaysia, Hawaii, and the South side of Chicago? Perhaps Senator Obama's presuppositions are different because, as Sara Palin, with her extreme intellectual acumen, accuses him of only having extensive community organizational skills? Perhaps we should assume that Senator Obama's presuppositions are different because he graduated from Columbia University and has a law degree from Harvard Law School? Are his presuppositions different because he is a former editor of the *Harvard Law Review* and University of Chicago Constitutional law professor? Perhaps Senator Obama's presuppositions are different because his hero is Martin Luther King? Remember, he's the civil rights and anti-war dude who died for America. You know, the person whose birthday John McCain did not want as a national holiday.

I have a question. With all of the above considered, how many times do you think Senator Obama has been called "nigger?" Presuppositions directly contribute to the thought process responsible for speech and behavior. Subsequently, speech and behavior of an individual directly influence the thought, behavior, and finally the presuppositions of others. It is reciprocal. That is the reason American government's spiritual health, ethics, morals, economy, international integrity, and physical infrastructure are crumbling as you read. Obama is America's Nehemiah standing on the wall watching for the enemy, prepared to sound the alarm, with a sword in one hand and a hammer in the other. *"And it came to pass from that time forth, that the half of my servants wrought in the work, and the other half of them held both the spears, the shields, and the bows, and the habergeons; and the rulers were behind all the house of Judah. They which builded on the wall, and they that bare burdens, with those that laded, every one with one of his hands wrought in the work, and with the other hand held a weapon"* (Nehemia 4:16-17). Obama appears to be God's anointed construction foreman for the rebuilding of America's crumbling wall.

McCain's Pain ━━━━━━━━━━━━━━━━━━━━━━━━━━━

It blew up! It is Sunday, October 26, 2008, nine days out and the McCain campaign is crumbling and crashing around Senator McCain's feet. The Republican campaign blunders have all but flushed any chance of a McCain victory down the crapper. The ill-advised and hasty selection of Alaska's governor Palin can no longer be whitewashed by GOP spin masters. The entire nation has seen the magnitude of her lack of readiness for the office of vice president, and the nation cringes when it considers her ascension to the presidency in the wake of tragedy. Palin is struggling not to become a joke, which is impossible when each week Tina Faye does such a fabulous mimic of her latest missteps on Saturday Night Live. It is obvious why the McCain campaign kept her insulated from the press. She is woefully ill-prepared, as evidenced in the tragically disastrous interview with Katie Couric. It was embarrassing. The irony is that while she criticizes Senator Obama for his alleged inexperience, when asked by Couric for three newspapers that she reads, Palin could not name one. This and her ignorance in calling Africa a country instead of a continent, questions her scholastic acumen, and after an eight-year Bush tragedy, America doesn't need another intellectually challenged leader. To continue her $150,000 clothes budget seems to cloud her image as a consignment shopping mom, and her homegrown regular girl hockey mom persona.

The Republican campaign did everything they could to validate this imposter. She obviously wasn't vetted thoroughly. Now that her inadequacies are glaring, the Republican campaign leadership is pointing fingers at her and each other while running for political cover. Members of her own Republican camp have publicly referred to her as a diva and a renegade, an irony considering how proudly Senator McCain and she wore their campaign mantra of maverick. Palin gave them what they asked for, but without control. At this point the Republican campaign is desperate, and their efforts have deteriorated into a comedy of errors and clown-like buffoonery. The nation now sees John McCain for what he really is and not what they thought he was. Gender pandering, political prestidigitation did not pan out for

"Mac is back," as he calls himself. Attractive hockey moms married to "Joe the plumber" apparently are not prepared to be vice President of the United States and potentially the leader of the free world. Please remember Senator McCain's accusation scolding Senator Obama for rather winning an election than a war. McCain would rather win an election than to protect a nation from the potential of dangerous leadership.

Although Senator Obama has a clear advantage, like a true champion he is turning up the pressure. His thirty-minute infomercial on Wednesday October 29, 2008, wooed America. Even the Republican pundits were impressed. He is crisscrossing America at a maddening rate, often making 12-15 stops in 20 hours. Champions leave nothing to chance. If Barack endeavors to secure and close international dealings with foreign leaders like he is shutting the door on this campaign, then America is in great hands. Obama is like a major league relief pitcher, the consummate closer. He's bringing the heat. God bless the colorless man.

For Further Discussion

1. What is the meaning of sovereignty?

2. Please explain the four attributes of God.

3. Have you experienced spiritual stigmata?

4. What is meant by "Winning may often cost you the victory"?

Glossary

Conflagration - a great fire; disastrous fire
Consanguinity - an inheritance or inherited privilege
Demagogue- a person who appeals to the emotions and prejudices of people

Diatribe - a portion of caustic, biting speech
Didactic- a moral lesson
Epithet - a term of abuse
Faux pas - a mistake
Homogenous - of the same kind
Inculcation - the process of forcing a habit; it is similar to brainwashing
Mendaciously - given to deception or falsehood
Metergemen - an interpreter similar to the holy men who translated the Hebrew Scriptures into Aramaic for the repatriated Israelites
Obscurantism - opposition to knowledge and enlightenment
Oligarchy - government ruled by a small group of people usually at the top of the "food chain"
Pejorative - placing in an unfavorable light
Salvific - the act of saving
Sophist - a manipulator of truth to win philosophical arguments
Symbiosis - a close mutual coexistence between two or more organisms or entities

References

Bible, King James Version.

Dyson, Michael Eric (2008). *April 4, 1968 Martin Luther King Jr.'s Death....* Basic Civitas Books. 387 Park Avenue South, New York, NY 10016-8810.

God's Little Instruction Book II (1994). Honor Books, Inc. P.O. Box 55388, Tulsa, Oklahoma 74155.

Lost Books of the Bible (1979). Crown Publishing, Inc.

Obama, Barack (2006). *The Audacity of Hope.* Crown Publishing Group, Inc., New York.

Epilogue

"Let every soul be subject unto the higher powers. For there is no power but of God: the powers that be are ordained of God." (Romans 13:1)

"Be ye followers of me, even as I also am of Christ."
(I Corinthians 11:1)

The epigraph of the epilogue details specifically how believers are to handle secular authority. In order to completely understand the meaning of Romans 13:1-3, one must read it in the original language. *"Let every soul be subject unto the higher powers. For there is no power but of God: the powers that be are ordained of God. Whosoever therefore resisteth the ordinance of God: and they that resist shall receive to themselves damnation. For rulers are not a terror to good works, but to the evil. Wilt thou then not be afraid of the power? Do that which is good, and thou shalt have praise of same."* Some may misinterpret this scripture passage to mean that believers should follow secular leadership without question. No! The operative words are *"For there is no power but of God,"* which means God gives rulers their power. "For rulers are not a terror to good works" implies that God will often use the sins of evil leaders for the good of His Kingdom. Scriptural validation lies in how God used Assyria and Babylon as implements of judgment to punish and cleanse the apostasy of the Northern and Southern kingdoms. *"In the ninth year of Hoshea the king of Assyira took Samaria, and placed them in Halah and in the cities of the Medes. For it was, that the children of Israel had sinned against the Lord their God, which had brought them up out of the land of Egypt, from under the hand of Pharaoh king of Egypt, and had feared other Gods"* (II Kings 17: 6-7). The Southern kingdom was not without fault, and God punished them similarly. *"And the king of Babylon smote them, and slew them at Riblah in the land of Hamath. So Judah was carried away out of their land. And as for the people that remained in the land of Judah, whom Nebuchadnezzar king of Babylon had left, even over them he made Gedalah the son of Ahikam, son of Shaohan, ruler"* (II Kings 25:21-22). When necessary, God will pass judgment on individual disobedience, but judgment is contrary to His nature. In Isaiah 28:21, the prophet calls judgment strange. Strange in this context means unfamiliar and not pleasurable. *"For the Lord shall rise up as in mount Perazim, He shall be wroth as in the valley of Gibeon, that He may do His work, His strange work; and bring to pass His act, His strange act."*

Jeremiah, upon direction from God, told Zedekiah, the king of the Southern Kingdom, to surrender to Nebuchadnezzar, the king of Babylon. Jeremiah told Zedekiah that if he didn't obey that the city and temple would be burned. Zedekiah did not obey, and subsequently God's Word came to fruition. *"Then saith Jeremiah unto Zedekiah, Thus saith the Lord, the God of hosts, the God of Israel; If thou wilt assuredly go forth unto the king of Babylon's princes, then thy soul shall live, and this city shall not be burned with fire; and thou shalt live, and thine house"* (Jeremiah 38:17-18). Resultant of Zedekiah's disobedience, he was taken prisoner and his family killed. Nebuchadnezzar executed his sons and immediately blinded him, so that Zedekiah's final vision and lasting memory would be their death. *"And the king of Babylon slew the sons of Zedekiah before his eyes: he slew also all the princes of Judah in Riblah. Then he put out the eyes of Zedekiah; and the king of Babylon bound him in chains, and carried him to Babylon, and put him in prison till the day of his death"* (Jeremiah 52:10-11). Do you remember the "pluck, slap, and the slug?" To whomever God gives the responsibility of His people, that person is held accountable. If the leader ignores that responsibility, the leader will be judged harshly. *"Woe be unto* the pastors that destroy and scatter the sheep of my pasture! saith the Lord" (Jeremiah 23:1). "Whosoever heareth the sound of the trumpet, and taketh not warning; if the sword come, and take him away, his blood shall be upon his own head. But if the watchman see the sword come, and blow not the trumpet, and the people be not warned; if the sword come, and take any person from among them, he is taken away in his iniquity; but his blood will I require at the watchman's hand" (Ezekiel 33:5-6). In order to thoroughly understand the responsibilities of a leader and a follower, one must consider I Corinthians 11:1 and Romans 13:1-3 in conjunction. "Be ye followers of me, even as I also am of Christ" (I Corinthians 11:1). Very simply, if the leader is not behaving in congruence with God's Word, then believers should not honor or follow the leadership. Do not follow unholy leaders. Extricate yourself as spiritually gracefully as possible. As believers we must respect the position; however, believers are not obligated to sin or defy God's Holy Word. Always remember, rank does not confer power. It imposes responsibility.

Please understand: there is often a vigorous challenge for the children of the Father to hold the faith. Do not fret. God never gives us more than we can handle. Usually we are prepared for His challenges before we are required to meet them. "There hath no temptation taken you but such as is common to man: but God is faithful, who will not suffer you to be tempted above that ye are able; but will with the temptation also make a way to escape, that ye may be able to bear it" (I Corinthians 10:13).

It is critical that the next American president be a man of God, a theoanthropoligical Christian. A secular-centered leader will expose Americans to the wrathful judgment of God. America must corporately repent and begin to live by the mantra written on our currency, "In God We Trust." Has America trusted God? Who better to trust? Pray for the country, and pray a colorless man!

The Second Most Important National Decision

This election may be the most defining event in American History since the Declaration of Independence and the Revolutionary War. Obama's election, for people of African descent in America and around the world, certainly will be as profound as the Emancipation Proclamation of 1865. God has called the citizens of this nation to strengthen the fabric of the American character. America has the opportunity to meet the inspired request of Barbara Jordan, "That America live up to its Promise." After 232 years, this nation will make a decision that is second only to America's choice to seize its independence. This election will change our nation's history. Regardless of the election's outcome, America has undergone a race and gender metamorphosis. America has the opportunity to grow from a bigoted, gender-biased, *xenophobic* slimy worm to a beautiful glorious butterfly.

It will not be easy. There will be a backlash. The racial tenor of this nation will be volatile. Racial, economic, social, political, and religious lines will be drawn after the election. Initially, the social and economic issues may deteriorate before they improve. America may experience a brief period of dormant rest, but as the bloom of the election's electricity wanes, the reality of America's fiscal circumstance will surface. Bigotry is heightened during times of economic challenge, and Americans must be prepared for a potentially nasty social upheaval. Whichever man secures the presidency will face conceivably insurmountable challenges, and minus divine direction is destined to fail. Americans must pray and exercise faith in the promise of God. *"Trust in the Lord with all thine heart; and lean not unto thine own understanding. In all thy ways acknowledge Him, and He shall direct thy paths"* (Proverbs 3:5-6). Although it appears that Senator Obama may be our next president, regardless of the outcome, McCain or Obama will have to be the American Moses. Our next president will need our prayers to continue to be, or become, the colorless man that this country requires. Consider an interesting footnote. Jeremiah Wright was Senator Obama's pastor for twenty years. For those who have forgotten, Pastor Wright was the minister that made several inflammatory statements from his pulpit that by association placed Obama's patriotism in question.

Perhaps the comments were not politically correct, but were they untrue? What is most important, the truth or appeasement?

Is he the One?

Is Barack the one who can lead America out of the quicksand of sin? The United States has had many reasonable facsimiles. Some thought it was George Washington. Some thought it was Abe Lincoln. Some thought it was Marcus Garvey. Some thought it was Teddy Roosevelt. Some thought it was Franklin D. Roosevelt. Some thought it was Kennedy. Some thought it was his brother Bobby. Some thought it was Martin. Some thought it was Malcolm. Apparently it wasn't time. Who will it be? As Martin Luther King said, "the urgency is now." It truly is! Only America can make the choice. God's Word promised, *"If my people, which are called by my name, shall humble themselves, and pray, and seek my face, and turn from their wicked ways; then will I hear from heaven, and will forgive their sin, and will heal their land" (II Chronicles 7:14).* America has a chance to repent and turn. Will America? Tomorrow, Wednesday November 5, 2008, America will know. The answer will be definitive and give a clear example of America's direction. Will America be restored via this election or will America continue the trek to destruction and national sin? The only hope of America rests in theoanthropology. Without a relationship with the Creator, America's spiraling decline will continue unchecked. All of America and the world are desperate for the "Audacity of Hope." God is hope.

In my opinion, and in the opinion of many other Americans, this nation's hope is grounded in the election of a spiritually sensitive man who has the audacity to think that America can again be a Godly nation. A Godly nation includes all of us regardless of appearance. Regardless of one's religious persuasion and the God of one's belief, spiritual discernment should tell us that God is not pleased. America has not heeded the pluck. America has not acknowledged the slap; what remains is the slug, and it will be mighty. Just as God did in the Old Testament, he is aligning His tools of judgment.

God has placed America in the global position of defender of the world. The Creator has selected America as His spiritual beacon of freedom, democracy, and righteousness, but to His chagrin America has metastasized into a degenerate example of frightful apostasy.

As evidenced by the fiscal treachery of our financial institutions and the flagrant imperialism of America, our God has become the "all mighty dollar." America's position parallels that of the northern and southern nations of Israel prior the Assyrian and Babylonian captivities. Look at America's threats; conspicuously Argentina, North Korea, and Pakistan lie in wait. Saudi Arabia, although touted as an ally, if given an opportunity will pick our bones clean, as evidenced by the international dominance of oil production, price, and the manipulative leadership of the O.P.E.C. nations. Afghanistan, Iraq, and Iran are the obvious and the most immediate threats. Notice the geographical positions of these countries. They all come from the east, exactly like they did in the Old Testament. Also, be careful to realize that the most threatening are contemporary Assyria, Iran, and Babylon, Iraq. America, wake up! The handwriting is on the wall. We are headed for the same fate as Belshazzar and Babylon (Daniel 5:1-31).

Before America can reassume its Godly position, we must clean the stench of home. The United States of America is still the most powerful nation in the world, but that power has significantly eroded, economically, politically, militarily, and spiritually. America's international integrity "sucks." Americans must unite as "One People in God We Trust." The critical question is, "Who is spiritually strong enough to unit America?" The next and more critical question is, "Will we let him?"

Differences Determine Destiny

Science, logic, God, and just plain common sense have taught us that there is less than a fifteen percent difference between all humans. The divine and phenomenal morphing mechanism that all humans possess, which makes humans identical but uniquely different, is unexplained. The uniqueness is simply God's preternatural way of keeping His divine images strong and able to adapt, much like how He maintains the perfect orbit of the moon that maintains the freshness of the waters of the world.

With limited knowledge, God allows us minimal insight into His miraculous perfection. Proof is unnecessary. It is a paradox. Our differences give us a diversity to determine our destiny, which is our decision. The universe, including humanity, is one infinite miracle. Look at a tree. Smell the flowers. Watch the grass grow. Listen to your children play. Breathe, and realize that every subsequent breath is a miracle. We are one. E Pluribus Unum. Out of many, one. Let's act like it!

Everybody's Mamma

Is more proof necessary? With the realization of Mitochondrial Eve and DNA tracking, tracing, timing, and tagging, it has been determined that every human being has the #168 gene. Again, every human being has this gene. The #168 gene has been traced to our "Mitochondrial Mamma." Mamma surfaced approximately 60-100 thousand years ago, not millions of years ago as some thought and taught. "Mamma" did not evolve from a one-celled animal or from lesser humans. Neanderthal man, Cro-Magnon man, and the others were hominids, humanlike but not human. They were facsimiles of humans, not human. Research has shown that every human's genetic mamma, black, white, Asian, Indian, Native American, Malaysian, or a combination thereof, has been genetically tracked, traced, and timed to have surfaced in the African region of Sudan, near Darfur. The resultant factual information confirms that we are all kinfolks, with the same genetic mother. The world is one gigantic family, and that's what God wants.

As all families, there is always a bully who thinks they can take liberties with the other siblings. Fights always occur, but it's time for us to grow up and be "big people." It always takes a bold brother or bold sister to break the mold, and change the routine. It's always difficult, and there will always be fights, sometimes physical and bloody. It is necessary because the oppressor will never willingly give up the key to the chains. Thus far, it appears that Barack Obama is America's mold breaker, and in Christ-like manner the retriever of the key to freedom.

The past 18 months, especially the final 10, have been an educational example of how to be a colorless man. Obama isn't perfect. Men will never be perfect. One can only try to be Christ-like. The chronicling of this presidential campaign, from the primaries to the general election, provided a stark example of the difference in candidates and campaigns. While Senators Clinton and McCain acquiesced to degrees of negativity as a viable campaign strategy and accepted tool, Obama struggled to remain positive. He only relented when forced to defend himself during the campaign prior to the general election. Please remember the power of entrainment.

Unfortunately, McCain supporters shamelessly sunk into racial and ethnic degradation, truth manipulation, and violent threats and epithets. McCain was reluctant to reprimand his supporters by confronting the issues at his rallies, and as a result the last six weeks of the campaign grew increasingly embarrassing, bigoted, and ugly. Again, Obama was not without fault. He stumbled under the assault; however, America appreciated his commitment to an obvious reach for integrity. Even if Senator Obama loses the election, the American public will appreciate his struggle to remain honorable. Politics is a difficult avocation. It's a "dog fight." Unfortunately, when one is in a "dog fight," one must fight like a dog. Read your Bible and consider David. Dave was a priest, prophet, king, and warrior. David was perhaps the fiercest righteous man that ever lived, and next to Christ he was God's favorite! The profoundness of the following statement rings clear. Often accompanied with an "amen" from Deacon Macio, the great urban philosopher James Brown often said, "Sometimes ya gotta git funky!" "Hit me, I can't stand myself."

Both Senators McCain and Obama entered into this presidential battle viewed as honorable men. Only one man will leave with his honor intact. By now, America has made its choice. As you read, we now know if the distorted American mantra, "win at all costs," won. If it has, hopefully it doesn't cost too much. Regardless of the election's outcome, McCain's honorable status as war hero will forever be tarnished. This was reflected in the final, but major, endorsement of Senator Obama by General Colin Powell.

American voters, especially the undecided, have patiently anticipated General Colin Powell's presidential endorsement. His explanation was slightly *truncated* due to time constraints, but he criticized Senator McCain in four major areas that he perceived as national concerns. The first was the lack of a clear and steady economic recovery plan. The second was the less than a complete economic grasp on the critical conditions of contemporary America. General Powell's third issue was the less than thoughtful selection of Sara Palin, whom he considered completely unprepared for the vice-presidency. Finally, he was uneasy with the erratic behavior and decisions of Senator McCain during the campaign.

However, judging from the tone and inflection of his voice, General Powell was more concerned with the disturbing tenor of Senator McCain's negative campaign. "And I've also been disappointed frankly, by some of the approaches that Senator McCain has taken recently, or his campaign ads, on issues that are not really central to the problems that the American people are worried about." General Powell was referring to the Bill Ayers *hyperbole* erroneously associating Senator Obama with the '60s terrorist. Although Senator Obama's association with Ayers was tertiary, the Republican election machine ignobly inferred that Senator Obama was a terrorist. At McCain rallies, there were disturbing racial epithets and frightening death threats directed at Senator Obama, which Senator McCain didn't quell. General Powell was clear: "Senator McCain is a friend. Now I understand what politics is all about. I know how you can go after one another, and that's good. But I think this goes too far. And I think it has made the McCain campaign look a little narrow." Please understand the connotation of narrow. General Powell was being gracious in his criticism. General Powell understands the character necessary to lead America, and he has decided that Senator McCain is lacking.

The African American Maturity Dynamic

One last "heads up" for African America. Black America can no longer rest on the excuse of discrimination as a reason not to succeed. The shackles are off. If a black man of mixed lineage with a white single mother and absentee Kenyan father, with white Midwestern grandparents, can rise to the heights of vying for the presidency of the United States, anything can be accomplished in America. Racism is no longer an excuse of African America. Get over it! If one fails now, it is most likely by choice.

This writer calls it "the African American Maturity Dynamic." In this case, maturity does not refer to chronological age, but to the ability to assume responsibility for one's success. Simply, the fact that Senator Obama is poised to assume the presidency is an indication of the glorious metamorphic change in this nation's racial attitude. The people, regardless of the outcome of the election, have indicated that the nation is ready for change. The change resides deeper in the American spirit than economic or political change. America begs a new spiritual, philosophical, and ethical direction.

Polls are no definite indication of how the nation will vote. However, today, November 3, 2008, Obama's lead varies from 4-10 percentage points. Senator Obama has amassed close to 60% more campaign funds than Senator McCain. The financial disparity indicates, however slightly, that he now is the nation's favorite. People tend to financially support those that they prefer. Please remember the ancient aphorism, "Put your money where your mouth is." If Obama is elected, this writer predicts that a minimum of 60% of the vote affirming his election will be white, which is a profound statement reflecting the nation's healed racial attitude. Like the Berlin wall, if Obama is elected, gradually the prejudicial barriers of racial, gender, religious, and sexual preference will crumble.

African Americans can expect and should look forward to being successful in all areas of American society. By reestablishing the desire for academic excellence, there will no longer be a reason for minorities to sublimate their ambitions with crime or related negative activities. In time, the marginalization of minorities will minimize, and the potential for political engagement will increase along with the corporate sharing of wealth. Perhaps even religious homogeneity will gradually and positively come to fruition for all Americans. Moreover, the new face of America will positively reconfigure the global profile. What this writer hopes to see is the spiritual resurrection of a spiritually dead nation. Let us pray that the righteous mantra proudly etched on America's currency is realized in the corporate spirits of the citizens of this nation. "In God We Trust" must not be an empty perfunctory recitation. "In God We Trust" must reflect the underpinnings of a Theoanthropologetic nation underpinned by God's Divine Word and led by colorless men and women.

Required Currency ━━━━━━━━━━━━━━━━━━━━━━

What have we learned? There were a few interesting "Did You Knows?" There were some interesting similes and parallels. There were some enlightening Bible lessons. Perhaps there were a few profound quotes. We have had thoughtful insight, and a little levity. However, the greater blessing has been witnessing the living definition of the theoanthropological man. We have seen history develop minute-by-minute, hour-by-hour, day-by-day, week-by-week, and month-by-month. America and the world now know how to recognize, appreciate, accept, and above all be a colorless person.

The greatest lesson is that righteousness costs. Anxiety, derision, disrespect, anonymity, and occasionally physical pain and death are the required currency when performing God's work. Righteousness costs, with a big "C" for Christ. Always remember the price Christ paid for our freedom and salvation. The price of being colorless is comparatively cheap. Compared to crucifixion, it is a bargain. America has an enormous opportunity, but it may be fleeting. Please remember. "If my people, which are called by my name, shall humble themselves, and pray, and seek my face, and turn from their wicked ways; then will I hear from heaven, and forgive their sin, and will heal their land" (II Chronicles 7:14). What a promise! Chronicles 7:14 is not a corporate challenge; it is an individual charge that every American must meet. Everyone, every American, must humble themselves with spiritual introspection and tolerance. Manifest your humility in prayer for this nation and its leadership. Leadership is amorphous minus God. America needs God's powerful anointing that will only be realized when we step as individuals into our colorlessness. It is Tuesday evening at 7:30 p.m. EST. My stomach is in knots, my head hurts, and my hands are shaking in joyous anticipation as I write these final lines. My body is wrenching in excitement, but my spirit is peaceful, because In God I Trust. Don't let me be the only one. Pray for each other and the colorless man. May God Bless America Again!

For Further Discussion

1. After a period of critical introspection, list what is necessary for you to develop into a theoanthropological/colorless person.

2. How do you plan to use your gifts to build God's Kingdom?

3. List five people to whom you will explain the difference between relationship and religion.

Glossary

Amorphous - shapeless; ill organized

Hyperbole - exaggerated statement not meant to be taken seriously

Ignoble - dishonorable; mean; base

Truncate - to shorten; to cut the top or the end

Xenophobic - deep dislike and/or fear of foreigners

References

Bible, King James Version.

"One reason the dog has so many friends:
He wags his tail instead of his tongue."

Unknown

"People will be more impressed by the depth
of your conviction than the height of your logic."

Unknown

"I like a man who grins when he fights."

Winston Churchill

"It is difficult for men in high office to
avoid the malady of self-delusion."

Calvin Coolidge

"We content ourselves with appearing to be what we are not,
instead of endeavoring
to be what we appear."

Henry Home
In *Introduction to the Art of Thinking* (1761), "Friendship"

"Allow others to discover your merit:
They will value it the more for being
their own discovery."

Henry Home
In *Introduction to the Art of Thinking* (1761)

"The most important thing in communication is to hear what isn't
being said."

Peter Drucker

"A man becomes a man, and a woman becomes a woman when
we realize that often loyalty
supersedes security."

Gregory G. Ogle

"Society sets the norms, which are often not normal."

Gregory G. Ogle